Learn Java™

Sunrise Midday Sunset

In a Weekend®

Sunset Evening Sunrise

Learn Java™

Joseph P. Russell

Premier Press

The Premier Press logo, top edge printing, and related trade dress is a trademark of Premier Press, Inc. and may not be used without written permission. All other trademarks are the property of their respective owners.

Java and all Java-related technologies are trademarks of Sun Microsystems, Inc. Microsoft, Windows, Internet Explorer, and Notepad are trademarks or registered trademarks of Microsoft Corporation. Netscape is a registered trademark of Netscape Communications Corporation. TextPad is a registered trademark of Helios Software Solutions. Red Hat is a registered trademark of Red Hat, Inc. All other trademarks are the property of their respective owners.

Important: Premier Press cannot provide software support. Please contact the appropriate software manufacturer's technical support line or Web site for assistance.

Premier Press and the author have attempted throughout this book to distinguish proprietary trademarks from descriptive terms by following the capitalization style used by the manufacturer.

Information contained in this book has been obtained by Premier Press from sources believed to be reliable. However, because of the possibility of human or mechanical error by our sources, Premier Press, or others, the Publisher does not guarantee the accuracy, adequacy, or completeness of any information and is not responsible for any errors or omissions or the results obtained from use of such information. Readers should be particularly aware of the fact that the Internet is an ever-changing entity. Some facts may have changed since this book went to press.

ISBN: 1-931841-60-8

Library of Congress Catalog Card Number: 2001099844

Printed in the United States of America

02 03 04 05 RI 10 9 8 7 6 5 4 3 2 1

Publisher:
Stacy L. Hiquet

Marketing Manager:
Heather Buzzingham

Managing Editor:
Sandy Doell

Acquisitions Editor:
Stacy L. Hiquet

Project Editor:
Melba Hopper

Editorial Assistant:
Margaret Bauer

Technical Reviewer:
Roseanne Russell

Copy Editor:
Elizabeth A. Barrett

Interior Layout:
Shawn Morningstar

Cover Design:
Christy Pierce

Indexer:
Kelly Talbot

Proofreader:
Jenny Davidson

For my father.
You enjoy these books even more than I do.

ACKNOWLEDGMENTS

Thanks to everyone at Premier Press for their excellent work on this project. Being a computer geek at heart makes it hard to write a book that isn't too technical for normal people to enjoy reading. That's why it's great to have editors! They're there to tell me when I'm being too boring or if I'm not making any sense. The whole team worked hard to get the information out of my head and onto paper in such a form that other people might actually consider reading it. A special thanks to Rosie, my sister firstly and technical reviewer lastly, for her superior job. Thanks to my kids, Brianne and Tyler, for making me laugh, keeping me happy, and making my life worth living.

ABOUT THE AUTHOR

Joseph P. Russell is an Information Systems Engineer for a Fortune 100 corporation, where he develops Java applications based on the current J2EE (Java 2 Enterprise Edition) technology. Russell is a Sun certified Java programmer for the Java 2 Platform. He graduated from Rhode Island College, where he majored in computer science. While attending RIC, Russell was a Web developer for their Web site (http://www.ric.edu). In his spare time, he enjoys playing video games, programming computer games, painting, and playing his bass guitar. He is a father of two and truly loves his kids. You can visit his Web site at http://members.cox.net/j.p.russell or drop him an e-mail at j.p.russell@cox.net.

CONTENTS AT A GLANCE

CONTENTS

SATURDAY AFTERNOON
Getting Beyond the Basics **97**

SUNDAY MORNING
More GUI, Graphics, and Exception Handling 243

Introduction

When I got my first Atari system, I fell in love with computers. I wanted to know how they worked. Even more, I wanted to be able to *make* them work. I wanted to tell the computer what to do and have it obey my every command. Now, I'm all grown up and that's what I do for a living. Computer programming gives you the power to write programs that control your computer. Have you ever wanted a piece of software that doesn't exist? When you know a programming language, you can write your own software—and maybe even sell it to others! Right now, Java is very hot. Chances are that if you go on an interview for a programming job, they're going to ask you if you know Java.

The title of this book is *Learn Java In a Weekend*. You might be thinking to yourself, "Yeah right! I'm not going to be able to learn Java in a single weekend." While it is true that to become really good at Java programming, you're going to need a lot more than just a single weekend's time to get there, you can, in fact, learn the basics pretty quickly. This is especially true if you already have some programming experience. If you're new to programming in general and this is your first programming book, take as long as you need. Read everything, especially the code samples, very carefully. Try coding all of the samples to really get a feel for the Java programming language.

If you already know a programming language or two and you're in a hurry to learn Java for a job interview or something, try a different approach. Try reading through the book and instead of coding each and every sample for yourself, just make sure that you fully understand the code as you're reading it. Then, when you're not in such a rush, try coding the samples. Or try tackling the calculator project, which spans the bulk of this text. Just keep in mind that the best way to learn something new is by doing it. Have fun!

Who Should Read This Book

This book is for anyone who needs or wants to start programming using the Java 2 programming language. Although this book doesn't assume that you have any prior programming experience, you should have a basic understanding of computer science terminology. You should also be familiar with your computer and its operating system.

This book is intended for beginners to intermediate-level programmers. The first couple of sessions are written at a fairly elementary level to get beginners up to speed with intermediates, and the sessions become increasingly advanced toward the end of the book. If you have prior programming experience with C or C++, you should be able to fly through the earlier sessions because there are a lot of syntactical similarities between those programming languages and Java. If you have no prior programming experience, you will need to read earlier sessions a bit more carefully, but everything is explained for you, so you won't get stuck.

What You Need to Begin

The great thing about Java is that everything you need to start programming, except for your computer, is free! To compile and run Java programs, you will need the Java Software Development Kit (SDK). For you to be able to download the SDK and the book's sample programs from Premier's Web site, you will need to have Internet access. You can visit the Web site at http://www. premierpressbooks.com/downloads.asp.

For installing the SDK, your computer should have a 166 MHz or faster processor and at least 32MB of RAM. Your operating system can be any of the following: Microsoft Windows 95/98/2000/ME/XP/NT 4.0, Linux (Red Hat Linux 6.2 is officially supported), or Solaris 2.6/7/8. The installed SDK size varies a bit among operating systems, but, generally, you should have about 75MB of available disk space.

For running Java applets, you should have a Java-compatible Internet browser, such as Microsoft Internet Explorer or Netscape. Such browsers are freely available to you. However, you can run the applets without a browser if you need to.

For writing Java code, you need to have a text editor, such as Notepad or TextPad. If you have a Java IDE (integrated development environment) like Forte, that's even better, but any text editor will do.

How This Book Is Organized

This book is written so that you can complete it in seven sessions over the course of a single weekend. Of course, you can read it anytime you want. The first session focuses on getting you going. The next two sessions go over all the rules and syntax of Java. Saturday Evening and Sunday Morning cover the Abstract Windowing Toolkit for GUI programming and graphics programming. The rest of Sunday focuses on applets, threads, and more advanced Java programming. Starting on Saturday Morning and continuing through to the end of the book, you'll be developing a calculator application. The calculator application starts out simple and small, and as you learn new things, you'll be adding to the calculator application. Eventually, you'll have a fully functional calculator application equipped with some cool features. The basic outline of the book is shown here:

➤ **Friday Evening: "Introducing Java"** provides an introduction to Java. It explains what Java is and provides a brief history of Java. After that, this session provides instructions for installing the SDK, which you'll need to have for the rest of the book. This session ends by showing you how to write your first Java program and your first Java applet.

➤ **Saturday Morning: "Learning the Basics of Java Programming"** provides you with a Java programming foundation that you will build upon in the later sessions of the book. It covers data types, variables, arrays, and methods. It also covers object-oriented programming (OOP), which is an extremely important concept in Java. Toward the end, this session shows you how to begin the calculator application.

➤ **Saturday Afternoon: "Getting Beyond the Basics"** covers conditional operators, conditional statements, loops, command-line arguments, and the `java.util` package. Just about every nontrivial Java application implements all these things. This session also covers the `Math` class, which Java programs use to perform all kinds of mathematical functions. This session concludes by showing you how to build upon the calculator application using the knowledge you gain in this session.

➤ **Saturday Evening: "Graphical User Interface Programming"** starts the real excitement! You'll learn how to program graphical user interfaces, or GUIs, using the abstract windowing toolkit (AWT). The session begins with an introduction to GUI programming and moves on to show you the AWT components, such as `Buttons`, `TextFields`, and `Labels`. You'll also learn how to handle events, such as when someone clicks a button. Next, the session covers layout managers, which help you lay out the AWT components inside a Frame. Finally, at the end of this session, you will start to program the calculator's appearance.

➤ **Sunday Morning: "More GUI, Graphics, and Exception Handling"** continues to show you how to program GUIs. This session begins by showing you how to do graphics programming. This session moves beyond the AWT to cover lightweight GUI components. You'll program your own graphics for a lightweight component to create digits that have a liquid crystal appearance for the calculator, like that of a real calculator. Continuing with lightweight components, this session explains the Swing package, which defines a set of lightweight GIU components. Once you learn about Swing, you'll convert the calculator application to Swing. This session gets to more advanced topics—inner classes and exception handling. Finally, you'll update the calculator application by creating a digital display panel using the skills you gain in this session.

➤ **Sunday Afternoon: "Interfaces, Applets, and Threads"** increases your Java programming skills by covering interfaces, applets, and threads. You'll use interfaces and your knowledge of event handling to develop an event model for the calculator application. This session shows you how to program applets and shows you how to modify the calculator application, so that you can also run it as an applet. Threads are also covered in this session. Threads allow you to do two or more things at the same time in a Java program.

➤ **Sunday Evening: "Packages, File I/O, JARs, and Javadocs"** covers advanced Java programming and Java utilities. You'll start off this session by learning about packages. You'll learn about the benefits associated with packaging Java classes, and then this session will show you how to package the calculator application classes. Next, you'll learn how to perform file input and output using the `java.io` package. You'll add some features to the calculator application that allow it to access the filesystem to read and write files. The last two topics that this session goes over are the `jar` tool and the `javadoc` tool. The `jar` tool lets you zip up multiple program files into a single compressed file, and the `javadoc` tool generates HTML documentation for your code. You'll complete the calculator application by applying both of these tools.

I have also provided two appendixes on the companion Web site. To download them, just direct your browser to http://www.premierpressbooks.com/downloads.asp. You'll need Appendix B to complete the calculator application in Friday Night's session, so be sure you get at least that one. Here are descriptions of the two appendixes:

➤ **Appendix A: "Java Language Summary"** provides the Java language summary that you can use as a quick reference while writing your own Java programs.

➤ **Appendix B: "Full Source Code Listings"** provides the full source code for all the classes of the calculator application. The code includes the `javadoc` comments, which are excluded in the source code listings in the book's seven sessions.

Special Features

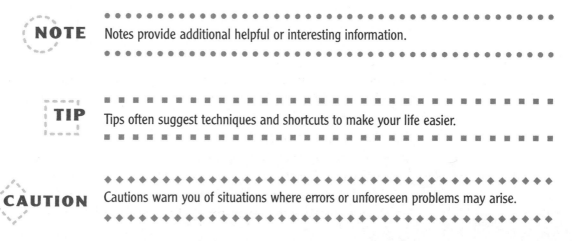

NOTE Notes provide additional helpful or interesting information.

TIP Tips often suggest techniques and shortcuts to make your life easier.

CAUTION Cautions warn you of situations where errors or unforeseen problems may arise.

Introducing Java

- ➤ What Is Java?
- ➤ Installing and Setting Up the Java 2 SDK
- ➤ Writing Your First Java Program
- ➤ Introduction to Applets

It's Friday evening, the beginning of your weekend—that is, if you're following the implied schedule for this book. Perhaps you've picked this weekend to learn Java because you have a job interview on Monday or your weekly schedule is hectic and the idea of learning Java in a single weekend appeals to you. While it's entirely possible to get through this book in a weekend, especially if you have some prior programming experience, feel free to work at your own pace. After all, you're trying to learn Java, so it really isn't to your advantage to rush through a particular section of the book just to stay on schedule. If you're struggling with a section of this book, take the time you need to understand the concepts. Each section builds upon previous sections, so make sure that you understand each concept before moving on to the next.

Tonight, I'll keep it light so that you can get oriented. In fact, you may find tonight's session a tad elementary. Feel free to skim through it. Just make sure you get the Java SDK installed and the first program working tonight. If you're a novice, you may find reading the entire session helpful. In this session, you learn exactly what the Java programming language is and get a brief history. Next, you set up the Java SDK (Software Development Kit) so that you can write and run your Java programs. Then you get your hands dirty with your first Java program, `HelloWorld`. You also write a quick Java applet and run it using your Web browser. All this sound like fun, right? I hope it's as much fun for you as it is for me. Here we go.

What Is Java?

With all of the hype surrounding Java and the fact that you're reading this book, you might already have a good idea what Java is. Just to be sure we're on the same page, I'll give you my definition of the language. *Java* (by Sun Microsystems, Inc.) is an object-oriented programming (OOP) language that can run in any environment that has a Java interpreter installed. With Java, you can accomplish many things, such as building standalone applications or applets that run within a Web browser.

Java Is a Programming Language

Like C, C++, COBOL, FORTRAN, and BASIC, Java is a programming language. Computers are merely machines; they don't think for themselves. Someone, at some point, has to give the computer a detailed set of instructions to follow for the computer to be of use. At the operating system level, the computer basically knows how to read, write, process, and store information using the computer's hardware. To do more complicated tasks, such as sending and receiving e-mail, writing formatted documents, or even balancing your checking account, you need a program. Programming languages allow you to tell the operating system what you want it to do. Java is one language that a programmer can use to communicate to the computer just how to accomplish these tasks.

Java is a *high-level* programming language. High-level programming languages resemble human languages. When you look at Java code, you will actually see English words—even if you don't know Java, you can make guesses as to what's going on based on the words you recognize. Computers "speak" machine language, which is a very different type of language than we humans use. Programming languages that more closely resemble machine language, such as assembly languages, are cryptic (not very readable by humans) and are called low-level programming languages. Unlike Java and other high-level programming languages, without studying assembly language, there's no way you can understand what the program is supposed to be doing.

Java is a *compiled* programming language. You write a somewhat English-like text file, called a *source code file,* but the computer doesn't understand how to interpret it in that format. Being able to read and write program code that makes sense to humans benefits the programmer, but the computer needs for it to be translated in such a way that it can make sense of the language, too. That's where compiling comes in. When you compile your source code, a new file called a *byte code file* is created. The computer knows how to interpret it and follow the instructions it contains, but if you were to open it and try to read it, you wouldn't be able to make any sense of it.

Some Java History

Sun Microsystems started developing Java in 1991 as part of what they called the Green Project. The goal for the project was basically to enable electronic appliances to communicate with each other. The team experimented with C++, but determined that it was inadequate for their specific purposes, which is why they decided to develop a new language—Java. Java was originally named "Oak," after a tree outside a team member's office window. The name was later changed to Java because of copyright issues associated with the name "Oak." The team came up with the name Java while visiting a local coffee shop!

NOTE Some people ask, "What does JAVA stand for?" The computer science world is chock full of acronyms. Java is not actually an acronym for anything, although some programmers joke that it stands for Just Another Vague Acronym!

Java really got its boost from the big Internet boom. In order for the Web to be successful for a wide audience, it had to be reliable, secure, and able to run on any platform. These nonfunctional requirements were directly in line with Java's design. Sun developed a Web browser called HotJava, which showcased Java's potential usefulness to Internet developers.

On May 23, 1995, Sun Microsystems officially introduced the Java language, and Netscape announced support for Java in its Netscape Navigator Web browser. Prior to the Web's adoption of Java, the Internet was full of static Web pages that essentially could only display information. With Java, Web designers could do more than merely display information; they could build applications to process data, adding a whole new dimension to Web technology. Java continues to evolve and become an evermore powerful Web-centric application development language.

What Is Platform Independence?

One of Java's biggest selling points is its *platform independence*. Platform independence refers to a program's capability to run on any platform. You may have heard the phrase "Write once, run anywhere" in reference to Java's features. This means that Java programmers need to write and maintain only one set of source code. Java programs can be written and compiled on any system that supports Java and can be run without any modification on any other system that supports Java. Why is this such a great thing? Other languages rely heavily on the underlying system's native APIs (Application Programming Interface). APIs act as an interface between the operating system and a program. When programmers write a program in C++, for example, they need to know a great deal about the operating environment to be able to utilize the native APIs in their program. The downside to this is that it becomes very difficult to port an application from one system to another. APIs are different for each operating system. In order to be ported from one operating system to another, a program needs to be rewritten to make use of the new APIs. It takes time, and therefore money, to accomplish such a task. With Java, this is not a problem at all.

When program code written in most other languages is compiled, it is translated into a file that the computer can directly execute. Because each platform has its own machine language, one platform cannot interpret a different system's executable files. It must be compiled separately for each platform. As an analogy, consider different spoken languages. Say that a

Chinese man invited an Italian and an Irishman to his home and provided directions, written in Chinese, from the airport to his house. Without using a translator to translate the directions into Italian and English, the Chinese man probably would be without his guests.

How does Java's platform independence work to overcome this "language" difficulty? Well, each platform has its own Java interpreter, or JVM (*Java Virtual Machine*), installed on it. Java programs are compiled to Java byte code. A computer cannot directly interpret Java byte code; instead, byte code is interpreted by the JVM. Each platform-specific JVM knows how to communicate instructions to the platform on which it is installed. Any JVM can interpret any Java byte code file and communicate platform specific instructions to the underlying operating system. While this JVM system does well to overcome platform differences, there is one side effect to this approach: Because the operating system uses a JVM middleman instead of directly interpreting the code, it takes a bit longer to execute.

Object-Oriented Programming Overview

As I mentioned earlier, Java is an object-oriented programming language. To better understand what this means, you need to first understand what a *procedural programming language* is and then compare the two. Some examples of procedural programming languages are C, FORTRAN, and COBOL. With these types of languages, programs are constructed by listing steps in the order in which the computer is to execute them. Each program is a procedure, hence the term procedural programming language.

As an example of the drawbacks of this type of language, consider writing a data entry program used to enter products into a nationwide retail chain database. If such a program were built with a procedural programming language, the concept of a product would be vague—just a collection of data fields, such as product name, item number, price, and so on. It would all be defined within the program and would not be an independent identity. You're probably thinking, "So what? It gets the job done, right?"

Yes, it does; but every other program that processes product data, such as a cash register, an inventory program, and promotion scheduling programs, would have to rewrite the same programmatic definition of a product within their code. A seemingly simple task such as changing the item number from six to seven digits could potentially cause a lot of work, as each of these separate programs would need to be updated to reflect the change.

Object-oriented programming languages, such as Java, and to some extent C++, have the added capability of grouping sets of related characteristics and functions together to describe *classes*. Continuing with the same example, with an OOP approach, the concept of a product is defined in a class. Product fields, such as first product name, item number, price, and so on, are grouped together along with operations that can be performed on products, such as validating item number input. Specific products are instances of the product class, or, in other words, *product objects.*

In this case, if you need to change the item number length from six to seven digits, the task will be a significantly easier one if you are using OOP. You would only need to update the product class file. Programs that use the product class only need to process the concept of a product, and don't care about the details of the product class's programmatic implementation. Programs that need to make sure item numbers are valid, just call upon the validate function defined in the product class. When the item number format is changed, the validate function is updated, but the programs use it exactly the same and don't need to be updated at all if the programmer uses good OOP design to build applications.

Object-oriented programming is a very important concept. Java is strictly object-oriented. Every Java program must be defined as a class. Since this is such a huge topic, don't worry if you don't quite get it yet. This section is just meant to be an overview so that you get your wheels turning in the right direction. Tomorrow morning, you'll read a lot more about OOP.

Installing and Setting Up the Java SDK

Before you can write and run Java programs, you need to install the Java SDK on your computer. The SDK consists of the Java compiler, the JVM, and many other useful tools. Getting set up correctly is very important. I'll be as thorough as possible in this section. Programmers new to Java tend to find it difficult just to get set up because it involves not only installing the software, but also manually setting up the environment. If you follow the instructions for your system, you should be all set.

Windows Installation and Setup

If you are running Windows 95/98/Me or XP/NT/2000, follow the steps in this section to set up the SDK. When you finish these steps, you will be ready to compile and run Java.

1. Run the installer program. The file `j2sdk-1_3_1_01-win.exe` is the installer program. Go to http://www.premierpressbooks.com/downloads.asp to find the program.

   Double-click on the `j2sdk-1_3_1_01-win.exe` icon to start the installation process. To avoid confusion, just accept the default installation directory: `c:\jdk1.3.1_01`. (Just keep clicking on OK.)

2. Update the `PATH` variable. The `PATH` variable specifies where your computer can find executable files. Your computer looks at this variable when trying to run executable files that are in directories other than the current directory. First, it checks the current directory; if the executable file is not there, your computer checks the `PATH`. If the location of the executable files is not specified in the `PATH`, your computer won't know what to do. Here, you're updating the `PATH` so that you can run the compiler and Java programs from any directory you choose. You can do this in a few different ways, depending on your preferences and your version of Windows, as shown in the following list:

_bin\
Javac
Javadoc
jdb

➤ **For any version of Windows:** You can create a batch file (.bat) that updates your path. Open a text editor, such as Notepad, and type the following text:

```
SET JAVA_HOME=C:\jdk1.3.1_01
SET PATH=%PATH%;%JAVA_HOME%\bin
```

Then save it as env.bat. (Actually, you can save it using any file-name, as long as it ends with the .bat extension. Just remember where you save it.) Anytime you want to compile or run Java programs, you need to run this batch file. First, open a command prompt.

➤ **For Windows 95/98/Me:** Click on the Start button, select Run from the menu, then type **command** and press Enter. An MS-DOS Prompt window should appear.

➤ **For Windows XP/NT/2000:** Instead of typing command, type **cmd** and press Enter.

Next, you need to go to the directory in which you saved your env.bat file. Use the CD DOS command to change directories. If you're unfamiliar with DOS, just type **CD**, type the name of the directory (folder) you want to get into (where _foldername_ appears in the following example), and press Enter.

```
CD foldername
```

To back out of a folder, type **CD**. Then press Enter. If you're still confused, try typing **CD /?**

When you issue the CD/? command, some versions of DOS will print a help message for using the CD command. Another place to look for tips on using DOS is on the Internet. Further details about using DOS are beyond the scope of this book.

Once you are in the proper directory, just type the name of the .bat file (you can omit the .bat file extension). If you named your file env.bat, just type **env**.

Now you are all set to compile and run your Java programs. It is important to understand that this does not change your PATH variable permanently. You need to run this batch file separately for each command prompt session you open. It changes the variable only for the session in which it is run and doesn't affect any other session.

If you want to change your PATH permanently so that you don't have to constantly run this file, follow these instructions for your specific operating system:

➤ **For Windows 95/98/Me:** To permanently update your PATH variable, you need to edit your autoexec.bat file. Your computer automatically executes this file each time it is turned on. Part of the autoexec.bat file's responsibility is setting up environment variables such as PATH. This file is extremely important. Make a backup of the file before you edit it. Create a copy and name it autoexec.bak or any other name you'll remember. Using Notepad, open the original autoexec.bat file. It can be found in your root directory at C:\autoexec.bat. (Don't double-click on the autoexec.bat file to open it. That will just cause your computer to run it and not open it for editing.) Now, find the line within that file that sets your PATH variable. For example, that PATH line typically looks like the following:

```
SET PATH=C:\WINDOWS;C:\WINDOWS\COMMAND
```

If there isn't a line that begins with SET PATH like this in your autoexec.bat file, you need to create a new one. Just know that it must appear on a line of its own. To set up a variable that keeps track of the location of the Java installation, type the following code on any line before the one where your PATH is set:

```
SET JAVA_HOME=C:\jdk1.3.1_01
```

Now add it to your PATH like this:

```
SET PATH=C:\WINDOWS;C:\WINDOWS\COMMAND;%JAVA_HOME%\bin
```

➤ **For Windows NT/2000/XP:** Open your control panel by clicking on the Start menu and selecting Settings, Control Panel. Double-click on the System icon. Next, click on the Environment tab. Instructions for XP are a little different. From the Start Menu, open the Control Panel and double-click on the System icon to open System Properties. In System Properties, select the Advanced tab and click on the Environment Variables button. Under System Variables, click on Path and then click on the Edit button. Update the PATH variable by appending the path to the Java executable files to it. For example, if your PATH looks like

```
C:\WINNT;C:\WINNT\SYSTEM32
```

update it to

```
C:\WINNT;C:\WINNT\SYSTEM32;C:\jdk1.3.1_01\bin
```

To be able to do this, you must have administrator privileges for your system. If you do not have administrator privileges, you must create a new user environment variable named PATH. If one is already there, just append the Java bin directory as just shown. If not, create a new one and set its value to the following:

```
%PATH%;C:\jdk1.3.1_01\bin
```

NOTE No matter what operating system you're using, you should reboot your system after you install the Java SDK.

Solaris Installation

Follow these instructions for installing the SDK on Solaris SPARC or Solaris x86 (Intel) platforms:

1. Copy the self-extracting binary to the directory where you want to install the SDK. You can find it at http://www.premierpressbooks.com/downloads.asp. Use the `j2sdk-1_3_1-solsparc.sh` file for SPARC or `j2sdk-1_3_1-solx86.sh` for the Intel platform.

Make sure that the execute permissions are set by using the following commands:

- **For SPARC:**

```
chmod +x j2sdk-1_3_1-solsparc.sh
```

- **For Intel:**

```
chmod +x j2sdk-1_3_1-solx86.sh
```

2. Run the SDK self-extracting binary. This will create a subdirectory called j2sdk1_3_1.

Linux Installation

There are two different Linux installation options. You can install the SDK using the self-extracting binary file or the RPM file.

Follow these instructions if you are using the self-extracting binary file:

1. Copy the self-extracting binary file to the directory in which you want to install the SDK. The file can be found at http://www.premierpressbooks.com/downloads.asp. The file is named j2sdk-1_3_1-linux-i386.bin.

2. In the directory containing the copy of the self-extracting binary, use the following commands to run the installer:

```
chmod a+x j2sdk-1_3_1-linux-i386.bin

./j2sdk-1_3_1-linux-i386.bin
```

Follow these instructions if you are using the RPM file to install the SDK in package form:

1. Copy the installer program to the directory where you want to install the SDK. You can find this file in the /SDK/ directory. The filename is j2sdk-1_3_1-linux-i386-rpm.bin.

2. In the directory containing the copy of the installer file, use the following commands to run the installer:

```
chmod a+x j2sdk-1_3_1-linux-i386-rpm.bin
./j2sdk-1_3_1-linux-i386-rpm.bin
```

3. This will create a file named `jdk-1.3.1.i386.rpm` in the current directory.

4. Become the root user by using the `su` command.

5. Use the `rpm` command to install the packages into the newly created `/usr/java/jdk1.3.1` directory.

6. Add the `/usr/java/jdk1.3.1/bin` directory to your `PATH` environment variable by using this command:

```
export PATH=/usr/java/jdk1.3.1/bin:$PATH
```

Troubleshooting

Let's make sure that you're set up properly, okay? First things first: As a quick check, type the following command at your command prompt:

```
java -version
```

Your computer should spit out the Java version information. If, instead, you get a message (for example, bad command or filename) indicating that the computer didn't understand you, you're having trouble. Your `PATH` may not be set up correctly. If you're sure that you set up your `PATH` correctly, there could be another problem. Some versions of Windows require you to use an 8.3 format when specifying files and directories in autoexec.bat. This format is basically a convention in which filenames are no more than eight characters long and have extensions that are no more than three characters long. Using 8.3 format, the directory name is `jdk1.3.1_01` is `jdk13~1.1_0`. Pretty weird, huh? Try using that directory name in your `PATH` instead. You can set the `PATH` manually at your command prompt. For example, at the Windows MS-DOS prompt, you can type

```
set PATH=C:\WINDOWS;C:\WINDOWS\COMMAND;C:\jdk13~1_1\bin
```

Now try checking your Java version again. You should now see the version information. You also might want to try typing the following command:

```
javac
```

If your path is set up correctly, you should get information about how to use this command. Figure 1.1 shows this example. If your screen corresponds to Figure 1.1, you're definitely all set. If you want to set your PATH permanently, make sure that you update your autoexec.bat file and reboot your system.

Take a Break

Now that you're all set up and ready to program with Java, you deserve a break! Before tackling your first Java program, why not grab a drink and a snack? Sit back and relax for a few minutes and clear your mind so that you'll be fresh and ready to learn something new. After your short break, you're going to write a complete Java program, learn how to compile it, and run it using the SDK you just installed. It's not all that complicated, but it's important that you're refreshed. You will use what you learn in the next section throughout the rest of this book.

Figure 1.1

This figure shows how the MS-DOS prompt reacts to a successful PATH test.

Writing Your First Java Program

Now you're going to do some hands-on Java programming! What do you need to get going? You need a text editor for writing your Java source code. Any simple text editor, such as Notepad, will do, but if you have a more Java-friendly text editor such as TextPad or an IDE (*Integrated Development Environment*) such as Forte, feel free to use it. This book does not cover how to use compiler tools other than the one included with the Java SDK, so if you choose to use another compiler, you'll have to consult the corresponding user manuals or help documentation. For the examples in this book, I assume that you're using a plain old text editor and the SDK compiler so that you're not tied to any specific IDE. As long as you were able to get the SDK set up and you have a text editor, you're ready to go.

Hello, World!

If you've ever taken a programming course or have ever read a programming book, you're probably familiar with the "Hello World" example program. Although not a groundbreaking application, it does serve an important purpose—to acclimate you to a new programming language. In writing this program, you are introduced to the way a source code file is created, how to compile it, and also how to run it. You will follow the steps outlined in this section for every program you write throughout the rest of this book.

Writing the Source Code

The best way to learn something is by actually doing it. I'll walk you through writing, compiling, and running `HelloWorld.java` from start to finish. First, you need to open whatever program you're using as a text editor. Next, type the source code listed here into your text editor. Don't worry; I'll explain it all in detail later on.

```
/*

 * HelloWorld
```

```
 * This is a very simple Java program that prints a message
 */

public class HelloWorld {

    public static void main(String args[]) {
        //print a message to standard output
        System.out.println("Hello, World!");
    }

}
```

Make sure that you type the source code exactly as you see it here. Now, save it as `HelloWorld.java`. The filename is very important. If you don't name the file correctly, you won't be able to compile or run it. After you're certain that your source code file matches the preceding listing, move on to the next section to compile your program.

Compiling HelloWorld.java

Now that you've written the source code for `HelloWorld`, you're ready to compile it. The command used to compile Java programs is `javac`. Like all other Java utility programs, `javac.exe` is a program that lives in the `bin` directory that you added to your PATH environment variable. The syntax for our use of the `javac` command is as follows:

```
javac JavaSourceCode.java
```

At the command prompt, type the name of the actual compiler program, `javac`, to run the compiler. Then add a space, followed by the name of your source code. In this case, you need to replace `JavaSourceCode.java` with `HelloWorld.java`. Now you can go ahead and compile `HelloWorld`. First, you need to open your command prompt window. For example, in Windows 95, 98, or Me, click on the Start menu, select Run, type **command** into the text field, and press Enter. For Windows NT, 2000, or XP, type **cmd** rather than `command`. At the command prompt, change to the directory that contains your source code (HelloWorld.java) and type the following command to compile HelloWorld.java:

```
javac HelloWorld.java
```

Did anything happen when you pressed Enter? If not, that's a good thing, as long as your command prompt completed compilation. As long as you didn't get any error messages and your command prompt is awaiting a new command, you should be all set. Just make sure that it created a HelloWorld.class file in the same directory as HelloWorld.java. In Windows, type **dir** to get a listing of the contents of your current directory. In UNIX/Solaris, type **ls** to accomplish the same thing. At the very least, you should see two files listed in your current directory. These files are HelloWorld.java and HelloWorld.class. Congratulations! You've just compiled your first Java program!

If things did not turn out as expected, you're probably having a problem with one of two things. You might be having trouble with your SDK setup, or you might have some errors in your source code file. Check the error message you received when you tried to compile. If you received an error to the effect that the command is not recognized or is a bad command, make sure that you set up your SDK properly. Remember, if you chose not to permanently change your environment variables when you installed the SDK as described in the earlier section "Installing and Setting Up the Java 2 SDK," you need to set them up for each command prompt session you start. Refer to that section and the "Troubleshooting" subsection to make sure that you are set up correctly.

If your command prompt accepted the javac command but spit out some other error message, then there are errors in your source code or your source code filename. Don't worry; you can fix this. Open HelloWorld.java in your text editor (if it's not already open) and double-check the following things:

➤ Make sure that your filename is exactly HelloWorld.java. It's case sensitive, so check your uppercase and lowercase lettering!

➤ Make sure that class name appears exactly as HelloWorld in the line

```
public class HelloWorld {
```

➤ Make sure that all your source code matches exactly my source code listing in the section "Writing the Source Code." Sometimes dots (.) look like commas (,), so be sure that you're reading carefully.

Checking and fixing these things should take care of the situation. Other problems you could be having may be non-Java errors. For example, be sure you are in the same directory as your source code when you're compiling at the command prompt. Figure 1.2 demonstrates how three different compilation scenarios look from the Windows command prompt. First, it shows how the screen should look when compilation is successful. Next, it shows what happens if you compile an erroneous program. For this I used an intentionally buggy program, HelloWorldBad.java. Finally, it shows what happens when your environment is not set up correctly. You can see where I set the PATH incorrectly. Hopefully, you'll see the first scenario more often than not when you code the examples throughout this book!

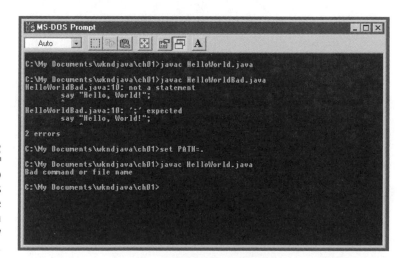

Figure 1.2

It's important to note the differences between the compilation responses you may experience.

Running the HelloWorld.class File

Earlier tonight, I mentioned that compiling a Java program creates a new byte code file that the JVM can interpret. `HelloWorld.class` is the byte code file for the `HelloWorld` program. When you run `HelloWorld`, the JVM will interpret `HelloWorld.class` and completely ignore the `HelloWorld.java` source code file. In fact, you could delete it if you wanted to, but that would make it hard for you to make any changes to your program, wouldn't it? If you still have the command prompt session open that you used to compile it, then you're ready to run `HelloWorld`. If not, open a new command prompt session and change to the directory that contains the `HelloWorld.class` file. To run the program, simply run the `java` command. The syntax for the `java` command is

```
java JavaMainClass
```

At the command prompt, type the Java application launcher program name (**java**), followed by a space, and then the name of the program that you want to run. In this case, you just want to replace `JavaMainClass` with `HelloWorld`, so at the command prompt, enter the command

```
java HelloWorld
```

Okay, what happened? Your program output should look something like the output shown in Figure 1.3. On the line immediately following the `java` command line, you should see text that says, `Hello, World!`, and underneath that, you should see another command prompt ready to accept another command. If you received an error message, make sure that your `PATH` variable is set up and that you typed the source code exactly as it appears earlier in this book. Then recompile and try to run your program again.

Learning Java Syntax Basics

You've already written and run your first Java program! Now, take another look at the source code for `HelloWorld`, and I'll explain what all that code

Figure 1.3

When you run
`HelloWorld`,
the output should
appear as shown in
this figure.

means and expand on it a bit. The first three lines of `HelloWorld.java` are
simply a multi-line comment. These three lines don't actually do anything:

```
/*
 * HelloWorld
 * This is a very simple Java program that prints a message
 */
```

A programmer uses comments to explain things about the source code.
You can write anything you want in your comments, and the compiler
will completely ignore them. The syntax for a multi-line comment is

```
/* Comments including spaces, multiple lines, or whatever,
   go here. */
```

You start a comment using a forward slash followed by an asterisk (`/*`).
This combination tells the compiler to ignore everything that follows it.
You can type anything you want in there and can use as many lines as you
want in doing so. To end your comment section, use an asterisk followed
by a forward slash (`*/`). That tells the compiler to stop ignoring your code

so that whatever follows your comment is compiled. You can have as many multi-line comments in your code as you want.

NOTE In `HelloWorld.java`, I preceded each new comment line with an asterisk, but that is not required. I put the asterisks there just for the sake of readability. The asterisk makes the comment section more visible so that it's not confused with actual code.

The multi-line comment is not the only type of comment line in `HelloWorld.java`. The following excerpt is a single-line comment:

```
//print a message to standard output
```

To create a single-line comment, simply precede the comment line with two forward slashes (`//`). The compiler will ignore the remainder of that single line. Compilation will resume on the following line. Single-line comments don't have to be on lines of their own. They can also be on the same line as Java code. For example, the following line is valid:

```
System.out.println("Hello, World!"); //print a message
```

The part of the line preceding the double slashes will be compiled, while the rest of it will be ignored.

The compiler also ignores the blank line that follows the multi-line comment. *Whitespace*, spaces and blank lines that are between pieces of Java code, don't matter. You should use them to format your code so that it is readable.

TIP It's a good idea to skip lines between significant pieces of code so that you can visually separate pieces of functionality. Skipping lines is definitely not required when writing a program, but it makes it easier for someone else, or even for you, to read and understand the source code.

The next line is the class declaration. You'll learn more about what a class is tomorrow morning. For now, just think of it as the way you name your program. The following line from `HelloWorld.java` indicates that you're creating a program named `HelloWorld`:

```
public class HelloWorld {
```

The words `public` and `class` are *reserved* words. You don't need to know their meaning right now, but on a very basic level, they indicate this class's accessibility from other classes. `HelloWorld`, the name of this program, follows them. Remember that the name of the program is case sensitive and must exactly match the part of the source code filename that precedes the `.java` extension. The open curly brace (`{`) indicates that the code that follows it belongs to the `HelloWorld` class. For every open curly brace you have in a Java program, there must be a corresponding closing curly brace (`}`). The very last line of `HelloWorld.java` is the closing curly brace that corresponds to the one that follows the class declaration. Everything that you see between the opening and closing curly braces belongs to the `HelloWorld` class.

Two lines below the class declaration, the `main()` method begins:

```
public static void main(String args[]) {
```

Don't worry about the words `public static void` at this point. They're just more keywords that we'll get to eventually. `main` is the name of the method that drives the `HelloWorld` program. Actually, every standalone Java application needs a `main()` method to drive it. The `main()` method is the entry point for the JVM. It is where you list the steps that the computer must follow to execute Java programs. The part in parentheses that comes after `main`, (`String args[]`), is a way that you can pass information, called *arguments*, into the program from the command line. We didn't use it here, and you haven't learned about arrays or variables yet, so that's another thing we'll just have to put off until tomorrow. Tonight, I'm just getting you up and running. Another significant part of the `main()` method declaration is the open curly brace. Similar to the class's open curly brace, this one indicates that everything between it and the corresponding closing curly brace three lines below belongs to the `main()` method. The line immediately following the `main()` method declaration is just a single-line comment. The following line is the line that tells your computer to print "Hello, World!" to the screen:

```
System.out.println("Hello, World!");
```

This entire line constitutes one Java statement. Every Java statement must end with a semicolon (;). If you leave it out, the compiler will yell at you. Figure 1.4 shows what happens when you forget the semicolon. With the semicolon intact, the statement gets your system's output stream and tells it to print "Hello, World!" as one line of output. Anything that you put in between the quotation marks in this statement will be printed. Go ahead and see if you can get it to print something different. Just edit the source code and replace `Hello, World!` with whatever you want to print. Another thing you can try is getting your program to print more than one line. Just copy the entire statement, `System.out.println("Hello, World!");` and paste a second copy of the line below the original, change the text to whatever you want, recompile it, and then run it. If you can do all of this, then you're up to speed and right where you need to be in terms of understanding this chapter.

Figure 1.4

The compiler tells you that it expects a semicolon after your Java statement.

Introduction to Applets

So, you've written a standalone program. What else can Java do? Well, a lot of things, actually. Another major Java use covered in this book is Java *applets*. Java applets are Java programs that run inside another application, such as a Web browser, instead of on their own. In this section, you'll write a simple applet and see what it looks like running inside your Web browser.

What Is an Applet?

As I mentioned, a Java applet is a Java program that is run by Web browsers, such as Microsoft Internet Explorer or Netscape Navigator. Browsers that support Java include their own Java Runtime Environment (JRE) or have plug-ins that can interpret Java applets. Applets are typically embedded within a Web page and are usually some sort of graphical user interface (GUI) that has buttons, textfields, and so on that provide a user with some way of entering and manipulating data. Applets can also be games or anything else that a Java program can be. There are, however, security restrictions. Applets can't access a computer's local file system. This prevents hackers from doing nasty things to your computer when you visit their Web pages. Sunday morning, I'll go over applets in detail. Right now, I'll just give you an introduction so that you'll have an idea about how to write a simple applet.

Writing a Simple Applet

Now that you're clued in to what an applet is, you're going to write one. Writing the source code is a breeze. Just follow the same process you used to write `HelloWorld`. Open your editor and create a new file named `HelloWeb.java`. As always, it's important that you're careful when copying the source code. Make sure that you don't make any mistakes. It's hard to debug your code when you're not that familiar with Java. Look closely at the source code listing and make sure that you can clearly make out all the characters. Here is the source code listing for `HelloWeb.java`:

```
import java.awt.Graphics;
import java.applet.Applet;
```

```
public class HelloWeb extends Applet {

    public void paint(Graphics g) {
        g.drawString("Hello, Web!", 100, 50);
    }

}
```

After you type and save the source code, you're ready to compile it. Again, you do this exactly as you did for HelloWorld, except that you specify the HelloWeb.java file instead of HelloWorld.java:

```
javac HelloWeb.java
```

Now things start to differ from your first program. Once everything's compiled, you're still not ready to go, unlike the way things worked with HelloWorld. Figure 1.5 shows what happens if you try to run this applet as though it is an application. The JVM is looking for a main() method so that it can run your program as an application. Since there is no such method, you'll get an error message.

In order to run your applet, you need to include it in a Web page. The Web browser runs the Applet for you.

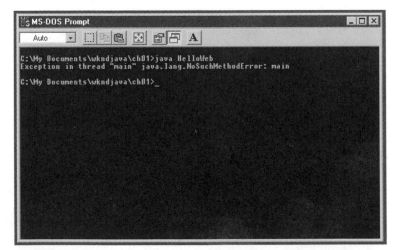

Figure 1.5

You cannot run HelloWeb using the java command.

Writing the HTML

Now you need to create a Web page so that your Web browser can run the HelloWeb applet. If you're not familiar with HTML (*hypertext markup language*), trust me when I say that it's not as complicated as it might sound. On the other hand, if you already know some HTML, you understand that this is actually very easy to do. You don't need to know HTML at all to read this book; you can just blindly copy the source code if you want, but I will explain the HTML source code anyway. HTML is a simple language that is used to create Web pages. HTML gives you a set of *tags* that you can use to specify certain formatting attributes for different parts of Web pages. For example, to make text bold, you use the `<b>` tag:

```
This is how you make <b>bold</b> text.
```

Like many other tags, the `<b>` tag has an opening tag and a closing tag. Closing tags look just like opening tags with the addition of the slash in front of the tag name. Only the text between `<b>` and `</b>` is bold. Here, just the word "bold" is bold. HTML provides the `<applet>` tag, which you can use to embed an applet within a Web page. To do so, open your editor, type the following `helloweb.html` source code and then save it.

```
<html>
<body>
<h1 align="center">HelloWeb Applet</h1>
<center>

<applet code="HelloWeb.class" width=250 height=100>
Your browser does not support Java Applets.
</applet>

</center>
</body>
</html>
```

The source code starts with the `<html>` tag, which just indicates that this document is in HTML format, rather than some other format such as XML or whatever. The content of your Web page must fall between the opening `<html>` tag and its corresponding closing `</html>` tag, which is the last line of `helloweb.html`. The `<body>` and `</body>` tags contain the body of the Web page, which is the main displayable content. Next comes the `<h1>` tag, which is used for text headings. The `<center>` tag does just what you'd think; it aligns content in the center of the Web page. The most significant HTML tag in this example is the `<applet>` tag, which is what actually pulls the applet into the Web page. I used three *attributes* in the `<applet>` tag. HTML tag attributes enable you to specify how a Web browser interprets the tags. Here, the `code` attribute specifies the name of the Java class that defines the applet, `HelloWeb.class`. The `width` and `height` attributes specify the width and height of the applet in pixels. The area in between the opening and closing `<applet>` tags can be used to display information in browsers that do not support Java applets. Browsers that do support applets ignore text entered here, but browsers that do not support Java blindly display it. Both of the major Web browsers, Internet Explorer and Navigator, support Java.

Running the Applet

Now you're ready to run the applet. In this section, I'll show you how to run it in two different ways. First, I'll show you how to run the applet using your Web browser, and then I'll show you how to run it using the appletviewer tool, which is included in your Java SDK installation. To run the applet in your Web browser, browse to the place you saved the `helloweb.html` file and double-click on the icon associated with that file. If you're using Windows and you have Internet Explorer, you can save yourself a second or two by typing the following command at the command prompt:

```
explorer helloweb.html
```

Figure 1.6 shows how the applet looks when it's running in Internet Explorer.

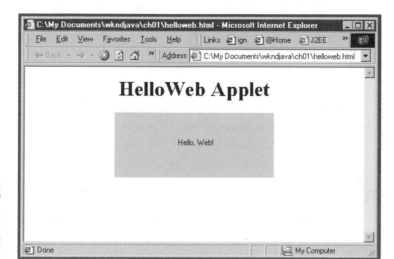

Figure 1.6

Applets run within Web browsers such as Microsoft Internet Explorer.

You don't have to have a Web browser to test your Java applets. The Java SDK includes a tool, appletviewer, that can run applets outside a Web browser. The appletviewer tool takes an HTML document as an argument, so the syntax for using it is

```
appletviewer HTMLDocument.html
```

Replace HTMLDocument with the actual name of the HTML document. The HTML document must have tags in it that reference an applet like helloweb.html does. The appletviewer tool searches the HTML document for references to applets and runs each applet in its own window. To run HelloWeb using appletviewer, enter the following command:

```
appletviewer helloweb.html
```

The Applet Viewer window will pop up and display "Hello, Web!" just like the browser did. The only difference is that appletviewer displays only the applet and none of the other HTML. Did you notice that the "HelloWeb Applet" heading didn't show up even though it was included in the HTML? Well, now you know why. The appletviewer tool is not meant to replace your Web browser, only to test run applets. Figure 1.7 illustrates the way appletviewer looks when it is running the HelloWeb applet. Sweet! You've run your first Java applet.

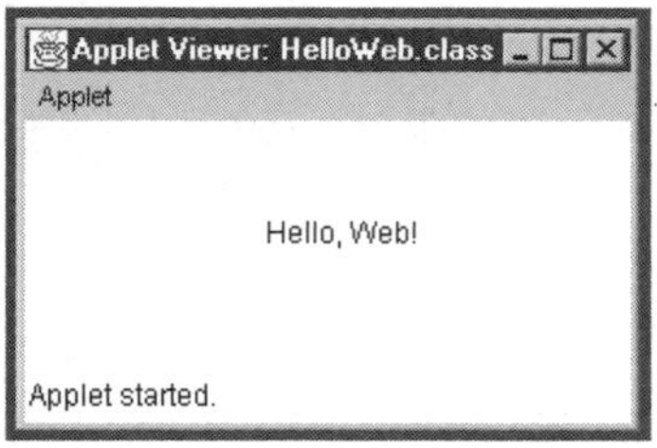

Figure 1.7

Use the appletviewer tool to quickly test your applets independent of a Web browser.

```
Applet Viewer: HelloWeb.class
Applet

                    Hello, Web!


Applet started.
```

Wrapping Up

Tonight, you accomplished more than you may think. Although you've written only two simple programs so far, it took a lot to get there. First, you learned what Java is, which prepared you to get going. Then you installed the SDK, which is a formidable task by itself. The most common problem Java *newbies* come across is installing the SDK and properly setting up their environment. Congratulations for getting this far! Getting your first two programs running is very significant as well, even if you don't completely understand them yet. Unfortunately, or fortunately, depending on your perspective, even the simplest Java programs have a lot to them. It's not that they're overflowing with code, but there is a lot to them conceptually. You'll be learning these concepts throughout the rest of this book. You'll also be using what you have already learned.

Tomorrow morning, you're going to dive deeper into the Java language. You'll learn about data types and variables. You'll also learn about arrays and methods. Tomorrow, I'll also go over one of the most important concepts in Java, object-oriented programming. I gave you a brief introduction to it in this chapter, but tomorrow you'll learn much more about the topic. If you're following the book's implied schedule, make sure that you get a good night's sleep. *Good night.*

Learning the Basics of Java Programming

- ➤ Learning about Data Types and Using Variables
- ➤ Using Arrays
- ➤ Learning about Methods
- ➤ Object-Oriented Programming

Good morning! It's Saturday morning, and you're going to learn the basics of Java programming. This morning I'm assuming that you're okay with creating Java source code, compiling it, and running it. Before proceeding, make sure that you remember what you did last night and have a pretty good understanding of it all. Of course, if at any point you find that you have forgotten something, such as how to compile your code, you can refer back to last night's session. It all works the same—just the class names and, therefore the filenames, are different. The compile and run commands work the same way. So, if you were able to complete last night's session, that means you also were able to install the Java SDK and that you should be ready to learn some real Java programming.

In this session, you're going to learn the real basics of Java programming. To start off, I'll introduce you to primitive data types. Primitive data are simple bits of information, such as numbers, characters, and Booleans. Specific types of primitive data, such as integers, long integers, floating-point values, and double floating-point values, are called *primitive data types*. Next, you'll learn about variables, which are Java's way of storing values. You'll also learn how to perform mathematical operations. After that, you'll learn how to store multiple values, actually a list of values, in a single variable with arrays. You'll then move on to learn about methods, which you use to perform specialized functions. Finally, you'll learn more about object-oriented programming, which is very important in the world of Java programming.

Learning about Data Types and Using Variables

For any program to be useful, it must be able to store and manipulate data. After all, that is the only reason you'd ever want to write a program, right? To put yourself in the right mindset, think of an ATM (*automatic teller machine*). When you want to withdraw money from your checking account to go out on a Friday night, you go to the ATM and get your cash. When you put your card in, the ATM reads your account number, but it needs some way to remember your account number throughout the transaction, so the ATM program stores it in a variable. Once it authenticates that you are who you say you are by asking you for your PIN number and crosschecking it with the bank's database, it asks you what you want to do. You tell the ATM that you want to withdraw money from your checking account. The ATM accesses your checking account data. It then asks you how much you need. You're only going to the movies and out for a drink, so forty dollars should do, but you decide to take out sixty dollars just in case. The ATM checks your balance data. Do you have enough dough in there to cover it? Of course you do, so it decrements your checking account balance, stores your new balance in the bank's database, spits out your cash, and thanks you for your business. So you see, you get the money that you need because the ATM program processed some data. That's what all programs do.

Primitive Data Types

Java programs are no different than programs written in any other language in that they all need to work with data to be of any use. There are basically two major categories of data in Java—*primitive data types* and *object references*. In this section, you'll learn about primitive data types. (You'll learn about object references later this morning.) Primitive data types are specific types of data that can easily be stored by a computer. To simplify this idea, think of a primitive data type as something as simple as a number. A single, specific number takes up a specific amount of memory in a computer. That specific number is very simple for the computer to store and use directly. Something more complex, such as a video game program, is not a simple, small piece of data, but more like a huge collection of small pieces of data. These small pieces of data are primitive data types. They're just numbers, characters, and Boolean values that the computer accesses directly.

Java has eight primitive data types. They are `byte`, `short`, `int`, `long`, `float`, `double`, `char`, and `boolean`. Whenever you need to process a piece of data in your Java program, you need to specify what type it is. The first four primitive data types that I listed (`byte`, `short`, `int`, and `long`) are types of integers. Integers are whole numbers such as `1`, `2002`, and `-33`. They don't have a fractional portion. They are listed in order by size, smallest to largest. The two real number (floating-point) data types are `float` and `double`. They are also listed in order from left to right by size. Real numbers have a fractional portion. Some examples are `98.6`, `0.007`, and `-1.0`. The `char` primitive data type is for character data. When you open a text editor, anything you can type into it is a character. For example, `'a'`, `'&'`, and `'5'` are all characters. Note that I included the number `'5'` as a character. Isn't that a number? Well, when you type it into your text editor, it's interpreted as a character, just like letters, symbols, punctuation, spaces, and carriage returns. The `boolean` type is for true and false values. Any Boolean value is either `true` or `false`, and nothing else. Refer to Table 2.1 for a convenient listing of all the primitive data types.

Computers see all information as a series of binary magnetic *bits* that are either *on* or *off*, (`0` or `1`). When you need to process a piece of data in a program, you have to specify what type it is because the computer needs to know how much memory to allocate for that piece of data. For example, if you need to use an `int`, by looking at Table 2.1, you'll see that Java uses 32 bits to store it.

TABLE 2.1 PRIMITIVE DATA TYPES

Data Type	Description	Size	Range
Byte	Byte-size integer	8-bit	-2^7 to $2^7 - 1$
short	Short integer	16-bit	-2^{15} to $2^{15} - 1$
int	Integer	32-bit	-2^{31} to $2^{31} - 1$
long	Long integer	64-bit	-2^{63} to $2^{63} - 1$
char	Character	16-bit	0 to $2^{16} - 1$
boolean	True or false	1-bit	N/A
float	Single-precision floating point	32-bit	N/A
double	Double-precision floating point	64-bit	N/A

Note: The range for boolean is not applicable because the value must be either true or false. The ranges for float and double are not applicable because the confusing details as to how the computer stores these is beyond the scope of this book.

Expressing Literals

You use *literals* to express specific data values. A literal stands for itself, meaning that what you type is what you get. A literal does not represent anything else, such as a function or variable. It is a specific value that you express literally by using that value directly. For example, if you express the number 1 as a literal, the computer sees that as the value 1, which is exactly what you would type in your program. Literals aren't just for integers. There are ways of expressing literals for each of the eight primitive data types, as well as for character strings. For a listing of some literal expressions and their corresponding data types, see Table 2.2.

TABLE 2.2 EXAMPLES OF LITERAL EXPRESSIONS	
Literal Expression	Data Type
27	int
033	int (octal)
0x1B	int (hexadecimal)
27L	long
27.0	double
27.0D	double
27.0e3	double
27.0F	float
'@'	char
'\n'	char
'\u003F'	char
true	boolean
false	boolean
null	null

As you can see in Table 2.2, some of the numerical literals contain both letters and numbers. There is a good reason for those letters being there. The letters are used to express data types for literals that would otherwise be ambiguous. For example, if you type the number 27, you know that it's an integer, but how does the computer know how much memory to allocate for it. Is it an `int`? Is it a `long`? The default data type for unspecified integer literals is the smallest data type that fits the value. So, if you want to express a long literal, you have to specify that fact by suffixing the number with the letter L. 27 is an `int`, but `27L` is a `long`. Similarly, the default data type for floating point numbers is `double`, so if you need to specify a literal as being a `float`, you have to suffix the literal with the letter F. 27.0 is a `double`, but `27.0F` is a `float`. Also, integers can be expressed in octal or hexadecimal notation. If you don't know what this means, that's okay, because you'll hardly ever see it, if at all.

I'll explain hexadecimal and octal numbers briefly here, but to really understand this, you should refer to a computer science text that covers binary mathematics. Our normal decimal number system is based on the number 10. Basically, octal and hexadecimal notations are ways of expressing integers using bases that are powers of 2. Octal is base 8 (it uses digits 0 through 7), and hexadecimal is base 16 (it uses digits 0 through F, where A=10, B=11, C=12, D=13, E=14, and F=15). In Java, octal integers are expressed by prefixing the literal with a zero (0). For example, `033` is the octal number 33 (which in our familiar decimal notation is 27). Hexadecimal numbers are expressed by prefixing the number with zero, followed by x (0x). For example, `0x1B` is the octal number 1B (which is also 27 in decimal notation). *hex*

CAUTION

◆◆◆

Be careful when expressing `long` primitive data type literals. The lowercase letter l can easily be mistaken for the number 1, especially when it immediately follows a bunch of numbers. For example, the number 11, when expressed as a `long` literal using a lowercase l is `11l`. It looks like `111`, doesn't it? Using the lowercase l makes it harder to read the source code. You can fix this problem by using an uppercase L instead. `11L` wouldn't be confused with `111`. Try to remember to use uppercase letters when expressing `long` primitive data type literals.

◆◆◆

Character literals are expressed by enclosing the character within single quotes. For example, `'B'` is the character literal for the letter B. The data type for character literals is `char`. To be a valid `char` literal, only a single character or an escape code can appear within the opening and closing single quotes. For example, `'goat'` is not a valid character literal, and the Java compiler won't know what you mean if you try to use it. Because some characters can cause the compiler to be confused if they are typed in directly, we use *character escape codes* as a special way of expressing those confusing characters. For example, say that you wanted to change the `HelloWorld` program you created last night so that it would print `"Hello, "World"!"` including the quotation marks around `"World"`. You couldn't do it this way:

```
System.out.println("Hello, "World"!");
```

Recall that this is the line that tells the computer what to print, and it will print anything that appears within the opening and closing double quotes. Here, you can see how the compiler could get confused and not know exactly where the quotation opens and closes. It would correctly interpret the very first quotation mark as the opening quotation mark, but it would see the second one as the closing quotation mark, rather than as part of the quotation as you intended. Instead, you'd need to use the character escape code for double quotes (`'\"'`) to tell the compiler that you want the double quotes to be interpreted literally as characters rather than interpreting them as Java code that opens and closes character string data. This is how you'd do it:

```
System.out.println("Hello, \"World\"!");
```

Refer to Table 2.3 for a listing of character escape codes and a description of the way Java interprets them.

Character literals can also be expressed as Unicode characters. Actually, all Java characters are Unicode characters. Unicode is a specification for

TABLE 2.3 CHARACTER ESCAPE CODES	
Escape Code Literal	**Description**
`'\''`	Single quotation mark
`'\"'`	Double quotation mark
`'\b'`	Backspace
`'\f'`	Form feed (page break)
`'\n'`	Newline
`'\r'`	Carriage return
`'\t'`	Tab
`'\\'`	Backslash

character representation in which every character has a unique numerical code. The syntax for a Unicode character literal is

`'\uNNNN'`

Use the \u prefix and follow it with a four-digit hexadecimal representation of the unique number that corresponds to the desired character. The Unicode specification is beyond the scope of this book, but I included the syntax here so that you'll be familiar with it and recognize it if you ever see it in a Java program, or if you ever need to know how to specify Unicode characters in your own Java code.

 NOTE For more information about Unicode, visit http://www.unicode.org.

Boolean literals are self-explanatory. Booleans can only be true or false. The literal expressions `true` and `false` are always of the `boolean` primitive data type. The `null` literal is not any specific data type. It is assigned to object reference variables, which are described later this morning. Basically, `null` is used to make object reference variables not refer to any actual object.

Understanding Strings

You've learned about all of the eight different primitive data types that are used in Java, so now it's time to tackle strings. Strings are not primitive data types, though at times Java syntax seems to treat them like primitives. `string` is a Java class and any `string` instance is a Java object, not primitive data. We'll get back to that later this morning. For now, you just need to understand what a character string is. Basically, a string consists of a sequence of characters, known as a *character string*. You express a Java `string` literal by enclosing zero or more characters within double quotes. A few examples follow:

```
"Hello, World!"
"123"
 "\n\n"
"  "
""
```

You should recognize the first example. You used that `string` literal in the `HelloWorld` program. The second example demonstrates that a sequence of numbers can be interpreted as a character string. Each *digit* is interpreted as a *character*, not a number. You can also use character escape codes, as demonstrated in the third example. The last two examples show the difference between a space character and the empty string. A space *does* count as a character, even though you can't see it. You express the empty string by opening and closing the double quotes without putting any characters between them, so it is possible to have a string of zero characters.

TIP

■ ■

A neat thing about Java `strings` is that you can add them together to create bigger Java `strings` with the plus symbol (+).

```
"Happy" + " New " + "Year!"
```

The preceding code adds the three `strings`, `"Happy"`, `" New "`, and `"Year!"` together to create a new `String`, `"Happy New Year!"`. Actually, you can add any data type to a `String` literal, and the result will be interpreted as a `String`.

```
"The year is" + 2002
```

This creates a new string, even though the number 2002 isn't enclosed in quotation marks. Java interprets anything that's added to a `String` literal as if it were itself a Java `String` literal. The preceding code creates a new Java `String`: `"The year is 2002"`.

You can add the empty string to a primitive data type to convert it to a `String`, like this:

```
5 + ""
```

The result of this operation is the `String` value, `"5"`.

■ ■

Declaring and Using Variables

Now that you've got primitive data types and `string` literals down pat, you're ready to take the next step and learn how to store them in variables. *Variables* are containers that hold specific types of data. Variables can contain primitive data types as well as object references. When you declare (create) a variable, you must specify what data type it can contain and give the variable a name. Also, you must end the statement with a semicolon. The syntax for declaring a variable is as follows:

```
data_type variable_name;
```

The data type can be any one of the eight primitive data types, or, as you'll see later, it can be any class name. Let's create an `int` variable named `myInt`:

```
int myInt;
```

After you declare `myInt` to be an `int`, you can start assigning `int` values to it. The equal sign (=) is the assignment operator. To assign a value to a variable, the variable name must go to the left of the assignment operator, and the value goes to the right side. To assign 2 to `myInt`, you do this:

```
myInt = 2;
```

You can actually take a shortcut by declaring a variable and initializing its value on a single line of code:

```
int myInt = 2;
```

● ●

There are specific syntax rules that you need to follow when naming variables. Java variables can start with any letter, an underscore (_), or a dollar sign ($) and can be followed by any letter or number, an underscore, or a dollar sign. A variable name cannot contain any spaces or any of the following characters:

```
#%&'()*+,-./:;<=>?@[\]`{|}~
```

Also, by convention, variables start with lowercase letters, and new words begin with uppercase letters, as the following shows:

```
thisIsAnExample
```

● ●

Now, here is an example program, called `VariableTest`, that you can write, compile, and run for yourself so that you can get a better feel for using variables. The source code for `VariableTest.java` is as follows:

```
/*
 * VariableTest
 * Demonstrates how to declare and access variables
 */


public class VariableTest {
```

```
public static void main(String args[]) {
    //Declare an int variable
    int age;
    age = 242;
    System.out.println("Age = " + age);

    //Declare a double variable and assign a value
    double ounces = 11.2;
    System.out.println("ounces = " + ounces);

    //Declare some String variables
    String name = "Guinness",
           origin = "Ireland",
           brewery;
    System.out.println("name = " + name);
    System.out.println("origin = " + origin);
    brewery = "St. James Gate Brewery";
    System.out.println("brewery = " + brewery);

    //Assign a value of one variable to another
    int yearsOld = age;
    System.out.println("yearsOld = " + yearsOld);

    //Declare a boolean variable and assign a value to it
    boolean tastesGood = true;
    System.out.println("tastesGood = " + tastesGood);
}

}
```

In `VariableTest`, I just declared some variables, assigned some values to them, and printed their values to standard output. Recall that Java `String` class literals can be added together to create bigger `String` literals. Recall from last night that you can print `String` values to standard output using the `System.out.println()` method. The line

```
System.out.println("Age = " + age);
```

just prints "`Age = `" followed by the value of `age`. I did that for all of the variables. You should also notice that I declared some `String` variables. You do this exactly the same way that you declare variables of primitive data types. Actually, I declared multiple `String` variables in a single statement:

```
String name = "Guinness",
                origin = "Ireland",
                brewery;
```

You can do this for any variable type; just specify the data type and then specify each variable separated by commas. After the last variable, you need to use a semicolon. You can optionally initialize each variable as well, as I did for `name` and `origin`, but not `brewery`. You can see the output for this program in Figure 2.1.

The data that a variable contains can vary—which is why they are called variables—but the data type cannot vary. A variable that holds `int`s, can hold only `int`s, and nothing else. You can store the value of a smaller data type, such as a `byte` or `short`, but it is converted to an `int` automatically. You can't assign a value of a larger data type such as `long` to an `int` variable, because it literally won't fit; 64 bits of data can't be crammed into a 32-bit area of memory. The Java compiler won't let you do this. However, there are ways around this with data type *casting*. Casting is the act of explicitly changing the data type of some value to another data type. The syntax for casting is

```
(new_data_type) value
```

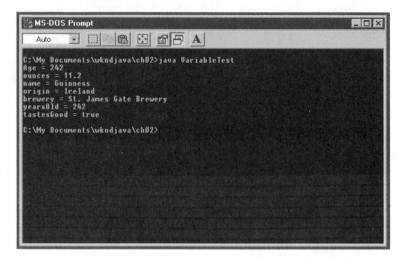

Figure 2.1

The
`VariableTest`
program prints the
values of different
types of variables.

You specify the new data type in parentheses and place it in front of the value you want to cast. For example, you might create a `long` and assign a small number, such as 10, to it.

```
long longInt = 10;
```

You, as the programmer, know that the value 10 can fit in an `int` variable. Elsewhere in your program you might want to assign the value of `longInt` to an `int` variable. You must explicitly cast it to an `int`. Here's how you do that:

```
int myInt = (int) longInt;
```

This code takes the value of `longInt` and converts it to an `int` by discarding the extra 32 bits and storing the resulting value in `myInt`. If you don't explicitly cast it and use, for example, the following code instead, the compiler will yell at you:

```
int myInt = longInt;
```

If this happens, you'll get a message similar to the following:

```
Incompatible type for declaration. Explicit cast
    needed to convert long to int.
```

Make sure that when you cast values of larger data types to smaller data types you don't corrupt your data. If you cast a number that is too large to fit into the space allocated for the smaller data type, your data can become garbage. As an example, what do you think the value of myByte should be after this snippet of code executes?

```
int myInt = 242;
byte myByte = (byte) myInt;
```

I'll give you a hint. It's not 242. The byte data type can hold values ranging only from -128 to 127; 242 is just too big to fit. Without going into the details of how computers interpret binary integers using two's complement, I'll just tell you that the computer gets confused and interprets the value as -14, not 242. Keep this in mind when you're casting data types.

When you assign a floating point literal to a float, you must make sure that you're assigning a float literal rather than a double literal. Sometimes this can be misleading. The following code won't compile:

```
float f = 1.0;
```

Java interprets the literal 1.0 as a double, not a float. If you try to compile your code with this line in it, you'll get an error message indicating that you can't convert a double to a float without an explicit cast. Instead you must either explicitly cast the double to a float:

```
float f = (float) 1.0;
```

Or you need to specify that you're using a float literal by using the letter F notation that you learned earlier:

```
float f = 1.0F;
```

Performing Mathematical Operations

Java provides mathematical operators that you can use to perform simple numeric mathematical operations. The five operators are used for addition, subtraction, multiplication, division, and modulus operations. (Refer to Table 2.4 for a listing of these operations and some examples.) The remainder of this section goes over each of these operators in more detail, introduces other operators, and explains operator precedence.

The addition operator (+) is used to add two numbers together. As you can see in Table 2.4, adding the integers 20 and 15 together results in the value 35. The subtraction operator (-) subtracts the second number from the first number, as you would expect. Subtracting the integer 15 from 20 results in the value 5. Multiplication also works exactly as you'd expect it. Multiplying the two integers 20 and 15 together results in the value 300. Java uses the asterisk (*) as the multiplication operator. Division can sometimes be confusing when applied to integers. The result of an integer division operation is always an integer, so the remainder is truncated, not rounded to the nearest integer. Although you learned in math class that 20 divided by 15 is 1 and ⅓, the result in Java is 1. The extra one-third is discarded. Similarly, if the result of an integer division operation is technically

TABLE 2.4 MATHEMATICAL OPERATORS			
Operator	**Description**	**Example**	**Result**
+	Addition	20 + 15	35
–	Subtraction	20 - 15	5
*	Multiplication	20 * 15	300
/	Division	20 / 15	1
%	Modulus (remainder after division)	20 % 15	5

1.99999, the result in Java would still just be 1. It wouldn't round the value to 2. On the other hand, if you were performing the division operation on real numbers, such as floats or doubles, the fractional portion would be retained. The modulus operator is the percent symbol (%). The result of a modulus operation is the remainder after a division operation. So, when you divide 20 by 15, the result is 1, with a remainder of 5. Because the result of a modulus operator is the remainder, the result of the modulus operation 20 mod 15 is 5. The SimpleMathTest program demonstrates these five operations.

```
/*
 * SimpleMathTest
 * Performs simple mathematical operations on integer and
 * double operands
 */


public class SimpleMathTest {

    public static void main(String args[]) {
        int x = 10,
            y = 7;
        //be careful not to confuse math operators with string
        //operators
        System.out.println(x + " + " + y + " = " + (x + y));
        System.out.println(x + " - " + y + " = " + (x - y));
        System.out.println(x + " * " + y + " = " + (x * y));
        System.out.println(x + " / " + y + " = " + (x / y));
        System.out.println(x + " % " + y + " = " + (x % y));

        //would be more readable with explicit casting
        //i.e. double a = (double) x, b = (double) y;
```

```
double a = x,
       b = y;
System.out.println(a + " + " + b + " = " + (a + b));
System.out.println(a + " - " + b + " = " + (a - b));
System.out.println(a + " * " + b + " = " + (a * b));
System.out.println(a + " / " + b + " = " + (a / b));
System.out.println(a + " % " + b + " = " + (a % b));

//emphasizes that floating point modulus ops can
//result in real numbers
System.out.println("1.1 % 1.0 = " + (1.1 % 1.0));
    }

}
```

This program declares two int variables, x and y. It assigns the values 10 and 7 (respectively) to these variables. Then it proceeds to perform addition, subtraction, multiplication, division, and modulus operations on them and prints the results, which you can see in Figure 2.2.

There are also two other operators that are used as shortcuts for adding and subtracting 1 from a variable. They are called the increment operator (++) and the decrement operator (--). The increment operator adds 1 to the variable on which it is used and then assigns the incremented value to the variable. For example, this code adds 1 to x:

```
x++; //same as x = x + 1
```

If the value of x was 1 before the operation took place, then after the operation, the value will be 2. The comment just lets you know that x++ causes the same result as x = x + 1. The decrement operator subtracts 1 from the variable on which it is used and assigns that value to the variable. For example, this code subtracts 1 from x:

```
x--; //same as x = x - 1
```

Figure 2.2

The result of the modulus operation is not exactly 0.1 because computers can't store real numbers with absolute precision, so there is always a minute margin of error.

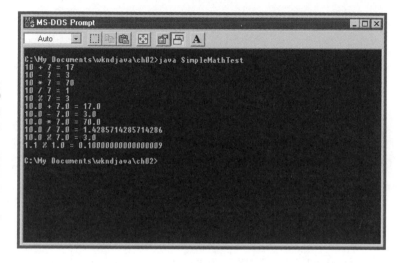

```
MS-DOS Prompt
Auto

C:\My Documents\wkndjava\ch02>java SimpleMathTest
10 + 7 = 17
10 - 7 = 3
10 * 7 = 70
10 / 7 = 1
10 % 7 = 3
10.0 + 7.0 = 17.0
10.0 - 7.0 = 3.0
10.0 * 7.0 = 70.0
10.0 / 7.0 = 1.4285714285714286
10.0 % 7.0 = 3.0
1.1 % 1.0 = 0.10000000000000009

C:\My Documents\wkndjava\ch02>
```

If the value of x was 1 before the operation, then the decrement operation causes the value of x to become 0.

The increment and decrement operators can be used after the variable (postfix), as in the previous examples, but they can also be used in front of them (prefix). For example, this code also adds 1 to x and x stores that new value:

```
++x; //same as x = x + 1
```

On the surface, prefix and postfix seem to be identical, but there is an important difference in the way they work. Prefix increment and decrement operations are evaluated *before* any other assignments or operations are performed, while postfix increment and decrement operations are evaluated *after* any other assignments or operations are performed. Two examples should help here. After the following code executes, the value of both x and y is 2:

```
int x = 1, y;
y = ++x;
```

The reason for this is that x is incremented to 2 *before* the value is assigned to y. However, after this next bit of code executes, the value of y is 1 and the value of x is 2.

```
int x = 1, y;
y = x++;
```

The reason is that x is not incremented until after y gets its value. Because x is 1, y gets that value, afterward x is incremented to 2.

There are also some other shortcuts for assignment and math operations. The five shortcuts that correspond to the five mathematical operations are +=, -=, *=, /=, and %=. The syntax for these operators is as follows (replace *<op>* with the operation to be performed—that is, +, -, *, /, or %):

```
variable <op>= value;
```

The result of this is the same as

```
variable = variable <op> value;
```

Here are some examples with in-line comment explanations:

```
int y = 10;
y += 3; //result y = 13; same as y = y + 3
y = 10 ;
y -= 3; //result y = 7; same as y = y - 3
y = 10;
y *= 2; //result y = 20; same as y = y * 2
y = 10;
y /= 2; //result y = 5; same as y = y / 2
y = 10;
y % = 3; //result y = 1; same as y = y % 3
```

When performing mathematical operations in Java, it's also important to understand operator precedence. Generally, mathematical operations are performed from left to right, but Java will perform operations with higher precedence first. Multiplication, division, and modulus operations take precedence over addition and subtraction, as illustrated here:

```
int x = 10 - 4 + 14 / 2;
```

The value of x after this code is evaluated is 13. If operator precedence didn't play its part and operations were done strictly left to right, then the value of x would be 10 (10 - 4 = 6; 6 + 14 = 20; 20 / 2 = 10). But, because division takes place before subtraction and addition, Java evaluates 14 / 2 = 7 first and then performs 10 - 4 + 7 from left to right, (subtraction and addition have the same precedence), resulting in 13. You're not stuck with this, however. You can tell Java how to evaluate your expressions via parentheses. If you've ever taken an algebra class, you should be familiar with the way parentheses are used in mathematical operations. Placing parentheses around parts of an expression changes the precedence of the expression within the parentheses. All things within parentheses are treated as one unit and evaluated before operations outside the parentheses are performed. For example, the following code results in x being assigned the value 10:

```
int x = (10 - 4 + 14) / 2;
```

The parentheses tell Java to evaluate 10 - 4 + 14 before dividing 2. It's like saying "divide the value of the entire expression 10 - 4 + 14 by 2." See if you can figure out the value of x after the following code executes and then read on to see if you're right.

```
int x = 10 - (4 + 14 / 2);
```

The preceding example says, "Take the value of the expression 4 + 14 / 2 and subtract it from 10." Remember that division takes precedence over addition, so 14 / 2 = 7 is done first, then 7 is added to 4, which is 11. Then 10 - 11 is evaluated, and the result is -1. If you came up with -1, give yourself a pat on the back.

Using Arrays

An *array* is a variable that stores not only one value but also a list of variables, as long as every value in the list is of the same data type. Using an array is convenient in instances where you need to maintain a set of similar data. For example, you might have an array that you use to store a list of CDs that you own. Instead of creating a separate variable for each of your CDs, you need to create only one variable that stores them all. As you'll see this afternoon when I go over loops, operations such as listing all of your CDs are easy if they're stored together in an array.

Declaring Arrays

Declaring arrays is very similar to declaring variables of primitive data types. The only noticeable difference between the two is the use of square brackets ([and]). For example, to declare an array of ints named myArray, you do the following:

```
int[] myArray;
```

The square brackets follow the data type. Any value that you add to myArray must be an int. You can also put the square brackets after the variable name, like this:

```
int myArray[];
```

Both of these declarations declare an array of integers named myArray; there is no difference between the two.

Initializing Arrays

You can declare an array and initialize its values in a single Java statement. The syntax for this is as follows:

```
data_type[] array_name
    = { value_0, value_1, value_2, [el], value_n };
```

Declare the array by specifying the data type and the array name (don't forget the square brackets) and then assign it a list of values. The list of values is a comma-delimited list of values that have the same data type as the array specifies. This list goes between opening and closing curly braces. The number of items in the list determines the length of the array. If you put 10 items in the list to initialize the array, the length of the array will be 10. Once an array's size has been set, it can never be changed because Java allocates the correct amount of memory for the array as soon as its size is determined. Here is an example of a declaration of an `int[]` array:

```
int[] list = { 1, 2, 3, 4, 5, 6, 7, 8, 9, 10 };
```

The size of `list` after it is initialized is 10, because I assigned a list of 10 `int`s to it. You can programmatically determine the length of an array by using its length attribute. To access its length attribute, specify the array name, followed by a dot (.), followed by the word `length`:

```
int len = list.length;
```

The value of `len` after this assignment takes place is 10 because the length of `list` is 10.

You can also initialize an array's size before you assign it any values. The syntax to accomplish this is

```
data_type[] array_name = new data_type[array_size];
```

You have to use the `new` keyword to specify that you're creating a new array. After `new`, specify the data type, followed by the size of the array (which must be an integer) within square brackets. To initialize a new `int[]` array of length 10 named `myNewArray`, you do this:

```
int[] myNewArray = new int[10];
```

Or you could do this on two separate lines, like so:

```
int[] myNewArray;
myNewArray = new int[10];
```

When you initialize the size of an array of numbers without initializing any of its values, every value in the array defaults to zero.

Using Array Elements

Each individual value stored in an array is referred to as an array *element*. Each array element is indexed (subscripted) by an integer. It's intuitive to think of each item of a list as having a number associated with it (as a numbered list does), so this shouldn't be too difficult to grasp. The first element of an array is always indexed by the number 0, not 1, so to get the value of the very first element of any array, the syntax is

```
array_name[0]
```

Use the variable name for the array and use square brackets to enclose the index number of the element you're trying to access. Note that the very last element of an array is accessed like so:

```
array_name[array_name.length - 1]
```

The length of an array having 10 elements is of course 10, but the last element is indexed by the number 9. You can also assign values to array elements, one at a time, this way. Here is an example of assigning the values of a `boolean[]` array one at a time by specifying their indices:

```
boolean[] tfList = new boolean[3];
tfList[0] = true;
tfList[1] = false;
tfList[2] = true;
```

I've included the following sample program, called `ArrayTest`, so that you can get a better feel for how to use arrays in Java. Feel free to read over it or even tackle it on your own, if you want the extra help.

```
/*
 * ArrayTest
 * Demonstrates declaring, initializing, and using arrays
 */

public class ArrayTest {

    public static void main(String args[]) {
        //declare an array
        double[] temps;
        //initialize the array size
        temps = new double[3];
        //assign some values to array elements
        temps[0] = 103.2;
        temps[1] = 101.9;
        temps[2] = 98.6;
        //get its length
        System.out.println("temps length: " + temps.length);
        //print out its contents
        System.out.println("values: "
            + "\ntemps[0] " + temps[0]
            + "\ntemps[1] " + temps[1]
            + "\ntemps[2] " + temps[2]);

        //declare and initialize an array in a single
        //statement
        int[] primes = { 1, 2, 3, 5, 7 };
        System.out.println("primes length: " + primes.length);
        System.out.println("values: "
```

```
                    + "\nprimes[0] = " + primes[0]

                    + "\nprimes[1] = " + primes[1]

                    + "\nprimes[2] = " + primes[2]

                    + "\nprimes[3] = " + primes[3]

                    + "\nprimes[4] = " + primes[4]);


        //arrays aren't just for ints and doubles

        byte[] myByteList;

        short[] myShortList;

        long[] myLongList;

        float[] myFloatList;

        boolean[] myBooleanList;

        char[] myCharList;

    }

}
```

You can see the output of this sample program in Figure 2.3. Feel free to try to change the values in your own program. Play around with it! That's the best way to learn new things.

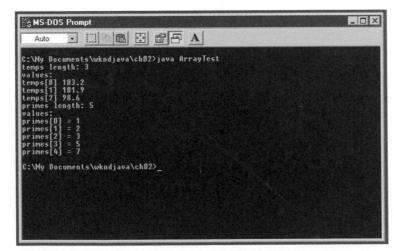

Figure 2.3

`ArrayTest`
sets up two arrays
and then displays
their values to
demonstrate how
Java handles arrays.

Multidimensional Arrays

In Java, *multidimensional arrays* are actually arrays of arrays, or lists of lists. Multidimensional arrays use multiple sets of square brackets. There is one set of brackets per dimension of the array. The following is an example of a two-dimensional array:

```
int[][] table = new int[12][12];
```

The preceding array declares a two-dimensional array of 12 by 12 elements. `table[0]` is an array of 12 elements, `table[1]` is an array of 12 elements, `table[2]` is an array of 12 elements, and so on. There is a way to declare a multidimensional array and initialize its values in a single statement. The following example does just that:

```
char [][] mda = { { 'a', 'b', 'c' }, { 'd' }, { 'e', 'f'} };
```

This example creates a two-dimensional array named mda and initializes its values. Table 2.5 provides the values of this array listed by its indices.

TABLE 2.5 MDA VALUES	
Element	**Value**
mda[0][0]	a
mda[0][1]	b
mda[0][2]	c
mda[1][0]	d
mda[2][0]	e
mda[2][1]	f

As you can see, it is possible for the lengths of each of the secondary arrays to vary. In this example, mda is an array of three arrays. The first array is three elements long, the second array is one element long, and the third array is two elements long. Because a multidimensional array is an array of arrays, you can find out the length of each sub-array. This is best demonstrated as an example and then explained. To get the three different lengths of mda's three sub-arrays, your code should look like this:

```
int len1 = mda[0].length;
int len2 = mda[1].length;
int len3 = mda[2].length;
```

After this snippet of code executes, len1 is three, len2 is one, and len3 is two. The MultidimensionalArrayTest program uses a multidimensional array. For a bit of practice, try writing it yourself and getting it to run. Here is the source code:

```java
/*
 * MultiDimensionalArrayTest
 * Demonstrates how to use multidimensional arrays
 */

public class MultiDimensionalArrayTest {

    public static void main(String args[]) {
        //Declare a multidimensional array
        double[][] grid = new double[2][3];
        //assign some values
        grid[0][0] = 0.0;
        grid[0][1] = 0.1;
        grid[0][2] = 0.2;
        grid[1][0] = 1.0;
        grid[1][1] = 1.1;
```

```
        grid[1][2] = 1.2;


        //Another way to do the same thing
        double[][] grid2 = { { 0.0, 0.1, 0.2 },
                             { 1.0, 1.1, 1.2 } };
        //The proof:
        System.out.println("grid2[0][0] = " + grid2[0][0]);
        System.out.println("grid2[0][1] = " + grid2[0][1]);
        System.out.println("grid2[0][2] = " + grid2[0][2]);
        System.out.println("grid2[1][0] = " + grid2[1][0]);
        System.out.println("grid2[1][1] = " + grid2[1][1]);
        System.out.println("grid2[1][2] = " + grid2[1][2]);
    }
}
```

The `MultidimensionalArrayTest` program declares a two-dimensional
array, `grid[][]`, and assigns values to its elements one at a time. It also
declares a second two-dimensional array and initializes its values in a single
Java statement. I did that to demonstrate that there's more than one way
to accomplish the same task. The second way uses less code, but may be
harder for programmers who are not familiar with that type of multidimensional array initialization. The first method uses more code, but is,
arguably, easier to follow. The output, shown in Figure 2.4, proves that the
values of `grid2[][]` are the same as the values I assigned to `grid[][]`.

Learning about Methods

You've actually already used a method. `System.out.println()` is a
method that prints a string to standard output. *Methods* are a way of iso-
lating Java code that performs a specific function. Put more simply,
methods are lines of Java code that execute when you tell them to execute.

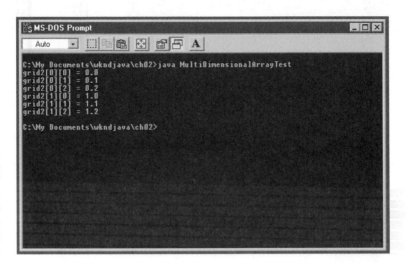

Figure 2.4

This program
demonstrates
how to use
multidimensional
arrays.

Methods also allow for code reuse. For example, you might define a method that adds tax to a retail product purchase and gives you back the total. In Rhode Island, tax is seven cents on the dollar, so the method would incorporate something like this:

```
double total = itemPrice * 1.07;
```

In the preceding example, the code multiplies the item price by 1.07 to get the total cost. Any time you need to calculate the total cost of an item, you just call the method to do the work for you, instead of having to perform the calculation directly each time. This example has only one line of code, so it's not really a big deal—unless you need to change the way tax is calculated. What if the tax rate changes? If you had not defined this method previously, you'd have to search for and update the tax calculation throughout your code. With the method defined, you need to change only the calculation in the method. The rest of your code simply makes calls to the updated method, so no further modification is necessary. That's the general idea of methods and their usefulness. Next, I'll get more specific and show you how to define and call methods.

Declaring Methods

When you *declare* a method, you define its access modifier, its method modifier(s), its return type, its name, any exceptions it might throw, and the method body itself. Modifiers are covered later this morning in the section titled, "Object-Oriented Programming." I'll go over exception handling tomorrow morning. For now, you just need to get the syntax down and understand how to define and call methods. The syntax is

```
access_modifier_opt method_modifiers_opt return_type name(args_opt) {

    method_body;

    return_statement;

}
```

The subscript $_{opt}$ denotes optional components of a method declaration.

In this section, we're going to use the `public` access modifier for our methods. We're also going to use the `static` method modifier. Without going into specifics, I am using `static` just to make it easier to explain how to call a method without having to use object-oriented Java syntax.

You specify the method return type after method modifiers (for example, `public` and `static` are modifiers). The return type of a method is the data type that the method will return after it completes its execution. You can return any primitive data type or object reference. If a method does not return any value, instead of specifying a data type, use the `void` keyword as the return type.

Following the return type, you specify the method name. By convention, method names should be verbs or verb phrases. As with variable names, method names should begin with a lowercase letter and any subsequent word in the method name should have initial capitalization. For example, `calculateTax` would be a good method name. (This is just a programming convention and is in no way required.)

You define any arguments that the method can accept within parentheses placed after the method name. If the method accepts no arguments, you still need the parentheses, like this: *method_name()*. If there is more than one argument, use commas to separate each argument. Arguments are also called *parameters*.

The method body consists of the statements that do the actual work, and they are placed within opening and closing curly braces. If the method returns a value, you need to include a return statement in the method, which is typically the last line in the method. The value that you return must be of the same data type that you define in the method signature (the part that comes before the method body). For example, to declare the addTax() method, you do this:

```java
public static double addTax(double itemPrice) {
    double total = itemPrice * 1.07;
    return total;
}
```

The argument that this method accepts, itemPrice, is actually defined the same way a variable is declared. In fact, it is a variable declaration; therefore, you must specify the data type. Any variable that you specify as an argument is *only* accessible within the method body. You can't access the variable from outside of the method. In this way, you can think of itemPrice as *belonging* to the addTax() method. Lastly, this sample method declares a double variable, total, and stores the result of the tax calculation in it. Then it returns the value of total back to the caller.

Calling Methods

Let's see how the addTax() method can be called:

```java
double totalCost = addTax(10.00);
```

The preceding line declares totalCost, a double variable, and calls the addTax() method, assigning the returned value to totalCost. The value of totalCost after this statement executes is 1.07. As you can see, you call a method by using the method name and placing any arguments inside the parentheses. When you call `addTax(10.00)`, the value `10.00` is assigned to the `itemPrice` variable that is defined in the `addTax()` method. The method then takes that value and does its thing and returns the value 1.07, which is assigned to `totalCost`. To better understand the way methods are used, read (or run!) `MethodTest`, the sample program that follows:

```
/*

 * MethodTest

 * Demonstrates the basics of how methods work

 */


public class MethodTest {

  //main() is also a method
  public static void main(String args[]) {
      double addResult, first, second;
      first = 10.0;
      second = 17.0;
      //call the add() method and store the result in addResult
      addResult = add(first, second);
      //print the result
      System.out.println(first + " + " + second + " = "
          + addResult);
      //take a shortcut:
      //call methods & pass results directly to output
      System.out.println("4.0 - 3.0 = " + subtract(4.0, 3.0));
      System.out.println("12.0 * 12.0 = "
          + multiply(12.0, 12.0));
      System.out.println("100.0 / 4.0 = " + divide(100.0, 4.0));
  }


    public static double add(double a, double b) {
```

```
        //methods can declare their own variables
        double result;
        //add the first and second arguments together
        //remember these variable names aren't the same
        //as the ones that were passed too this method,
        //but their values are the same
        result = a + b;
        //return the value back to the caller
        return result;
    }


    public static double subtract(double a, double b) {
        //get it all done in one line of code
        return a - b;
    }


    public static double multiply(double a, double b) {
        return a * b;
    }


    public static double divide(double a, double b) {
        return a / b;
    }
}
```

MethodTest has four methods (actually five, if you count the main()
method). The four methods are add(), subtract(), multiply(), and
divide(). Each of these methods accepts two double arguments, performs mathematical operations that correspond to the method names,
and returns the result. The main() method calls these methods and displays the results in standard output, as shown in Figure 2.5.

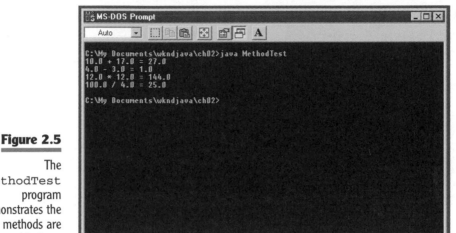

Figure 2.5

The `MethodTest` program demonstrates the way methods are used in Java.

Now you have the basic idea of what methods are and how to declare and call them in the Java programming language. There is more to learn about methods, including how methods work in object-oriented programming. But first, let's take a break.

Take a Break

So far this morning, you've learned about data types, arrays, and methods. We've already covered a lot in just a short time, so it's a good idea for you to take a break before moving on to the next section. When you come back, you'll read about object-oriented programming, which is arguably the most important aspect of programming in Java.

Object-Oriented Programming

Object-oriented programming, or OOP for short, is a central Java programming concept. Every Java program must be defined as an object. In that respect, Java is strictly an object-oriented programming language. The remainder of this morning's session covers the concepts of object-oriented programming and how they are applied in Java.

Understanding Object-Oriented Programming Concepts

Object-oriented programming is a way to organize Java code so that it mimics actual real-world objects. Objects in the real world are made up of smaller objects, have specific attributes or properties, can do certain things, and interact with other objects. A ball, for example, might be made of rubber and be filled with air molecules. A ball can bounce, it can be thrown, it can be used in a sporting event, and so on. A person, for the purpose of this example, is another real-world object. A person is made up of a body, complete with arms, legs, a head, and so on. The person can interact with the ball by throwing it or kicking it. The basic idea that objects are entities in and of themselves, with their own properties and abilities, and that different objects can interact with each other is what object-oriented programming is all about.

There are many benefits to using object-oriented programming. One obvious benefit is code reuse. For example, you can create a `CashRegister` object that at its core just provides for totaling a sum of items, adding the tax, and cashing the customer out. You can create another object that takes care of inventory. Then you can turn around and write a POS (point of sale) program for a retail chain. The retail chain might have really good things to say about your program and ask—well hire—you to write another POS program for a subsidiary of theirs. After all, you wouldn't do it for free, unless you're one of those weirdoes like me who thinks it's fun to code. You have to earn a living, right? Anyway, getting back to the example, say that the program has to be slightly different for the subsidiary company, but the `CashRegister` and `Inventory` objects might not have to change at all. If that's the case, you can just plug them into the new application, and you're good to go!

Encapsulation is another benefit of object-oriented programming. When you define a class, you put a common set of properties and functionality into it. You give other objects access to the class's properties through the class's fields (variables) and write methods to give other objects access to the class's functionality. Wrapping common properties and functionality into separate classes and hiding their implementation is known as encapsulation. The code within the methods is hidden from other objects. Other objects just call the class's methods and expect the functionality to work properly. You can change the way you implement a class internally by changing the code inside the methods, but not have to change the programs that make use of them as long as the class's method signatures, such as the return type and the number and types of arguments it accepts, don't change.

Defining Classes in Java

Every source code file you've seen up to this point is a Java class. Remember the `HelloWorld` program? It started like this:

```
public class HelloWorld {
```

The `class` keyword signifies that you are defining a class. Everything that goes between the opening curly brace and the corresponding closing curly brace belongs to the class. I think it's about time to use another Java code example to clarify what I'm talking about. Let's create a Java class that defines an automobile. First, some brainstorming is in order. What sort of properties does an automobile have? No need to overdo it here, so I'll keep it simple. An automobile can have an engine that is either running or not running, wheels, seats for the driver and some passengers, mileage, and a color. Here are some variables that keep track of these properties:

```
public boolean engineRunning;
public int numWheels;
public int numSeats;
public double mileage;
public String color;
```

The `public` access modifier will be described momentarily, so let's ignore that for now. Because these variables are declared at the class level and not in any method such as `main()`, the scope of these variables includes the entire class, which is everything enclosed by the class's opening and closing curly braces. This means that these variables are accessible from any methods you declare in the class. Speaking of methods, let's think about how to create Automobile's methods. What can you do with an automobile? You can start and stop the engine, and most importantly, you can drive it. Here are some method signatures for the methods that provide this functionality:

```
public void startEngine()
public void stopEngine()
public void drive(double numMiles)
```

Constructor Methods

Another thing that we need to provide in the Automobile class is a way of creating an Automobile *object*. The Automobile class defines what an automobile is, while an Automobile is an instance of the Automobile class as well as an actual object. An Automobile object is a specific automobile and has values for the properties that the Automobile class defines. For example, the Automobile class defines the color property, but an Automobile object would give a value such as "green" to the property as well as the other properties in the class. Java has specialized methods that allow you to create instances of classes. They are called *constructor* methods. Here is the constructor method for the Automobile class:

```
public Automobile(int wheels, int seats, String theColor) {
    numWheels = wheels;
    numSeats = seats;
    color = theColor;
    mileage = 0.0;
    engineRunning = false;
}
```

NOTE Constructor methods are optional. Java does not force you to write a constructor method; however, if you don't include one, the Java compiler will create one for you. The compiler creates the default no-argument constructor. It accepts no arguments and doesn't initialize any variables. Java doesn't change your source code. It defines this constructor only in the class file, but it works exactly as though you had defined a constructor like this:

```
public MyClass() { }
```

There are some differences between constructor methods and normal methods that you should note. First, there is no return type. No constructor method has a return type. Second, the method name `Automobile()` corresponds to the class name. It is similar to regular methods in that it can accept arguments. This constructor accepts arguments used to initialize the `numWheels`, `numSeats`, and `color` properties. It also takes the liberty to initialize the `mileage` property to `0.0` and the `engineRunning` property to `false`. Here is the full source code listing for `Automobile.java`:

```
/*
 * Automobile
 * Demonstrates Object Oriented Programming Concepts
 */


public class Automobile {
    //Declare fields that belong to the Automobile class
    public boolean engineRunning;
    public int numWheels;
    public int numSeats;
    public double mileage;
    public String color;

    //define the constructor
    public Automobile(int wheels, int seats, String theColor) {
```

```java
        //initialize the instance variables with the given
        //values
        numWheels = wheels;
        numSeats = seats;
        color = theColor;
        //initialize the remaining variables
        mileage = 0.0;
        engineRunning = false;
    }


    //define methods that belong to the Automobile class
    public void startEngine() {
        engineRunning = true;
    }


    public void stopEngine() {
        engineRunning = false;
    }


    public void drive(double numMiles) {
        mileage += numMiles;
    }


    //This method defines the String representation of this
    //object
    public String toString() {
        String s = "Number of wheels: " + numWheels;
        s += "\nNumber of seats: " + numSeats;
        s += "\nColor: " + color;
        s += "\nMileage: " + mileage;
        s += "\nEngine running: " + engineRunning;
```

```
        return s;

    }

}
```

Did you notice that there is no `main()` method defined in the `Automobile` class? That's because it's not an application. It's just a class definition. Not every Java source file has a `main()` method defined in it. Only classes that need to run as Java applications need to define a `main()` method. Also, you should notice that none of the methods are static methods. Earlier this morning, the methods you defined were static, making it easier for you to call them without having to know object-oriented programming. Now that you have some object-oriented programming skills, we can drop the `static` keyword, which has a specific purpose of its own. (I'll cover the purpose of the `static` keyword in just a moment.) The `toString()` method returns a `String` representation of an object. If you define the `toString()` method in any object, Java will automatically call this method when it needs to interpret your class as a `String` literal. For instance, you can add an object to a `String` literal like this:

```
String s = "my object = " + myObject;
```

Java will call `myObject`'s `toString()` method and append the returned value to the `"my object = "` `String` and assign the result in s. Also, if you pass in an object as the argument to the `System.out.println()` method, Java will call the `toString()` method and print the returned value to standard output. You'll actually see this for yourself when you test the `Automobile` class.

Now let's create a program to test the `Automobile` class. In it, you'll see a bit of a difference between the way the methods are called here and what you learned previously. To begin, you need to know how to create an `Automobile` object. You create a new `Automobile` object by calling its constructor. This is how you create an `Automobile` object named `auto`:

```
Automobile auto = new Automobile(4, 2, "red");
```

This creates a new `Automobile` object that is red and has four wheels and two seats. The `new` keyword is used to tell Java to allocate enough space for a new `Automobile` object. The `auto` variable is assigned to the new `Automobile` object. Notice that it is declared to be of type `Automobile`. Remember earlier when I said that variables are declared to be one of eight primitive data types or an object reference? Well, here `auto` is an object reference that references an `Automobile` object. I'm using the word *reference* here because `auto` doesn't actually store the data associated with the `Automobile` object directly. Instead, it stores a reference to the object, which is a memory location where the object is actually stored. From that, Java knows where to get the object's data.

After the `Automobile` object is created, you can access its properties and methods. The `AutomobileTest` class tests the `Automobile` class by creating a new `Automobile` object, `auto`, and playing around with its properties and methods. `AutomobileTest` calls `auto`'s `startEngine()` method like this:

```
auto.startEngine();
```

It uses *dot notation*. The syntax for calling an object's methods is as follows:

```
object_Name.method_name(args);
```

First, you use the object name to specify which object's method you want to call; then you use a dot (.) to separate the object name from the method name. Then, within the parentheses after the method name, you can pass in any arguments that the method accepts. You also use dot notation to access an object's properties. For example, to set `auto`'s color to black, the `AutomobileTest` program uses the following statement:

```
auto.color = "black";
```

The syntax for accessing an object's property is

```
object_name.property_name;
```

It's just like using regular variables, but with the addition of the object name and the dot to separate the object name from the property name. Pretty simple, don't you think? Here is the full source code listing for AutomobileTest.java:

```
/*
 * AutomobileTest
 * Tests out the Automobile class
 */


public class AutomobileTest {

    public static void main(String args[]) {
        //create a new Automobile object
        Automobile auto = new Automobile(4, 2, "red");
        System.out.println("Created new automobile:");
        System.out.println(auto);
        auto.startEngine();
        System.out.println(
          "Started Engine");
        //I see a red automobile and I want to paint it black
        auto.color = "black";
        System.out.println("Painted it black");
        auto.drive(12.8);
        System.out.println("Drove it 12.8 miles");
        System.out.println("Here are the results:");
        System.out.println(auto);
    }

}
```

AutomobileTest isn't complicated at all. In fact, it's pretty simple. It just creates an Automobile object, calls its methods, and accesses its member variables (properties). It also prints stuff to standard output so you can see the results of the method calls and property manipulation, as shown in Figure 2.6.

Understanding Modifiers

Modifiers specify different class, variable, and method attributes. Access modifiers define how fields and methods are accessed from other classes. The access modifier keywords are `public`, `protected`, and `private`. A class can directly access another class's public property or method through dot notation, just like you saw earlier when `AutomobileTest` accessed the properties of the `auto` object's properties and methods. The protected access modifier makes properties and methods accessible only to subclasses and other classes within the same package. (You'll learn about subclasses in the next section, "Creating Subclasses," and you'll learn about packages Sunday evening.) The most restrictive access modifier, *private,* makes properties and methods available only within the class that defines them. For example, if you create a class, `Foo`, and define a private variable, `x`, within that class, it will look like this:

```
public class Foo {

    private int x = 1;

}
```

Figure 2.6

This sample program takes the `Automobile` class for a test drive.

Then, if you create another class, ManChu, you will not be able to directly access Foo's x property from ManChu, and the following code will not compile:

```
public class ManChu {

    public static void main(String args[]) {

        Foo f = new Foo();

        System.out.println(f.x);

    }

}
```

A common practice in object-oriented programming is to make most of a class's properties private variables and provide public access methods for getting and setting their values. For example, Foo would provide a getX() and a setX() method so that other classes could indirectly access the x property, like this:

```
public class Foo {

    private int x = 1;


    public int getX() {

        return x;

    }


    public void setX(int value) {

        x = value;

    }

}
```

The ManChu class would change its System.out.println(f.x) statement to

```
System.out.println(f.getX());
```

The preceding is the most basic example of how encapsulation works. Why would anyone go to the extra trouble? Well, here it makes no difference because this is just a simple example. What if, instead, you declared a private variable named `age` in a class called `Person`? You wouldn't want to let anyone set that value to a negative number, would you? "How old are you?" "Well, I'll be -5 next month." No, it doesn't make any sense. So, in your `setAge()` method, you would test the value of the argument that gets passed in and make a special effort to screen out any negative numbers before assigning that value to `age`. You'll learn how to direct the flow of your program based on the value of variables later when you learn about conditional statements. For now, know that you'll be writing a whole bunch of Java objects, so just stick with it, and it will all come together.

There is one more modifier I need to cover here. The `static` modifier makes a class's variables and methods accessible without you having to create any instances of the class. Non-static variables and methods are called *instance variables* and *instance methods* because they are specific to a particular instance of a class. Static variables and methods are called *class variables* and *class methods* because they belong to a particular class, but are not specific to any particular instance of a class. Consider the following code as an example:

```
public class Foo {
    public static int myStaticInt = 1;
}
```

You don't have to create an instance of `Foo` to get the value of `myStaticInt`. You can do it using the class name in place of an object name:

```
int i = Foo.myStaticInt;
```

You can also access it through an instance of `Foo`, like this:

```
Foo f = new Foo();
int i = f.myStaticInt;
```

However, this is not a good practice because someone else who is reading your code wouldn't necessarily know that `myStaticInt` is static, whereas in the first example it is obvious. By convention, you should always access static variables and methods using the class name, and not through a specific object. The following code shows you why accessing static variables and methods through a specific object gets confusing:

```
Foo f1 = new Foo(), f2 = new Foo();
f1.myStaticInt = 5;
System.out.println("f2.myStaticInt = " + f2.myStaticInt);
```

The output of this code is

```
f2.myStaticInt = 5
```

This happens because `myStaticInt` doesn't belong to `f1` or `f2`; it belongs to the `Foo` class itself. Because all instances of `Foo` access the same value, if one `Foo` object changes the value, then all of the other instances will see the effects of the change as well. Rewriting the code this way makes it clearer that you're dealing with a static variable:

```
Foo f1 = new Foo(), f2 = new Foo();
Foo.myStaticInt = 5;
System.out.println("f2.myStaticInt = " + f2.myStaticInt);
```

`static` methods also belong to the class rather than a specific object. Because no specific instance is necessary to access the method, only `static` variables are directly accessible from within a `static` method. The `main()` method is static; therefore, if, for example, you create a `main()` method in the `Automobile` class, you can't access `Automobile`'s variables or other methods without first creating an `Automobile` instance. In other words, you can't do this:

```
public class Automobile {

...
```

```
public static void main(String args[]) {
startEngine();
color = "black";
}
...
}
```

Neither of the two statements in the main() method are valid because there is no Automobile instance to work with, and both startEngine() and color require a concrete instance. If startEngine() and color were static, it would be fine, but they're not. Instead, you have to create a new Automobile object and access them this way:

```
Automobile auto = new Automobile();
auto.startEngine();
auto.color = "black";
```

Now you know why I declared the methods in MethodTest to be static—so you wouldn't need to create an object to call the methods. That's all for modifiers for this morning. There are others, but I'll explain the others as you encounter them.

Creating Subclasses

Another great benefit of object-oriented programming is that you can extend a class by creating a subclass, thereby increasing functionality. The added subclass inherits the super-class's preexisting functionality. Any code that you write in the subclass is added to the super-class's functionality. Let's think about this in terms of the Automobile class you wrote earlier. The Automobile class is a fairly vague class that only generally defines an automobile. If you want to write a class that defines a more specific type of automobile, such as a truck, and another one that defines yet another type of automobile, such as a motorcycle, then you don't have to redefine the stuff that's already defined in Automobile. For instance, you don't have to redefine the variables that hold the number of wheels, the number of seats, the color, and so on. You don't have to redefine the methods either. Instead, you can create a subclass of the `Automobile` class. This concept is known as *inheritance*.

To create a subclass, you use the `extends` keyword in the class signature. When you extend a class, you automatically get the super-class's stuff, so you just need to add to it. Here is the syntax for extending a class:

```
public class subclass_name extends superclass_name { … }
```

For example, this `Truck` class is a subclass of `Automobile`:

```java
/*
 * Truck
 * Demonstrates how to create a subclass by extending
 * Automobile
 */

public class Truck extends Automobile {
    //already has all fields that it inherited from Automobile
    //add some more that are specific to Truck:
    private boolean hasTrailer, trailerFull;
    private double trailerMileage;

    public Truck(String color) {
        //call Automobile's constructor, 10 wheels and 2 seats
        super(10, 2, color);
        //now take care of the remaining variables
        hasTrailer = false;
        trailerFull = false;
        trailerMileage = 0.0;
    }
```

```java
//override Automobile's drive() method
public void drive(double numMiles) {
    super.drive(numMiles);
    trailerMileage += numMiles;
}


//already has all methods that it inherited from Automobile
//add some more that are specific to Truck:
public void attachTrailer() {
    hasTrailer = true;
    numWheels += 8;
}


public void detachTrailer() {
    hasTrailer = false;
    numWheels -= 8;
}


public void load() {
    trailerFull = true;
}


public void unload() {
    trailerFull = false;
}


public String toString() {
    //call Automobile's toString method
    String s = super.toString();
    //add more info
```

```
        s += "\nHas trailer: " + hasTrailer;
        s += "\nTailer full: " + trailerFull;
        s += "\nTrailer mileage: " + trailerMileage;
        return s;
    }
}
```

The `Truck` class defines two `boolean` properties, `hasTrailer` and `trailerFull`, and another `double` property, `trailerMileage`, to keep track of the number of miles put on the trailer. A typical `Truck` without a trailer has 10 wheels and 2 seats; so, instead of allowing those properties to be passed into the constructor, I removed them from the constructor's argument list and passed the hard-coded values to `Automobile`'s constructor.

The `super()` method is Java's way of allowing you to make a call to a super-class's constructor method. When using the `super()` call, it must be the very first line of your subclass's constructor method. However, there are a few exceptions. If the super-class has a default no-argument constructor, you can omit the `super()` call because Java will generate it for you in the class file. Another instance in which you don't have to use `super()` is if you use `this()` instead. Use the `this()` method to tell Java to call another constructor of the same class. No matter what, though, eventually the super-class's constructor will be called.

If you want to define more than one constructor, you can—as long as the argument list is different. In short, the number, order, and/or types of arguments cannot be the same. Here's a quick example:

```
public class Monkey extends Primate {

    public Monkey() {
        this(false, false, false);
```

```
        }

    public Monkey(boolean hearEvil, boolean seeEvil,➡
boolean speakEvil) {

        super(hearEvil, seeEvil, speakEvil);

        ...

    }

}
```

The Monkey class defines two constructors: one that accepts no arguments, and another that accepts three booleans. If a new Monkey is created by calling the no-argument constructor, then the values for hearEvil, seeEvil, and speakEvil are set to false because the no-argument constructor calls the three-boolean constructor using three false arguments. The three-boolean-argument constructor can also be called directly by the program that is creating a new Monkey, just by passing in three arguments. So, this gives the option of creating a Monkey object by not specifying any arguments and getting default values or by specifying the values directly. The act of specifying multiple methods with the same name but with a different arguments list is known as *overloading*. You can do this with regular methods as well. The method that gets called depends on the number and types of arguments you pass.

Now that I've illustrated how to define more than one constructor, let's get back to our Automobile example. In addition to creating new constructors, Truck also overrides the drive() method. To override a super-class's method, in the subclass, define a method with the same signature. The subclass's method takes precedence and overrides its super-class's method of the same name. The Truck's drive() method calls the super-class's drive() method using the following code:

```
super.drive(numMiles);
```

Truck doesn't need to rewrite the method entirely. It's already defined in Automobile. Truck just wants Automobile to perform its drive()

method and then add one more thing to it. Truck wants to increment the number of miles on the trailer. Truck also adds some more of its own methods. The TruckTest program that follows tests the Truck class. You can see the program's output in Figure 2.7.

```java
/*
 * TruckTest
 * Tests out the Truck class
 */

public class TruckTest {

  public static void main(String args[]) {
    //create a new silver truck
    Truck truck - new Truck("silver");
    System.out.println("Created a new truck:");
    System.out.println(truck);
    truck.startEngine();
    truck.attachTrailer();
    System.out.println("Started engine and attached trailer");
    truck.load();
    System.out.println("Loaded trailer");
    System.out.println(truck);
    truck.drive(127.75);
    truck.unload();
    truck.drive(127.75);
    System.out.println("Delivered load 127.75 miles away "
        + "and drove back empty to get another load");
    System.out.println(truck);
  }

}
```

```
MS-DOS Prompt                                          _ □ X
Auto ▼  □ 🗋 🖺 🔳 🔁 🗗 A
C:\My Documents\wkndjava\ch02>java TruckTest
Created a new truck:
Number of wheels: 18
Number of seats: 2
Color: silver
Mileage: 0.0
Engine running: false
Has trailer: false
Trailer full: false
Trailer mileage: 0.0
Started engine and attached trailer
Loaded trailer
Number of wheels: 18
Number of seats: 2
Color: silver
Mileage: 0.0
Engine running: true
Has trailer: true
Trailer full: true
Trailer mileage: 0.0
Delivered load 127.75 miles away and drove back empty to get another load
Number of wheels: 18
Number of seats: 2
Color: silver
Mileage: 255.5
Engine running: true
Has trailer: true
Trailer full: false
Trailer mileage: 255.5

C:\My Documents\wkndjava\ch02>_
```

Figure 2.7

The `TruckTest` output shows us that we've successfully created the `Truck` class as a subclass of `Automobile`.

NOTE   All Java classes implicitly extend the `Object` class, which is defined in the `java.lang` package.

More about Strings

Earlier this morning, you learned that `String` is actually a Java class, not a primitive data type. There are some very useful methods defined in the `String` class that make it easier for you to deal with `strings` in your Java programs. See Table 2.6 for a listing of some of the more useful `String` methods.

TABLE 2.6 SOME USEFUL STRING CLASS METHODS

Method	Description
`char charAt(int index)`	Returns the character at the specified index.
`String concat(String str)`	Concatenates this `String` with another and returns the result.
`boolean endsWith(String str)`	Tests whether this `String` ends with the suffix `str`.
`boolean equals(String str)`	Compares this `String` to another and returns true if they're equal.
`boolean equalsIgnoreCase(String str)`	Tests whether this `String` equals `str`, ignoring case.
`int indexOf(char c)`	Returns the integer index of char `c` at its first occurrence.
`int indexOf(char c, int n)`	Returns the first index of `c` starting at index `n`.
`int indexOf(String str)`	Returns the index of the first occurrence of `str`.
`int indexOf(String str, int n)`	Returns the index of the first occurrence of `str` starting at index `n`.
`int length()`	Returns the length (number of characters) of this string.
`String replace(char c1, char c2)`	Replaces all occurrences of `c1` with `c2` and returns the result.
`String substring(int n1, int n2)`	Returns the substring of this `String` between index `n1` and `n2`.

continued

TABLE 2.6 SOME USEFUL STRING CLASS METHODS

Method	Description
`String toLowerCase()`	Converts all letters in this `String` to lowercase.
`String toUpperCase()`	Converts all letters in this `String` to uppercase.
`String valueOf()`	Converts the argument to a `String`. There are versions of this method that accept `boolean`, `char`, `double`, `float`, `int`, and `long` data types.

The `StringTest` sample program demonstrates how to manipulate `Strings`. Take a look at it and then check out the program's output in Figure 2.8.

```
/*
 * StringTest
 * Tests how Strings are used in Java
 */

public class StringTest {

    public static void main(String args[]) {
        //Declare String alphabet
        String alphabet = "a";
        System.out.println("alphabet = \"a\";");
        System.out.println("alphabet: " + alphabet);
        //append (concatenate) some more letters
        alphabet += "bcdefg";
        System.out.println("alphabet += \"bcdefg\";");
        System.out.println("alphabet: " + alphabet);
        //This will not change the value of alphabet
```

```
alphabet.concat("hijklmnop");
System.out.println("alphabet.concat(\"hijklmnop\");");
System.out.println("alphabet: " + alphabet);
alphabet = alphabet.concat("hijklmnop");
System.out.println("alphabet = "
    + "alphabet.concat(\"hijklmnop\");");
System.out.println("alphabet: " + alphabet);
//Complete the alphabet
alphabet += "qrstuvwxyz";
System.out.println("alphabet += \"qrstuvwxyz\";");
System.out.println("alphabet: " + alphabet);
//Play around with some String methods
int r = alphabet.indexOf('r');
System.out.println("alphabet.indexOf('r'): " + r);
System.out.println("alphabet.charAt(" + r + "); "
    + alphabet.charAt(r));
alphabet = alphabet.toUpperCase();
System.out.println("alphabet.toUpperCase(); "
    + alphabet);
System.out.println("Indices:..............."
    + "01234567890123456789012345");
System.out.println("alphabet.subString(7, 9); "
    + alphabet.substring(7, 9));
System.out.println("alphabet.startsWIth(\"a\"); "
    + alphabet.startsWith("a"));
System.out.println("alphabet.startsWith(\"A\"); "
    + alphabet.startsWith("A"));
System.out.println("alphabet.startsWith(\"Z\"); "
    + alphabet.startsWith("Z"));
    }

    }
```

Figure 2.8

The
`StringTest`
program
manipulates
`Strings` using
built-in Java
features.

Creating the CalculatorModel and CalculatorHelper Classes

Starting with this morning's session and continuing through the remainder of the book, you will be building a calculator program. As you learn new things, you'll add to your program. And by the end of the book, the calculator program will be complete. In this section, using what you've already learned about object-oriented programming and math, you'll create the `CalculatorModel` and `CalculatorHelper` class. For now, these classes will be very simple, but you will build on them and improve them as you expand your skills. The purpose of the `CalculatorModel` class is to keep track of the calculator's data. The source code follows:

```
/*
 * CalculatorModel
 * Encapsulates the data model used by the Calculator
 * Application
 */

public class CalculatorModel {
```

```java
    private double operand1;
    private double operand2;

    public void setOperand1(double value) {
        operand1 = value;
    }

    public double getOperand1() {
        return operand1;
    }

    public void setOperand2(double value) {
        operand2 = value;
    }

    public double getOperand2() {
        return operand2;
    }

    public String toString() {
        String s = "operand1 = " + operand1
                    + " operand2 = " + operand2;
        return s;
    }

}
```

CalculatorModel defines two private double variables, operand1 and operand2. These are the operands on which mathematical operations are performed. There are five methods in the CalculatorModel class. The first four in the source code listing—setOperand1(), getOperand1(), setOperand2(), and getOperand2()—are simply for getting and setting the values of the two operand variables. Since the variables are private, these setter and getter methods are the only means of accessing the variables.

The purpose of the CalculatorHelper class is to provide mathematical functionality for the calculator project. The CalculatorHelper class uses a private CalculatorModel object to keep track of the operands while the CalculatorHelper class performs mathematical operations on the operands. The source code for the CalculatorHelper class follows:

```java
/*
 * CalculatorHelper
 * A class that performs mathematical functions for a
 * Calculator program
 */


public class CalculatorHelper {
    //define mathematical operand variables

    private CalculatorModel calcModel;

    public CalculatorHelper() {
        calcModel = new CalculatorModel();
    }

    public void setOperand1(double value) {
        calcModel.setOperand1(value);
    }

    public void setOperand2(double value) {
        calcModel.setOperand2(value);
```

```
    }


    public double add() {

        return calcModel.getOperand1() +
calcModel.getOperand2();

    }


    public double subtract() {

        return calcModel.getOperand1() +
calcModel.getOperand2();

    }


    public double multiply() {

        return calcModel.getOperand1() *
calcModel.getOperand2();

    }


    public double divide() {

        return calcModel.getOperand1() /
calcModel.getOperand2();

    }

}
```

CalculatorHelper defines a private CalculatorModel variable, calcModel. The constructor is a no-argument constructor that simply initializes the CalculatorModel instance. CalculatorHelper provides two setter methods for CalculatorModel's two operands, setOperand1() and setOperand2(). The four remaining methods, add(), subtract(), multiply(), and divide(), perform their corresponding operations on CalculatorModel's operands and return the resulting values. The CalculatorHelperTest class, which tests the CalculatorHelper class, is listed here:

```
/*
 * CalculatorHelperTest
 * Tests the CalculatorHelper class
 */

public class CalculatorHelperTest {

    public static void main(String args[]) {
        CalculatorHelper calcHelper
            = new CalculatorHelper();
        double a = 100.0,
               b = 25.0;
        calcHelper.setOperand1(a);
        calcHelper.setOperand2(b);
        System.out.println(a + " + " + b + " = "
            + calcHelper.add());
        System.out.println(a + " - " + b + " = "
            + calcHelper.subtract());
        System.out.println(a + " * " + b + " = "
            + calcHelper.multiply());
        System.out.println(a + " / " + b + " = "
            + calcHelper.divide());
    }
}
```

CalculatorHelperTest declares two doubles, a and b, and initializes their values to 100.0 and 25.0, respectively. Then CalculatorHelperTest calls each of the four mathematical methods and displays their results in standard output. Figure 2.9 shows what the output of CalculatorHelperTest looks like.

Figure 2.9

Don't worry; the calculator project will get better!

Wrapping Up

Whew, that was a lot of work, but you did it! You learned the Java essentials, which you'll use throughout the remainder of this book. You also started the calculator project, which you'll continue to work on and improve this weekend. This afternoon, you'll learn about controlling the flow of your program using conditionals and loops. You'll also learn about the java.util package, which provides some very useful utility classes that will help you write Java programs. You'll also learn about the Math class, which provides mathematical functions for you. Right now, though, pat yourself on the back for a productive morning and take a break. We'll talk again this afternoon.

Getting Beyond the Basics

- ➤ Using Conditional Statements
- ➤ Repeating Code Using Loops
- ➤ The `Math` Class
- ➤ The `java.util` Package
- ➤ Continuing the Calculator Project

This morning you learned the basics of Java programming. Your goal for this afternoon is to get beyond the basics. First, you'll learn about conditional statements. *Conditional statements* allow you to direct the flow of programs based on certain conditions. When using conditional statements, you test a condition and then write some code that handles different situations. For example, you might have a method called `withdraw()` in an ATM program that accepts a dollar amount as an argument. You only want to allow a user to withdraw the money if there is enough money in the account to cover it. If there isn't enough money in the account, you probably will not allow the withdrawal, and you will display a message to the user indicating that there are insufficient funds in the account. To do this, you have to write code that handles both situations. In this instance, you test whether the given withdrawal amount is less than the amount in the bank account. If the withdrawal amount is less than the total amount in the account, you direct the program flow to the code that handles the withdrawal. Conversely, if the withdrawal amount is more than the total amount in the account, you direct the program flow to the code that displays the error message to the user. Java supports multiple types of conditional statements, all of which you'll learn about this afternoon.

Next, you'll learn about loops. *Loops* are sections of repeatable code. Loops have many different uses. To understand these uses, consider printing all of the elements of an array. You could do it the long way and print them one at a time; but, if there were one hundred elements in the array, it would take one hundred Java statements to accomplish the task. That's not very efficient! With loops, you can use a variable to store the array index and a single statement to print one element of the array. You put the statement in a loop so that the code repeats itself, incrementing the index variable each time until the entire content of the array has been printed. Java supports more than one type of loop, and you'll learn about them all this afternoon.

The remainder of this afternoon's session covers some useful classes that are included in the standard edition of the SDK. The `java.util` package includes utility classes that make your programming life much easier. The `Math` class defines methods that perform mathematical operations for you.

Finally, you'll wrap up this afternoon's session by applying some of what you learn this afternoon to the calculator project.

Defining Conditions

Java has three different types of conditional statements: the *if* statement, the *switch* statement, and the *ternary conditional* statement. In this section, you'll learn how all three of these statements allow your program to react to different situations (conditions). Before getting into the syntax and use of conditional statements, you should know about numerical comparison operators and conditional operators, which is why they are covered first. Comparison operators and conditional operators are used as part of a conditional statement. All conditions evaluate to one of the two `boolean` values, `true` or `false`. A condition can be expressed as a `boolean` literal, `boolean` variable, or any method or expression that evaluates to a `boolean` value. After you learn how to define conditions in Java, you'll move on to learn the actual conditional statements.

Numerical Comparison Operators

The four numerical comparison operators, also called *relational operators,* are <, <=, >=, and >. They are used for comparing numerical data. The type of each of the operands must evaluate to a primitive numerical type, such as int, long, float, or double. The operand on the left side of the operator is compared to the operand on the right side of the operator. The result is evaluated as a boolean value. There are also two operators that are used to test for equality. They are equal-to (==), and not-equal-to (!=). They can be used not only for numerical comparisons, but also for comparing booleans and object references. These operators are described in Table 3.1. Note that *x* and *y* in the first four rows of the table can represent any numerical value, and in the remaining two rows, they can represent any numerical value, boolean value, or object reference.

NOTE

When comparing the equality of object references, keep in mind that you are not comparing the states of the two objects. Instead, you are comparing whether the two variables reference the same object—that is, they point to the same memory location. If they are two identical objects, they are still considered unequal when compared using the == operator. There Is a way to test for equality of two objects using the equals() method, which you'll learn about a bit later.

TABLE 3.1 COMPARISON OPERATORS		
Operator	**Syntax**	**Description**
<	x < y	Result is true if x is less than y; otherwise, it is false.
<=	x <= y	Result is true if x is less than or equal to y; otherwise, it is false.
>=	x >= y	Result is true if x is greater than or equal to y; otherwise, it is false.
>	x > y	Result is true if x is greater than y; otherwise, it is false.
==	x == y	Result is true if x is exactly equal to y; otherwise, it is false.
!=	x != y	Result is true if x is not exactly equal to y; otherwise, it is false.

The syntax for these operands is fairly simple; the comparison operator is placed between its two operands. Here are some examples:

```
1 < 2
1 <= 2
1 <= 1
1 == 1
10 >= 1
1 != 2
true == true
false == false
true != false
```

The previous examples all evaluate to `true`. Here are some examples that are `false`:

```
10 < 5
4 >= 5
19.1 <= -10.01
4 == 5
5 != 5
true == false
false != false
true != true
```

As you know, the value of all conditional expressions is `boolean`. This means that you can assign the value of a conditional expression directly to a `boolean` variable. For example, you can create a `boolean` variable called `isXLessThanY` and assign the value of the conditional expression `x < y` to it, like this:

```
int x = 1, y = 2;
boolean isXLessThanY = x < y;
```

In this instance, the value `true` is assigned to `isXLessThanY`.

Conditional-AND and Conditional-OR Operators

The conditional-AND operator (`&&`) and the conditional-OR (`||`) operator are operators that link conditional expressions together to form compound conditional expressions. The results of these expressions are also `boolean` values. Both of the operands must also be `boolean` values. The syntax for the conditional-AND operator is as follows:

```
condition1 && condition2
```

The value of this expression is true if and only if both `condition1` and `condition2` are `true`. If either one or both of them are `false`, then the value of the entire expression is `false`. Take being a father as a conceptual example. To be a father, you must be a man, and you must have children. If either one of these conditions is `false`, you are not a father. A woman cannot be a father, nor can a man who is childless.

The conditional-AND operator has a short-circuit property. When you use the conditional-AND operator, the left side is evaluated first. If the left side of the conditional-AND operation is `false`, the right side is ignored. Once it is determined that the left side is `false`, there is no need to evaluate the right-hand side because the value of the expression is definitely going to be `false`.

TIP

You can use the short-circuit property of the conditional-AND operator to your advantage. For example, to avoid runtime errors that occur when you exceed the bounds of an array (`ArrayIndexOutOfBoundsException`), type

`myIntArray.length > 1 && myIntArray[1] == 4.`

If `myIntArray.length` is not greater than one, then `myIntArray[1] == 4` is never evaluated, which is a good thing. Your program will crash if you try to access an array element outside of the array's bounds.

The conditional-OR operator also must have `boolean` operands. At least one of the operands must be `true` for the result to be `true`. If both of the operands are `true`, then the result is also `true`. This differs from XOR (exclusive-OR), where the result is `true` if one and only one of the operands is `true`. As a conceptual example of the conditional-OR logic, consider what it takes to see an R-rated movie. You must either be over 17 or an adult must accompany you. One or the other (or both) will do fine. If you don't meet either of the two conditions, you'll be stuck watching Harry Potter.

The conditional-OR operator also has a short-circuit property to it. If the left-hand side is `true`, the right-hand side is ignored because no matter what the value of the right-hand side is, the result of the entire operation will be `true`. There is no need to check the right-hand side.

Boolean Logical Operators

There are some other operators that work similarly to the conditional-AND and conditional-OR operators. They can get confusing because they have other uses as well. These operators (logical-AND, logical-OR, and logical-XOR) are called *Boolean logical operators* or *integer bitwise operators,* depending on the type of operands on which they are operating. If the operands are `booleans`, then the operators are Boolean logical operators, but if the operands are integers, they are integer bitwise operators. I'll go over their Boolean logical uses first.

The logical-AND operator, which is represented as a single ampersand (`&`), works almost exactly the same way as the conditional-AND operator. It results in `true` if both of the operands are `true`. It results in `false` in any other case. The difference is that both operands are always evaluated, even if the left side is false. In short, the logical-AND operator does not have the short-circuit property of the conditional-AND operator.

Similarly, the logical-OR operator, which is represented as a single pipe character (`|`), also lacks the short-circuit property. The right-hand side of the logical-OR operator is always evaluated, even if the left side is true.

The logical-XOR (^) operator is like the logical-OR operator; however, there is an important difference. Exclusive-OR logic requires that one and only one of the operands is true for the result of the operation to be true. If both of the operands are true, the result is false. Check out Table 3.2 for an easy place to compare the conditional and logical operators.

When the operators &, |, and ^ operate on integers, in other words when they are used as integer bitwise operators, they work at the binary level. Computers represent all information as a series of bits that are either on (1) or off (0). To keep consistent with the logic used in this section, think

TABLE 3.2 CONDITIONAL AND BOOLEAN LOGICAL OPERATORS

Operator	Name	Examples	Results
&&	Conditional-AND	false && false	false
		false && true	false
		true && false	false
		true && true	true
||	Conditional-OR	false || false	false
		false || true	true
		true || false	true
		true || true	true
&	Logical-AND	false & false	false
		false & true	false
		true & false	false
		true & true	true

continued

TABLE 3.2 CONDITIONAL AND BOOLEAN LOGICAL OPERATORS			
Operator	Name	Examples	Results
|	Logical-OR	false | false	false
		false | true	true
		true | false	true
		true | true	true
^	Logical-XOR	false ^ false	false
		false ^ true	true
		true ^ false	true
		true ^ true	false

of 1 as being true and 0 as being false. Thinking of it that way illustrates the similarities between integer bitwise operators and Boolean logical operators. The bits are compared one at a time and the resulting bit is either one or zero, depending on the operator being used and the values of the bits of the operands. Here are some examples and the resulting values (note that these are binary representations of integers—for example, 1010 is 10, and 1100 is 12).

Operation	Result
1010 & 1100	1000
1010 | 1100	1110
1010 ^ 1100	0110

The operation 1010 & 1100 results in the value 1000. Here's why: The first bit of the first operand is 1, and the first bit of the second operand is also 1. If you think of the operation as true & true, then you can understand that the result is also true, (1). Following this logic pattern, 0 & 1 is 0, 1 & 0 is 0, and 0 & 0 is 0, so the result is 1000. You should be able to apply this logic to understand the bitwise-OR and bitwise-XOR results.

In the previous example, I represented the integers in their binary form. In case you're curious about their decimal values, here is the same example, but in decimal format.

Operation	Result
10 & 12	8
10 | 12	14
10 ^ 12	6

If you don't quite understand why these operators would ever be used, don't worry about it. In most Java programs, they are never used, and you won't see them anywhere else in this book. However, if you should ever encounter them, you'll at least have an idea of what they do.

The Logical Compliment Operator

The logical compliment operator is represented by the exclamation point (!). It is sometimes referred to simply as *not*. It reverses the value of a boolean. So, !true, said "not true," is false, and !false, said "not false," is true. It can be used in front of boolean variables like this:

```
myBoolean = !myBoolean;
```

This operation would reverse the value stored in myBoolean. The boolean compliment operator can also be used in front of anything that results in a boolean value, such as a call to a method that returns a boolean, or any conditional operation—for example:

```
!myObject.isOK() && ! (x < y)
```

In this example, the result will be `true` if `myObject.isOK()` (which represents a method that returns a `boolean`) returns `false` (the logical compliment operator will reverse the returned `boolean` to be `true`) and `x < y` returns `false`. The logical compliment operator will also reverse the right side of the conditional-AND operator and make it `true`.

Object Comparison: equals() and instanceof

Two other operations are commonly used in conditional statements, and they are used to compare objects. They are the `equals()` method and the `instanceof` operator. Recall that when the equality operator (==) is used on object operands, the result is `true` only if both variables reference the same exact object. But there is a way to test for value equality of two different objects. This is done through the use of the `equals()` method, which is defined in the `Object` class, the super-class of all Java objects. The syntax for this method is

```
object.equals(anotherObject)
```

The `equals()` method accepts an argument of type `Object` and returns `true` if the value of the given object is equal to *object*. The `equals()` method in the `Object` class is strict, however, and returns `true` if and only if the == operator also returns `true`. So, even if the values of all of the members of an object are identical, the `equals()` method will return `false`. To get around this, override the `equals()` method and define, for yourself, what makes two different objects equal to each other. Here is a simple example of this:

```
public class MyObject {
    int x;
```

```
public boolean equals(Object otherObject) {
    return otherObject instanceof MyObject
           && ((MyObject)otherObject).x == this.x;
    }
}
```

In this example, objects of the MyObject class are considered equal if the x member variables of both objects are equal to each other. The value that is returned is the result of a conditional operation, otherObject instanceof MyObject && ((MyObject)otherObject).x == this.x.

Notice the instanceof operator. The syntax for the instanceof operator is

anObject instanceof *aClass*

An object, represented here as anObject, goes on the left-hand side. The name of a class, represented here as aClass, goes on the right-hand side. If the object is an instance of the class, or a subclass of the class, the result is true; otherwise, it is false. I needed to use instanceof here because the argument to the equals() method is of type Object. This means that any Java object can be passed in. (For example, you can pass in a String.) So, the instanceof operator is used here to make sure that the argument given is at least an instance of MyObject. If it's not, then there is no way they can be equal. Remember that the conditional-AND operator has a short-circuit property, so the right-hand side is only evaluated if otherObject is an instance of MyObject. Before you can reference the x variable, you have to cast the given Object to MyObject with the code ((MyObject)otherObject).x. This is because the x variable is not defined in the Object class; it is defined in MyObject. It is a good idea to override the equals() method any time you create an object. I will not do this in the examples in this book for the sake of brevity, but keep this in mind, especially if you ever need to test for object equality in this way.

Using Conditional Statements

Now that you understand how to construct conditional operations using conditional operators and `boolean` values, you can put them to use in conditional statements. First, I'll go over the `if` statement and how to build `if-else` structures. Then I'll move on to `switch` statements. After that, I'll show you how to use the ternary conditional operator, which is a shortcut that you can use for some simple conditional assignments.

The if Conditional Statement

The `if` statement evaluates a conditional expression and directs the flow of the program so that a block of statements executes only if the condition evaluates to `true`. To write an `if` statement, use the `if` keyword. First, you specify a condition within a set of parentheses. Then you begin a block of code using the familiar opening curly brace. Within this block of code, you define Java statements that should execute only if the condition is `true`. Finally, you close the block with a closing curly brace and resume the remainder of your program. The syntax for an `if` statement is

```
if (condition) {

    ...

    //statements if condition is true

    ...

}
```

For the condition—any conditional expression that you've learned so far—a `boolean` or a method that returns a `boolean` will work. As a quick example, here's how you would print "My number is even." only if a number is, in fact, even:

```
if (myInt % 2 == 0) {
    System.out.println("My number is even.");
}
```

Here, `myInt` is an `int` variable that contains any integer value. You test whether it is even with the modulus operator. If an integer is evenly divisible by two, the remainder will be zero and the number is even. If the number is even, then the condition `myInt % 2 == 0` will be `true`, and the program will spit out the appropriate message. If not, then the program will keep its mouth shut.

If you want to test this for yourself, try writing the `IfTest` program. First, it generates a random number between zero and one hundred. Next, it tests whether that number would be considered a passing grade. If the grade is passing, it prints out that fact. If the grade is not passing, that message never gets printed. Here is the source code:

```
/*
 * IfTest
 * Demonstrates how to use the conditional if statement
 */

public class IfTest {

    public static void main(String args[]) {
        //Generate a random number between 0 and 100
        double grade = Math.random() * 100;
        System.out.println("I totally guessed the answers " +
            + " and got a " + grade);
        if (grade >= 60) {
            System.out.println("I actually passed!");
        }
    }
}
```

The `double` variable, `grade` gets a random number through the use of the `Math.random()` method, which generates a number greater than or equal to 0.0, and very close to but less than 1.0. This program multiplies that number by 100 so that the random number is greater than 0.0, but less than 100.0. The `if` statement tests `grade` to see whether it is greater than or equal to 60. If it is, then the condition `grade >= 60` is true, and the message "`I actually passed!`" is printed. If `grade` is not 60 or greater, then that code is skipped and the program ends. Later today, you'll learn more about the `Math` class and about some more of its useful methods. The output for the `IfTest` program can be seen in Figure 3.1.

To use a `boolean` variable as the condition of an `if` statement, just put that variable in the parentheses.

```
if (myBooleanVariable) {

    …

    //statements if myBooleanVariable == true

    …

}
```

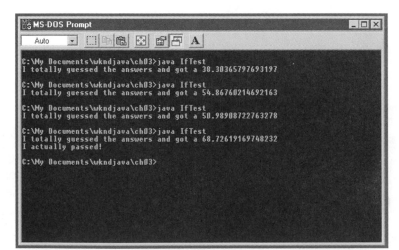

Figure 3.1

The message is printed only if the grade is greater than or equal to 60.

Using a method that returns a `boolean` is just as easy.

```
if (isMyBooleanMethod()) {

    …

    //statements if isMyBooleanMethod() returns true

    …

}
```

The if - else Structure

The `if` statement works pretty well to provide a fork in the program flow, but it only accommodates one situation: `true`. The `else` keyword is a way to define an alternate path for a program to follow if the condition defined in the `if` statement is `false`. The structure for using `else` is

```
if (condition) {

    …

    //statements if condition is true

    …

}
else {

    …

    //statements if condition is false

    …

}
```

First, write the `if` statement as you learned earlier. Then you must place the `else` keyword immediately following the closing brace of the `if` statement. Only white space and comments can be between the closing brace of the `if` statement and the `else` keyword—Java code doesn't belong there. After the `else` keyword, you define a block statement within curly braces. The statements in this block only execute if the condition passed to the `if` statement is `false`. For example, to print "My number is even." if a number is even or to print "My number is odd." do this:

```
if (myInt % 2 == 0) {

    System.out.println("My number is even.");

}

else {

    System.out.println("My number is odd.");

}
```

The `if` statement looks exactly as it did in a previous example. The difference here is after the `if` statement, in the `else` part. If `myInt` is even, then "`My number is even.`" is printed. If `myInt` is not even (therefore, it must be odd), "`My number is odd.`" is printed instead. Exactly one of these messages will be printed. There is no possibility for neither of them to be printed or for both of them to be printed. Here's a full example:

```
/*

 * IfElseTest

 * Demonstrates how to use the conditional if-else structure

 */


public class IfElseTest {


    public static void main(String args[]) {

        //Generate a random number between 0 and 100

        double grade = Math.random() * 100;

        System.out.println("I totally guessed the answers "

            + "and got a " + grade);    if (grade >=  60) {

            System.out.println("I actually passed!");

        }

        else {

            System.out.println("I bombed!");

        }

    }

}
```

This program is the same as the `IfTest` program shown earlier, with the addition of the `else` structure. This program prints "`I actually passed!`" if `grade` is greater than or equal to 60. If it's less than 60, then the message "`I bombed!`" is printed instead. You can see the output in Figure 3.2.

The `if-else` structure gives you two alternate paths based on a single condition. You can also define multiple paths by implementing multiple `if-else` structures back to back, like this:

```
if (condition) {

    ...

    //statements if condition is true

    ...

}
else if (condition2) {

    ...

    //statements if condition is false and condition2 is true

    ...

}
else if (condition_n) {

    // ...etc
```

Figure 3.2

The
`IfElseTest`
program uses the
`if-else`
structure to print
different messages
depending on the
value of the grade.

```
}

else {

    …

    //statements if all other conditions are false

    …

}
```

You start out with an `if` statement, and then follow with `else`. After the
`else` keyword, you can define another `if` statement, then another `else`
statement, and then another `if`, and then another `else`, and so on. When
a program reaches such a structure, it will execute only one of the conditional blocks of code. Basically, it will traverse through the structure until it
reaches the first `true` condition, and then it will execute the related block
of code. After it does so, it breaks out of the structure and continues on.
The `IfElseTest2` program demonstrates this. Here is the source code:

```
/*
 * IfElseTest2
 * Demonstrates a nested if structure.
 */

public class IfElseTest2 {

    public static void main(String args[]) {
        //Generate a random number between 0 and 100
        double grade = Math.random() * 100;
        System.out.println("I totally guessed the answers "
            + "and got a " + grade);
        if (grade >= 80) {
            System.out.println("I actually passed, "
            + "and did quite well!");
        }
        else if (grade >= 60) {
```

```
            System.out.println("I actually passed, "
                + "but didn't do that great.");
        }
        else if (grade >= 40) {
            System.out.println("I should have studied!");
        }
        else {
            System.out.println("I bombed!");
        }
    }
}
```

This program uses the if-else structure to print four different messages, depending on the value of grade. Take note that after the program reaches the first true condition and executes the corresponding block of code, it breaks out of the if-else structure altogether and does not evaluate any of the other conditions. So, if grade was 90, it will pass the first condition, grade >= 80, and "I actually passed, and did quite well!" will be printed. Even though the following condition, grade >= 60, is also true, it doesn't matter because it won't get evaluated if the first condition is true. Check out the results of the test program in Figure 3.3.

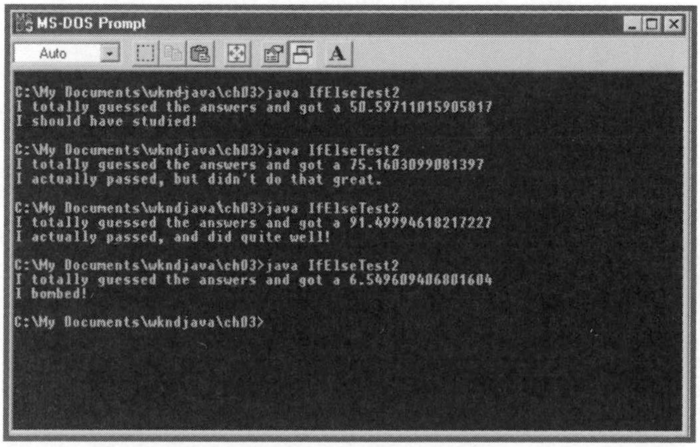

Figure 3.3

The
IfElseTest2
program shows
how to nest if-
else statements.

The switch Conditional Statement

Although the `switch` statement is like the `if` statement, it works a bit differently. The `switch` statement tests the value of an expression and executes different statements based on the value of that expression. The expression must evaluate to a `char`, `byte`, `short`, or `int`. If it doesn't, the program will not compile. This is different from the `if` statement, where the expression must evaluate to a `boolean`. Inside the `switch` statement, which is enclosed within curly braces, you define case labels using the `case` keyword followed by the value to test against the expression. If the expression is equal to the case value, all of the statements that follow the case value will be executed until the program encounters a `break` statement or the end of the `switch` statement. Here is the syntax for the `switch` statement:

```
switch (expression) {

    case value_1:

        statements_for_value_1;

        break; //(optional)

    case value_2:

        statements_for_value_2;

        break; //(optional)

    case value_3:

        statements_for_value_3;

        break; //(optional)

    default:

        statements_for_default;

}
```

The `switch` keyword is followed by an expression within parentheses. Then you open the `switch` block using the opening curly brace and put the `case` labels within the `switch` statement. To construct a `case` label, you use the `case` keyword and follow it with a possible value for the expression. After the possible value, you put a colon. The program will look for the first possible `case` value that matches the value of the expression and will execute the matching `case` statements that appear after the colon. The `break` keyword is used here to break out of the `switch` statement.

So, in the previous syntax example, if *expression* evaluates to the value *value_2*, the program will execute *statements_for_value_2;*. Then it will come to the `break` statement (which is optional) and completely break out of the `switch` statement. Finally, the program will execute any statements that come after the closing curly brace. The default case, specified by the `default` keyword followed by a colon, is optional. It's there for situations in which none of the `case` values match the expression. Statements that should execute by default are defined inside the `default` case. There are only two ways for a program to get to this point: either none of the `case` values match the expression or no `break` statements were used in the cases that precede the `default` case. The `SwitchTest` program demonstrates the use of the `switch` statement.

```
/*
 * SwitchTest
 * Demonstrates the use of the switch statement
 */

public class SwitchTest {

    public static void main(String args[]) {
        System.out.println("Rolling Die...");
        //get a random number between 1 and 6
        int die = (int) (Math.random() * 6 + 1);
        String s = "\n -------";
        switch (die) {
            case 1:
                s += "\n|        |";
```

```
        s += "\n|    *    |";
        s += "\n|         |";
        break;
case 2:
        s += "\n|      * |";
        s += "\n|        |";
        s += "\n| *      |";
        break;
case 3:
        s += "\n|      * |";
        s += "\n|    *   |";
        s += "\n| *      |";
        break;
case 4:
        s += "\n| *    * |";
        s += "\n|        |";
        s += "\n| *    * |";
        break;
case 5:
        s += "\n| *    * |";
        s += "\n|    *   |";
        s += "\n| *    * |";
        break;
case 6:
        s += "\n| *    * |";
        s += "\n| *    * |";
        s += "\n| *    * |";
        break;
default:
        //should never get here
```

```
                s += "\n|           |";
                s += "\n|     ?     |";
                s += "\n|           |";
            }
            s += "\n -------";
            System.out.println(s);
        }
    }
```

As you can see, the SwitchTest program generates a random number from 1 to 6 (inclusive) and stores it in the die variable. Then it uses a switch statement to construct a textual picture that represents the face of a die. If the random number value is 1, the program executes the statements within case 1:; if it's 2, then case 1: is skipped and case 2: gets executed, and so on. Each case includes a break statement to break out of the switch statement. This ensures that only one of the cases gets executed, no matter what. I used the default case to print a question mark if we get an unexpected value, but because all of the cases are handled within case statements, we should never reach the default statement. The SwitchTest output can be seen in Figure 3.4.

Figure 3.4

The SwitchTest program generates a random number and uses a switch statement to build a text picture to represent the rolling of a die.

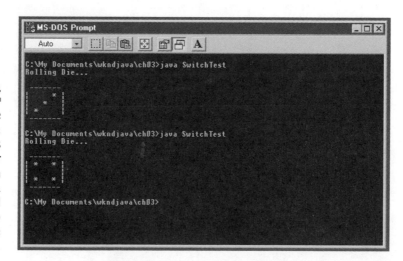

What happens if you don't use the break statements? In the event that there are no break statements, the switch statement will behave as follows: The program will search the switch statement for the very first correct case value and execute the statements defined there. Because there is no break statement to break out of the switch statement, the program will continue to execute all of the case statements that follow the first correct case value statements, including the default case. This behavior is better illustrated in the SwitchTest2 program code and its subsequent output:

```java
/*
 * SwitchTest2
 * Demonstrates how the absence of break statements affects
 * switch statements
 */
public class SwitchTest2 {

    public static void main(String args[]) {
        //create a random number between 1 and 5
        int n = (int) (Math.random() * 5 + 1);
        System.out.println("The number " + n + "...");

        switch(n) {
            case 5:
                System.out.println("...is greater than 4");
            case 4:
                System.out.println("...is greater than 3");
            case 3:
                System.out.println("...is greater than 2");
            case 2:
                System.out.println("...is greater than 1");
            default:
                System.out.println("...is greater than 0");
```

```
            }
        }
    }
```

In the `SwitchTest2` program, the `switch` statement doesn't use any `break` statements. The program generates a random number from 1 to 5 and stores it in the n variable. Then n is used as the expression for the `switch` statement. The program searches through the `case` statements for the value that matches n. All of the statements that follow the correct `case` will be executed. So, for example, if n is 3, the program will execute `case 3`, `case 2`, and `default`. If n is 4, the program will execute `case 4`, `case 3`, `case 2`, and `default`, and so on. Check out the results in Figure 3.5 to see what this means to your screen output.

The Ternary Conditional Operator

There is one more conditional statement that you need to learn: the ternary conditional operator. The ternary conditional operator is a short-cut for a conditional assignment operation. The conditional operator takes a `boolean` argument and executes one of two statements based on the truth or falsity of the `boolean` argument. The syntax is as follows:

```
condition ? expression_true : expression_false;
```

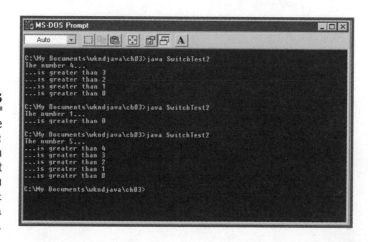

Figure 3.5

The `SwitchTest2` program demonstrates what happens when you don't use `break` in a `switch` statement.

As you can see, a conditional expression is followed by a question mark. Then two expressions follow the question mark. A colon separates these expressions. If the condition evaluates to true, the first expression (on the left side of the colon) executes. If the condition evaluates to false, then the second expression (on the right side of the colon) executes instead. The ConditionalTest program uses the ternary conditional operator. Here is the source code:

```java
/*

 * ConditionalTest

 * Demonstrates the ternary conditional operation

 */


public class ConditionalTest {
    private int myNum;
    //establish a min:max range for myNum
    public final static int MIN = 0,
                            MAX = 10;


    public static void main(String args[]) {
        ConditionalTest test = new ConditionalTest();
        System.out.println("Setting myNum to 5...");
        test.setMyNum(5);
        System.out.println("myNum = " + test.getMyNum());
        System.out.println("Setting myNum to -3...");
        test.setMyNum(-3);
        System.out.println("myNum = " + test.getMyNum());
        System.out.println("Setting myNum to 11...");
        test.setMyNum(11);
        System.out.println("myNum = " + test.getMyNum());
        System.out.println("Setting myNum to 10...");
        test.setMyNum(10);
```

```
        System.out.println("myNum = " + test.getMyNum());
    }


    /* This setter method enforces the range.
     * If the arg is out of range, MIN is used instead */
    public void setMyNum(int value) {
        myNum = (value >= MIN && value <= MAX) ? value : MIN;
    }


    public int getMyNum() {
        return myNum;
    }
}
```

The conditional statement in the `ConditionalTest` program appears in the `setMyNum()` method. It makes sure that the given argument, `value`, falls within the `MIN` / `MAX` range. If the argument does fall within that range, the program assigns `value` to `myNum`. If not, then it assigns the default valid value `MIN`.

TIP
I should also point out here that the `ConditionalTest` program is a good example of encapsulation. The variable `myNum` is hidden from the outside world with the `private` access modifier. The only access to this variable is given through the `getMyNum()` and `setMyNum()` methods. The conditional operator tests the given value in the `setMyNum()` method to make sure that it's valid. If the argument is valid, then the method happily sets `myNum` to the argument value. If not, it assigns a default valid value on its own. This is a very common practice in object-oriented programming.

Just to give you an idea of how the ternary conditional operator works as a shortcut, compare it to an `if` statement. If an `if` statement is used instead of the conditional operator, the code will look like this:

```
if (value >= MIN && value <= MAX) {

    myNum = value;

}

else {

    myNum = MIN;

}
```

See Figure 3.6 to examine the output of the `ConditionalTest` program.

A Note about Comparing Strings

You learned how to use the `==` operator to compare primitive data types. Comparing objects works a bit differently. This section goes over how to compare `String` objects. The information covered here actually applies to all objects (not primitives). I chose the `String` object in this case because some Java syntax makes it seem like `Strings` are primitive data types, when they're actually not. `String` is the only object that can be created without directly calling the constructor. For example, you can create a `String` object like this:

```
String myString = "You have six fingers on your right hand.";
```

Figure 3.6

The Conditional Test program uses the ternary conditional operator to assign only valid values to the myNum member variable.

Java does not force you to explicitly call the `String()` constructor method, but you can do so like this:

```
String myString = new String("Someone was looking for you.");
```

This second assignment is more intuitive because it shows that `String` is an object and not a primitive. But it's very uncommon to call the constructor because it's unnecessary. Just keep in mind that all `Strings` are objects, and you'll be fine.

There can be some confusion when comparing objects (especially `Strings`). You already learned the `equals()` method and know that you should not compare objects using the `==` operator unless you are testing whether both variables reference the same exact object in memory (where only one object exists, and both variables point to it). The reason for this is that object variables actually contain a memory location to the object, rather than the actual object itself. The confusion comes when `String` literals are involved in comparison operations. For example, it might seem like a good idea to test whether a `String` (`s` in this example) is equal to "Indigo," as shown here:

```
if (s == "Indigo") { //do something }
```

The problem is that this doesn't always work. Why did I use the word *always* here? Sometimes it works and sometimes it doesn't. No, it's not a bug in the Java interpreter! Understanding how Java handles `Strings` is the key to understanding why this works only sometimes. Java treats all `Strings`, including `String` literals, as objects. If two occurrences of the same `String` literal appear, only one `String` object is created from the two identical `Strings`. For example, the following code segment would print `true`:

```
String s1 = "To the pain";
String s2 = "To the pain";
System.out.println(s1 == s2);
```

Given the same assignments for `s1` and `s2`, the statement `System.out.println(s1 == "To the pain");` will print `true`. Nothing confusing yet, right? Okay, say that a third variable is declared and set this way:

```
String s3 = "To ";
s3 += "the pain";
```

Even though the values are equal, the following two statements both print `false`:

```
System.out.println(s1 == s3);
System.out.println(s3 == "To the pain");
```

The Java interpreter sees the two `"To the pain"` Strings and makes them one single object. `s1` and `s2` both store the memory location for the same object and are, therefore, equal to each other. `s3`, on the other hand, is constructed differently. It's constructed in two separate pieces, so even though the `String` that it references has the same value as the `String` that `s1` and `s2` reference, they point to two separate, but equal, objects. If you need to test the value of a `String`, use the `equals()` method instead of the `==` operator. Keeping with the same example, the following two statements both print `true`:

```
System.out.println(s1.equals(s3));
System.out.println(s3.equals("To the pain"));
```

To further illustrate this concept, check out the `StringCompareTest` program:

```
/*
 * StringCompareTest
 * Demonstrates why you should use equals() to compare strings
 */
```

```
public class StringCompareTest {

    public static void main(String args[]) {
        String str1 = "Hello";
        System.out.println("String str1 = \"Hello\";");
        System.out.println("str1 == \"Hello\" is "
            + (str1 == "Hello"));

        String str2 = "Hello";
        System.out.println("String str2 = \"Hello\";");
        System.out.println("str1 == str2 is " + (str1 == str2));

        String str3 = new String("Hello");
        System.out.println("str3 = new String(\"Hello\");");
        System.out.println("str3 == \"Hello\" is "
            + (str3 == "Hello") );
        System.out.println("str1.equals(\"Hello\") is "
            + str1.equals("Hello"));
        System.out.println("str3 == str1 is " + (str3 == str1));
        System.out.println("str3.equals(str1) is "
            + str3.equals(str1));
    }

}
```

Before you look at the output in Figure 3.7, try and figure out what the output should be based on what you just learned. Always keep in mind that you should use == for comparing object references only if you are checking to see whether two variables reference the same object. Use equals() if you want to check whether two different objects have the same values. Remember that whoever created the class for the object you're testing must have overridden the equals() method correctly for the return value to be accurate.

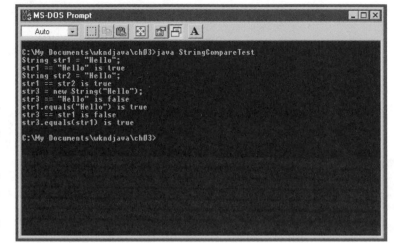

Figure 3.7

The `String`
`CompareTest`
demonstrates why
you should use
the `equals()`
method to compare
`String` objects.

Repeating Code Using Loops

Loops are repeatable blocks of code. Loops are very helpful because they allow you to get a lot of work done using a minimal amount of code. For example, you might write a loop in a payroll program that cuts a check for all employees. You'd start with the first employee to begin the loop. Inside of the loop, you write the code that generates a check for one employee, then you go to the second employee (for example, in an array of employees), and then go back to the beginning of the loop and generate a check for the second employee. The loop repeats to do the same thing for the next employee, and so on until all of the employees have a check waiting for them. This section covers how to create repeatable blocks of Java code using `for` loops, `while` loops, and `do-while` loops.

The for Loop

The `for` loop is used when a loop needs to repeat a determined number of iterations. For example, it is very common to use the `for` loop to loop through an array. The number of times the loop must repeat itself is equal to the length of the array. When looping through an array, you initialize an int variable that represents the index for the array elements. To begin, start the index at zero, which is the first array element index. Then each time you go through the loop, add one to the int variable so that the index references the subsequent elements of the array. You continue to do this until the index is equal to the array length. (Remember that the last index of an array is the array's length minus one.)

The for loop is designed especially for this kind of need. In a for loop, you declare a variable and set its initial value. You also specify what value of the variable should signify the end of the loop and the amount that the variable should change after each iteration of the loop. (Each time through a loop is called an *iteration*.) In short, to create a for loop, you use an initialization expression, a stop conditional expression, and an increment value. The syntax for a for loop is

```
for (initial_value; condition; increment) {
    repeated_statements;
}
```

The for keyword starts the for loop. Then the initialization expression, the termination condition, and the increment expression are defined within parentheses. First comes the initial value. Usually, this is where you declare and initialize the variable that is used as a loop counter. You end the initialization section with a semicolon. Next, you define the condition. Any condition that evaluates to a boolean value can go here. Before each iteration of the loop, this condition is tested. The loop will continue to repeat itself only while the condition evaluates to true. The condition usually compares the variable declared in the initialization section to some maximum value or cap value so that the loop continues to iterate only while the counter variable is less than the cap. The condition section is also ended with a semicolon. The increment section is next. This is where you define some change that should occur after each iteration of the loop. Normally, the counter variable is incremented here so that after each iteration of the loop, the counter increases. Eventually, the variable will be greater than the cap value, causing the condition section to evaluate to `false`. This condition will terminate the loop, and the program will start executing statements that follow the loop.

I'm probably giving you too much information upfront, but that's okay. An example is always good for clearing up some confusion, so take a look at this snippet of code that will print 1 2 3 4 5 6 7 8 9 10:

```java
for (int n = 1; n <= 10; n++) {
    System.out.print(n + " ");
}
```

In the initialization section, `int n = 1;`, the variable n is declared and initialized to 1. The condition section specifies that the loop should execute only while n is 10 or less. The increment section instructs the program to increment n by one after each iteration of the loop. The first time through the loop, n is equal to 1, which is less than or equal to 10, so the statement within the loop, `System.out.println(n + " ");` is reached. After the first iteration of the loop prints the value 1, n++ is evaluated, causing the value of n to increase to 2. Because 2 is less than or equal to 10, the loop repeats itself. This happens again and again until n is 10. After the value 10 is printed, n is incremented to 11. Because 11 is not less than or equal to 10, the loop terminates.

A more involved example of this is the `ForLoopTest` program.

```java
/*
 * ForLoopTest
 * Demonstrates how to use the for loop
 */

public class ForLoopTest {

    public static void main(String args[]) {
        //a loop that simply counts to 10
```

```
for (int n=1; n <= 10; n++) {
    System.out.print(n + " ");
}
System.out.println("\n");


//a loop that counts to 10 by 2s
for (int n=2; n <= 10; n += 2) {
    System.out.print(n + " ");
}
System.out.println("\n");


//create an array and loop on it
String str = "This is a String";
char[] charArray = str.toCharArray();
for (int i=0; i < charArray.length; i++) {
    System.out.print(charArray[i] + " ");
}


//see how fast the computer can count to a million
System.out.println("\nCounting to one million...");
System.out.println("Ready... GO...");
for (int i = 1; i <= 1000000; i++) {
    //no loop body
}
System.out.println("Done!");
    }
}
```

First, ForLoopTest counts to 10, just like in the previous example. Next, it demonstrates that the increment value doesn't have to be 1; it counts to

10 by twos. The program also demonstrates how to loop through an array. And, for fun, it also counts to one million to demonstrate just how fast a computer can do this. Depending on how new your system is, if you run this example, you probably won't even notice any delay.

`for` loops can be nested within one another to provide even greater utility. The `NestedForLoopTest` program demonstrates how to nest `for` loops (which, by the way, is good for looping through multidimensional arrays) by defining a `for` loop inside of another `for` loop. Each iteration of the outer loop causes multiple iterations of the inner loop. The following code illustrates a nested situation:

```
/*
 * NestedForLoopTest
 * Demonstrates how to create a nested for loop
 */


public class NestedForLoopTest {

    public static void main(String args[]) {
        for (int i = 0; i < 3; i++) {
            for (int j = 0; j < 3; j++) {
                System.out.println("i=" + i + ", j=" + j);
            }
        }
    }

}
```

The output for both the `ForLoopTest` program and the `NestedForLoopTest` program can be seen in Figure 3.8.

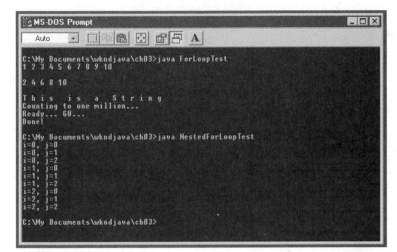

Figure 3.8

The
`ForLoopTest`
program
demonstrates the
use of the `for`
loop and shows
how fast the
computer can count
to one million.

CAUTION

Be careful when writing loops. If you don't construct a loop carefully, you can end up with the infamous infinite loop. An *infinite loop* will continue to repeat itself indefinitely. An infinite loop is caused when the condition that keeps the loop iterating never evaluates to false. This can occur if the condition is improperly constructed or the incrementation is wrong.

Here is an example of an infinite loop:

```
for (int n = 0; n >= 0; n++) {
    System.out.println("I will not chew gum in class.");
}
```

If you're running your Java programs from an MS-DOS prompt in Windows and you find yourself stuck in an infinite loop, you can terminate the process by pressing Ctrl+C.

The while Loop

Unlike the `for` loop, the `while` loop is typically used to loop an indeterminate number of times. Although you can immediately determine the size of an array and use it as a condition in a `for` loop, there are times when you won't always be able to know how many times you'll need to loop. Consider the ATM program loop: When you put in your card, the program doesn't automatically know how many transactions you'll need to make. So, after you complete your first transaction, it asks you, "Another transaction?" The program loop repeats itself while the customer answers yes to this question. The syntax for the while loop is

```
while (condition) {
    repeated_statements;
}
```

You start the while loop with the while keyword. Then you define the loop condition within parentheses following the while keyword. The loop will continue to repeat itself while the condition is true. Just like for loops, you can get stuck in an infinite loop. Be careful to make sure that within the loop, something happens that will cause the condition to eventually become false. The WhileLoopTest demonstrates how to use the while loop.

```
/*
 * WhileLoopTest
 * Demonstrates how to use the while loop
 */


public class WhileLoopTest {

    public static void main(String args[]) {
        int myNum = 0;
        //generate random numbers until we get 5
        while (myNum != 5) {
            System.out.print(".");
            myNum = (int)(Math.random() * 10);
        }
    }
}
```

The `WhileLoopTest` program declares an `int` variable, `myNum`, which it initializes to zero. Then it defines the `while` loop, which repeats itself while `myNum != 5`, so right away you know that the loop will iterate at least once. Inside the loop, it prints a dot; then a random number between 0 and 9 is assigned to `myNum`. This can happen at any time, so you don't ever know how many times this loop will iterate. Figure 3.9 shows that the loop doesn't always iterate the same number of times by showing the different numbers of dots for each run of `WhileLoopTest`.

The do-while Loop

The `do-while` loop is very similar to the `while` loop. The difference is that the loop's condition comes after the body of the loop, rather than before it. Because the loop body is executed once before the condition is even checked, the `do` loop is just a convenient way to define a loop that iterates at least once, even if the condition is never true. You very rarely see the `do` loop in real-world programs because anything that you can do within a `do` loop can be done just as easily with the more familiar `while` loop. Still, it's good to know what the loop does in case you ever encounter it. The syntax for the `do` loop is as follows:

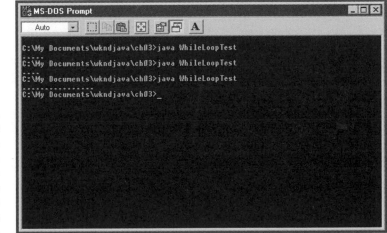

Figure 3.9

The `WhileLoop Test` program shows how to loop an indeterminate amount of times using the `while` loop.

```
do {
    repeatable_statements;
} while (condition);
```

You start the do loop with the do keyword and then immediately open the loop with the opening curly brace. Next, you define the loop statements within the curly braces. Then you end the loop body with the closing curly brace. After the body of the loop, you use the while keyword and specify the loop condition within parentheses. You finally end the loop with a semicolon. The DoLoopTest demonstrates the do-while loop. Here is the source code:

```
/*

 * DoLoopTest

 * Demonstrates how to use the do-while loop

 */


public class DoLoopTest {

    public static void main(String args[]) {
        int myNum;
        //generate random numbers until we get 5
        do {
            System.out.print(".");
            myNum = (int)(Math.random() * 10);
        }
        while (myNum != 5);
    }
}
```

The program does the same thing as the WhileLoopTest program, except it uses the do-while loop instead of a while loop. You can see the output in Figure 3.10.

Figure 3.10

The
`DoLoopTest`
program
demonstrates the
use of the `do-`
`while` loop.

Using break and continue to Control Loop Flow

You may recall that you've seen the `break` statement before, when you learned about `switch`. Now, it's time to take a more in-depth look at the utility of `break` and its counterpart, `continue`. The `break` statement transfers control from an enclosing statement. In other words, it is used to break out of a loop explicitly, taking control out of a `switch`, `while`, `do`, or `for` statement. If using `break`, you must make it appear within a `switch`, `while`, `do`, or `for` statement, or a compile-time error occurs. Here is an example:

```
while (true) {
    System.out.print("true");
    break;
}
System.out.println(" out of loop");
```

At first glance, this looks like an infinite loop, but it's not. The loop will iterate once because the condition is `true`, but the `break` statement takes the program right out of the loop as soon as `break` is reached. The output of this code is a single line: `true out of loop`.

The continue statement indicates that the loop should attempt to iterate again. If you want to use the continue statement, you must place it within an iteration statement such as a for, while, or do loop. Here's a simple example:

```
boolean b = true;
while (b) {
    if (b) continue;
    System.out.println("never gets here");
    b = false;
}
```

The continue statement doesn't break completely out of the loop. Instead, it causes the loop to stop where it is and loop again from the beginning. The condition for the loop is checked again, and if it is true, the loop iterates again. This example causes an infinite loop.

The break and continue statements can also be used in conjunction with labels. A label is an identifier, followed by a colon that precedes a block statement. For example, here is a block of code labeled myCode:

```
myCode : while (true) {
    statement_1;
    break myCode;
    statement_2;
}
```

I also sneaked in the break statement so that I could explain how it works when used with a label. The break keyword is followed by the label of the code that you want to break out of. In this example, statement_2 is never reached because the break myCode statement takes you out of the myCode block. This is a simple example, but imagine a larger block of code from which you might need to break.

When a label is used with the continue statement, instead of breaking out of the labeled loop, it takes the program back to the beginning. The break and continue keywords are not commonly used, but it's good for you to get some exposure to them in case you ever come across them.

CAUTION

If you are contemplating using these statements as a way to get tighter control of your loops, be careful. The use of these statements can make the program harder to trace and debug since it has program flow jumping all over the place. There is never a case where you are forced to use these statements, and if only for readability's sake, you should try to avoid using them.

Take a Break

Speaking of breaks, now's a good time for you to take a quick one. Almost all programs you'll ever come across will have both loops and conditional statements, so what you've covered so far in this session is very important. For the rest of this afternoon, you'll learn about accepting command-line arguments, the Math class, and some helpful java.util classes. After that, we'll revisit the calculator project and make some important updates using the skills covered in this session.

Accepting Command-Line Arguments

Command-line arguments are parameters that you specify and pass into a program at the command prompt when you execute a program. They are often used to set certain states of the program so that the program runs differently depending on the values you pass. For example, some programs accept the command-line argument verbose, which causes the program to spit out what it's doing while it's doing it. It becomes, in a word, *verbose.* This command-line argument helps you see the order in which the program performs operations. Because it does so, verbose can help you debug the program if it crashes. (You can see what the program was attempting to do when it crashed and then check the associated area of the source code and make appropriate adjustments.) Knowing where to start is very helpful when you're debugging programs, especially huge ones.

Debugging is just one example of the use of command-line arguments. You can use command-line arguments however you wish. If, for instance, you want to write a program that moves a file from one destination to another, you could accept two command-line arguments: the original location of the source and the destination location. In this section, you'll learn how to accept and handle command-line arguments in Java.

Passing Arguments at the Command Prompt

Passing in command-line arguments in Java is quite simple. When you start a Java program, you use the `java` command and follow it with the name of a class that contains a `main()` method. To pass in command-line arguments, you put a space after the program name and then start typing the command-line arguments. Each command-line argument is separated by a space. Here is the syntax:

```
java MyProgramName arg1 arg2 arg3 …
```

You can specify as many arguments as you wish. The program may or may not do anything with them. Here is an example where two command-line arguments are passed in:

```
java FileMove C:\source\myfile C:\dest\myfile
```

In this example, the program name is `FileMove`, and the two arguments are `C:\source\myfile` and `C:\dest\myfile`. It may be conceptually helpful to imagine that this program moves a file, `myfile`, from its source directory, `C:\source\`, to another directory, `C:\dest\`. At runtime, you can specify whatever source file and destination file you want. The program just takes the arguments you pass it and does its thing.

What if your command-line argument is a full sentence that contains spaces? In that case, you use quotation marks around the argument, like this:

```
java MyProgramName "this is one argument"
```

Without the quotation marks, the program will think that there are four arguments, but because the quotation marks are there, the program treats it as one argument, even though there are spaces.

Using the args[] Array

You know how the main() method always looks something like this:

```
public static void main(String args[]) {

    ...

}
```

Well, as you can see, args[] is an array of String objects. When you pass in command-line arguments, the program stuffs them into this array, so you can access them from within your code. The length of the array is always equal to the number of arguments you pass in, so if no arguments are passed in, args.length will be zero. The ArgsTest example program accepts as many command-line arguments as you want to give it. Then it just dumps them back out to the standard output stream. This program is a good demonstration of how to pass in command-line arguments and access them from within the program itself using the args[] array. Here is the source code:

```
/*
 * ArgsTest
 * Tests the use of command line arguments
 */

public class ArgsTest {

  public static void main(String args[]) {
    if (args.length > 0) {
      System.out.println("Command Line Arguments:");
      for (int a = 0; a < args.length; a++) {
        System.out.println("args[" + a + "]: " + args[a]);
```

```
        }
    }

    else {
      System.out.println("No command line arguments were "
          + "passed in.");
    }
  }
}
```

The output from the `ArgsTest` program is shown in Figure 3.11.

NOTE ●●

The `main()` method is just another method. There is nothing special about it except for the fact that when you instantiate a class from the command line and run it as an application, this is the method that is called automatically to start your program. Because it's just a method, you can name the `String[]` array argument anything you want. It is usually always named `args[]` by convention, and to avoid confusion, you should do the same, but don't take it for granted that everyone else will do that. If you're reading someone else's code, check the `main()` method signature for the name of the command-line argument array.

●●●

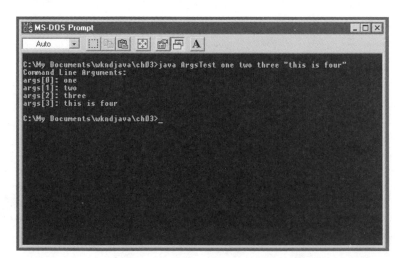

Figure 3.11

The `ArgsTest` program lists any command-line arguments that are passed in.

Parsing Data Types

The `args[]` array is an array of `String` objects. So, what if you want to accept other datatypes from the command line, such as `int`, `double`, or `char`? You can accomplish this, but not directly. You still have to adhere to the rule that command-line arguments initially get placed within a `String[]` array. However, you can parse the `String` to another data type. *Parsing* means converting the data type of an expression or literal. For example, if you passed in an integer as the first command-line argument, you can convert the `String` representation of that `int` from a `String` to an `int` like this:

```
int myArgInt = Integer.parseInt(args[0]);
```

The `parseInt()` method, found in the `Integer` class, accepts a `String` argument, which should be a valid representation of an `int` (or you'll get a runtime error). It returns the `int` value that corresponds to the `String` that you pass in. Table 3.3 shows some other useful methods that can be used to parse `String`s to primitive data types.

TABLE 3.3 STRING PARSING METHODS	
Method	**Description**
byte `Byte.parseByte(String)`	Parses a `String` to a `byte`.
double `Double.parseDouble(String)`	Parses a `String` to a `double`.
float `Float.parseFloat(String)`	Parses a `String` to a `float`.
int `Integer.parseInt(String)`	Parses a `String` to an `int`.
long `Long.parseLong(String)`	Parses a `String` to a `long`.
short `Short.parseShort(String)`	Parses a `String` to a `short`.

The Math Class

The Math class, defined in the java.lang package, is a nice utility class you can use to perform mathematical operations. The Math class is final, and there are no accessible constructors. This means that you can't subclass it or instantiate it (you can't create a Math object). All of Math's methods are static, so you don't need a Math instance to call them anyway. With the Math class, you can perform operations such as trigonometric functions, rounding functions, random number generation, square root, absolute value, and more. In this section, we'll play around with the Math class a bit and get a feel for its methods. Then at the end of this afternoon's session, we'll take advantage of some of the Math class's methods by adding them to the calculator project. Refer to Table 3.4 for a listing of some commonly used Math methods.

Using the Math Class's Methods

Because Math's methods are static, you call them using the Math class name, followed by a dot, followed by the method name. For example, to create a random number between 0.0 (inclusive) and 1.0 (exclusive), you call the random() method like this:

```
Math.random();
```

Or to get the square root of 100.0, you call the sqrt() method like this:

```
Math.sqrt(100.0);
```

Well, you get the idea. Now, let's go ahead with an example. The Math Test program makes use of some of the Math class methods. It optionally accepts two command-line arguments. Though, as you learned earlier, all command-line arguments are read in as Strings, they must be in a format that can be parsed to a double using the Double.parseDouble() method. If no arguments are passed in, the MathTest program generates two random numbers and performs the mathematical operations on them instead.

TABLE 3.4 MATH CLASS METHODS

Math Method	Description
`Math.abs(`*`int n`*`)`	Absolute value (*n* or *0-n*, whichever is greater)
`Math.acos(`*`double d`*`)`	Arc cosine of *d*
`Math.asin(`*`double d`*`)`	Arc sine of *d*
`Math.atan(`*`double d`*`)`	Arc tangent of *d*
`Math.ceil(`*`double d`*`)`	Ceiling (smallest value not less than *d* that is an integer)
`Math.cos(`*`double d`*`)`	Cosine of *d*
`Math.exp(double d)`	(e^d, where e=2.718...)
`Math.floor(double d)`	Floor (highest value not greater than d that is an integer)
`Math.log(`*`double d`*`)`	Natural Logarithm of *d*
`Math.pow(`*`double a, double b`*`)`	a^b
`Math.random()`	Generates a random number between 0.0 and 1.0
`Math.round(`*`float f`*`)`	Rounds *f* to the nearest *int* value
`Math.round(`*`double d`*`)`	Rounds *d* to the nearest `long` value
`Math.sin(`*`double d`*`)`	Sine of *d*
`Math.sqrt(`*`double d`*`)`	Square root of *d*
`Math.tan(`*`double d`*`)`	Tangent of *d*
`Math.toDegrees(`*`double d`*`)`	Converts *d* (in radians) to degrees
`Math.toRadians(`*`double d`*`)`	Converts *d* (in degrees) to radians

Here is the source code for the MathTest program:

```
/*
 * MathTest
 * Demonstrates some of the features of the Math class
 * Also uses the DecimalFormat class to limit the number of
 * fractional digits
 */
import java.text.DecimalFormat;

public class MathTest {

  public static void main(String args[]) {
    DecimalFormat form = new DecimalFormat();
    form.setMinimumFractionDigits(1);
    form.setMaximumFractionDigits(3);
    double n, n2;
    if (args.length == 2) {
        //get the numbers from the command line args
        n = Double.parseDouble(args[0]);
        n2 = Double.parseDouble(args[1]);
    }
    else {
        //get two random numbers between -10.0 and 10.0
        System.out.println("No command line args, "
            + "using randoms...");
        n = Math.random() * 20.0 - 10.0;
        n2 = Math.random() * 20.0 - 10.0;
    }

    //Math's methods are static and don't need a Math instance
    System.out.println("E = " + form.format(Math.E));
```

```
System.out.println("PI = " + form.format(Math.PI));
//print out the results of some Math functions
System.out.println("Math.abs(" + form.format(n) + ") = "
    + form.format(Math.abs(n)));
System.out.println("Math.floor(" + form.format(n) + ") = "
    + form.format(Math.floor(n)));
System.out.println("Math.ceil(" + form.format(n) + ") = "
    + form.format(Math.ceil(n)));
System.out.println("Math.rint(" + form.format(n) + ") = "
    + form.format(Math.rint(n)));
System.out.println("Math.max(" + form.format(n) + ", "
    + form.format(n2) + ") = "
    + form.format(Math.max(n, n2)));
System.out.println("Math.min(" + form.format(n) + ", "
    + form.format(n2) + ") = "
    + form.format(Math.min(n, n2)));
System.out.println("Math.pow(" + form.format(n)
    + ", 2.0) = " + form.format(Math.pow(n, 2.0)));
System.out.println("Math.sqrt(" + form.format(n) + ") = "
    + form.format(Math.sqrt(n)));
    }
}
```

Did you notice that I didn't have to import the Math class to gain access to it? That's because Math is defined in the java.lang class. All classes defined there are automatically imported and are immediately accessible in any Java program. Another thing you might notice is that I used the DecimalFormat class. The DecimalFormat class just formats a decimal number for nicer output. It is defined in the java.text package, so I had to import it before I could use it. The DecimalFormat object that the MathTest program uses, form, only restricts the number of fraction digits for printed decimal numbers. The two methods, setMinimumFractionDigits() and setMaximumFractionDigits(), set the minimum and the maximum number of digits that should appear after the decimal point when the formatted numbers are printed. I only used the DecimalFormat class to shorten the number of decimal digits because the Math.random() method creates numbers with a bunch of decimal digits. You can see the output of the MathTest program in Figure 3.12.

Using the java.util Package

The java.util package is a very important part of the standard Java Software Development Kit. It contains miscellaneous utility classes such as a random number generator, date and calendar classes, the collections framework, and more. This book doesn't cover all of these classes, but it does cover part of the collections framework, the Random class, and the Date and GregorianCalendar classes. The collection API (*application programming interface*), which defines collection classes such as Vector and HashTable, is very commonly used, as are many of the other classes in the java.util package. The java.util package also defines EventObject, the base class for all event classes. Tonight, you'll learn more about handling GUI events. For now, let's just take a look at some of the other java.util classes.

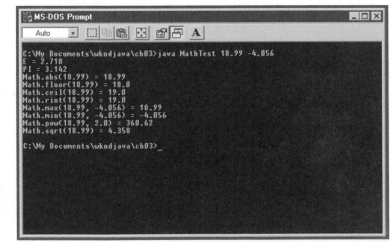

Figure 3.12

The MathTest program performs mathematical operations on two numbers (either passed in as arguments or random) using the Math class's methods.

Learning about Collections

The Java Collection API defines classes that group objects together. It might be useful here for you to recall what you already know about arrays and compare them to collection classes. Arrays are lists of objects or primitives. They are of a set, *unchangeable,* size. Once they're initialized, you're stuck with the size of the arrays as they were set. This is not true of the collection classes. The Vector class, for example, is an expandable list of objects. When you create it, you're not forced to declare its size. Anytime that you add an object to it, the size is automatically increased by one. All of the collection classes implement the Collection interface.

You'll learn all about interfaces tomorrow, but basically interfaces define a set of method signatures (without method bodies) that all implementing classes must provide bodies for. This means that all of the collection classes must have all of the methods defined in the Collection interface. Also, because the methods are not implemented in the interface itself, you can't instantiate a Collection object directly. Instead, you have to instantiate a class that implements the Collection interface to get Collection functionality. That's all you need to know about interfaces for now. Table 3.5 lists the methods found in the Collection interface.

NOTE The statement here that all of the collection classes must provide functionality for all of the methods declared in the Collection interface is not entirely true. Not all of the Collection interface methods are applicable to all of the collection classes. In those cases, the collections define the bodies of those methods to cause an UnsupportedOperationException to occur. It just causes your program to crash if you try to call an unsupported method on a collection class.

Each class that implements the Collection interface behaves in a slightly different way. For example, lists, like Vector, maintain an ordered set of Objects that can be accessed by a numerical subscript and typically allow duplicate elements. Sets don't allow any duplicate elements, nor do maps.

TABLE 3.5 METHODS OF THE COLLECTION INTERFACE

Method	Description
boolean add(Object)	Adds the given Object to the collection.
boolean addAll(Collection)	Adds all of the elements of the given Collection to this collection.
void clear()	Removes all of the elements from this collection.
boolean contains(Object)	Returns true if this collection contains the given Object.
boolean containsAll(Collection)	Returns true if this collection contains all of the elements contained in the given Collection.
boolean equals(Object)	Returns true if the given Object is equal to this collection.
int hashCode()	Returns the hash code number for this collection.
boolean isEmpty()	Returns true if this collection doesn't contain anything.
Iterator iterator()	Returns an iterator for this collection for iterating through this collection's objects.
boolean remove(Object)	Removes the given Object from this collection.
boolean removeAll(Collection)	Removes all of the elements contained by the given Collection from this collection.
boolean retainAll(Collection)	Removes all of the objects that are *not* contained by the given Collection.
int size()	Returns the number of elements contained in this collection.

TABLE 3.5 METHODS OF THE COLLECTION INTERFACE	
Method	**Description**
Object[] toArray()	Returns an array of the objects contained within this collection.
Object[] toArray(*Object[]*)	Returns an array of the same type as the given array that contains all of the objects within this collection.

The add(), remove(), and retain() methods that return boolean values return true if the collection changed as a result of the method being called. This happens because different collection classes have different rules for maintaining their objects. For example, some collections allow duplicate elements, while others do not.

Some lists are sorted, while others are not, and so on. The CollectionTest program tests two classes that implement the Collection interface, the Vector class and the TreeSet class. Here is the source code:

```
/*
 * CollectionTest
 * A short test of the Collection API
 */

import java.util.*;

public class CollectionTest {

    public static void main(String args[]) {
        Vector vect = new Vector();
        vect.add("Oranges");
        vect.add("Apples");
        vect.add("Limes");
```

```
        vect.add("Grapes");
        vect.remove("Limes");
        vect.add("Oranges");
        printContents(vect);
        TreeSet tree = new TreeSet(vect);
        printContents(tree);
        vect.addAll(tree);
        printContents(vect);
        //can also get an array:
        Object[] objArray = vect.toArray();
        System.out.println("Created an array of size: "
            + objArray.length + " from the Vector.");
    }


    public static void printContents(Collection collection) {
        Iterator i = collection.iterator();
        System.out.println("\nListing the "
            + collection.size() + " elements of a "
            + collection.getClass().getName());
        while (i.hasNext()) {
            System.out.println(i.next());
        }
    }
}
```

The Vector class simply maintains a list of Objects. It allows duplicate entries and does not sort its elements. The TreeSet collection does not allow duplicate entries and does sort its elements. The output, shown in Figure 3.13, demonstrates these facts.

In the printContents() method, I used an Iterator to loop through all of the collections' contents. You can get an Iterator from a collection

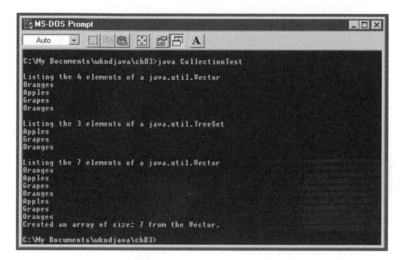

Figure 3.13

The Collection Test program uses the Vector and TreeSet classes from the Collection API.

by calling the `iterator()` method. An `Iterator` object has at least three methods: `hasNext()`, `next()`, and `remove()`. The `hasNext()` method returns `true` if there are more elements to iterate through. The `next()` method returns the next element (starting with the first and ending with the last) and moves to the next element. Using this logic, you can see that `hasNext()` will eventually return `false`, so it can be used as the condition for a loop, as was done in the `CollectionTest` program. In that program, the `while` loop in the `printContents()` method is basically saying, "while there are more elements, give one to me (until there aren't any more left)." The `remove()` method removes the last object returned from the `next()` method from the underlying collection.

Date and Calendar Utilities

The `java.util` package also defines some classes that you can use to perform date and calendar functions. A `Date` object represents a specific instance of time up to the nearest millisecond (that's one-thousandth of a second). The `GregorianCalendar` class allows for converting from the specific instance of time (a `Date` object) to calendar fields, such as month, date, year, hour, minute, second. The `Date` class doesn't handle this functionality on its own because the whole world doesn't use the same type of calendar. Most of us do, however, and that's what the `GregorianCalendar` class is for. The `DateTimeTest` program, listed next, demonstrates how to use these classes.

```java
/*
 * DateTimeTest
 * Demonstrates how to use dates and times.
 */

import java.util.*;
import java.text.DateFormat;

public class DateTimeTest {

  public static void main(String args[]) {
     Date date = new Date();
     System.out.println("Date: " + date);
     System.out.println("Seconds since "
        + "January 1, 1970, 00:00:00 GMT: " + date.getTime());
     GregorianCalendar greg
        = new GregorianCalendar(1879, Calendar.MARCH, 14);
     date = greg.getTime();
     System.out.println(date);
     DateFormat dateFormatter = DateFormat.getDateTimeInstance(
        DateFormat.FULL, DateFormat.FULL);
     System.out.println(dateFormatter.format(date));
     dateFormatter = DateFormat.getDateInstance(
        DateFormat.SHORT);
     System.out.println(dateFormatter.format(date));
  }
}
```

When you instantiate a new `Date` object using the no-argument constructor, the date is initialized to the current instance of time. There is also one other non-deprecated `Date` constructor that accepts a long representation of a `Date` as an argument. The `long` value that gets passed in is defined in milliseconds since January 1, 1970, at exactly midnight GMT. As you can see in the example, there are other ways to set a specific date using the `GregorianCalendar` class. I set the date to the day Einstein was born. I also used the `DateFormat` class. It's similar to the `DecimalFormat` class in that it parses something into a formatted `String` based on rules that you set on the `DateFormat` object. The only difference is that the `DateFormat` class formats dates instead of decimal numbers. You can see the output in Figure 3.14.

Another Way to Generate Random Numbers

The last `java.util` method that I cover here is the `Random` class. The function of the `Random` class is similar to the `Math.random()` method, except more robust. When you instantiate a `Random` object, you can do so by passing in a `long` as a random number key or call the no-argument constructor, in which case the current time, in milliseconds, is used as the key. Internally, the `Random` class uses algorithms to generate pseudorandom

Figure 3.14

The `DateTime Test` program demonstrates the use of the `Date` and `Gregorian Calendar` classes in the `java.util` package. It also demonstrates the `java.text. DateFormat` class, which is used to format date strings.

numbers using the key as an input value. The term *pseudorandom* is used here because the numbers are not technically random as their values are predictable if the key is known. In fact, if you always create Random objects with the same key, you'll always get the same sequence of pseudorandom numbers. The algorithms that are used by the Random class generate all possible numbers with extremely close to-equal probability. By the way, all of this also applies to the Math.random() method—it uses the Random class behind the scenes. You can see some common Random methods in Table 3.6.

The RandomTest program demonstrates how to use the Random class to generate random numbers. Here is the source code:

```
/*
 * RandomTest
 * Demonstrates how to use the java.util.Random class to
 * generate random numbers.
 */

import java.util.Random;

public class RandomTest {

    public static void main(String args[]) {
        Random randomGenerator = args.length == 0 ? new Random()
            : new Random(Long.parseLong(args[0]));
        System.out.println("Generating 5 random numbers "
            + "between 1 and 100 (inclusive)");
        for (int i = 0; i < 5; i++) {
            System.out.println(randomGenerator.nextInt(100) + 1);
        }
    }
}
```

TABLE 3.6 COMMONLY USED RANDOM METHODS	
Method	**Description**
boolean nextBoolean()	Randomly returns either true or false boolean values.
double nextDouble()	Returns a random double value ranging from 0.0 (inclusive) to 1.0 (exclusive).
float nextFloat()	Returns a random float value ranging from 0.0 (inclusive) to 1.0 (exclusive).
int nextInt()	Returns a random int value (all 2^{32} values are possible).
int nextInt(int *n*)	Returns a random int value ranging from 0 (inclusive) to n (exclusive).
long nextLong()	Returns a random long value (all 2^{64} values are possible).

The RandomTest program simply generates five random integers and prints them to the screen. Each time you run this program, the output should be different (see Figure 3.15).

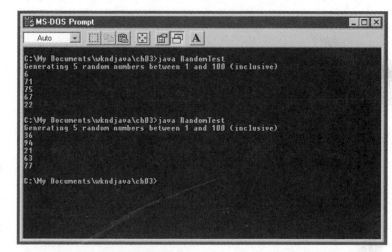

Figure 3.15

When you run the RandomTest program twice, you can see the way the numbers differ.

Updating the Calculator Project

You've learned quite a lot so far this afternoon. Now, it's time to put this knowledge to good use. In this section, you'll update both the `CalculatorModel` class and the `CalculatorHelper` class using some of what you learned this afternoon. After you update your classes, you'll see that the calculator project will actually start acting like a calculator. Lastly, before moving on to tonight's session, you'll test your classes to make sure that they're working correctly.

Updating CalculatorModel

The `CalculatorModel` class represents the state of a calculator—the data that a calculator uses to do its thing. It's been updated with some new and improved features. One difference is that the `CalculatorModel` class now keeps track of the operation along with the stuff it already had. It has constants (for example, `ADD`, `SUBTRACT`, `MULTIPLY`, and so on) that represent the calculator operations, and the `setCurrentOp()` method uses a `switch` statement to make sure that the given operation is a valid one. If it's not, the `setCurrentOp()` method sets the operation to `NONE`, which signifies no operation. There is also a new `isOpBinary()` method that returns true if the currently set operation is binary (that is, it takes two operands). The `CalculatorModel` class also keeps track of a memory value. Many calculators let you temporarily store a number in memory. The memory value for the `CalculatorModel` class is the same idea. Here is the updated source code:

```
/*
 * CalculatorModel
 * Encapsulates the data model used by the Calculator
 * Application
 */

public class CalculatorModel {
```

```java
private double operand1;
private double operand2;
/* Stores the value associated with a calculator's memory
 * function */
private double mem;
/* The current operand that appears in the calculator's
 * display */
private double currentDisplayValue;
/* Represents operation to be performed on the operands */
private char currentOp;
/* the following are possible values for currentOp */
public final static char ADD = '+';
public final static char SUBTRACT = '-';
public final static char MULTIPLY = '*';
public final static char DIVIDE = '/';
public final static char POW = '^';
public final static char SQRT = 'Q';
public final static char SIGN = '~';
public final static char NONE = '?';


/*
 * Constructs a new CalculatorModel object.
 * maxDigits - The maximum number of displayable digits
 */
public CalculatorModel() {
    currentOp = CalculatorModel.NONE;
}

public void setOperand1(double value) {
    operand1 = value;
```

```java
        currentDisplayValue = operand1;
    }


    public double getOperand1() {
        return operand1;
    }


    public void setOperand2(double value) {
        operand2 = value;
        currentDisplayValue = operand2;
    }


    public double getOperand2() {
        return operand2;
    }


    public void setMem(double value) {
        mem = value;
    }


    public double getMem() {
        return mem;
    }


    public void setCurrentDisplayValue(double value) {
        currentDisplayValue = value;
    }


    public double getCurrentDisplayValue() {
        return currentDisplayValue;
    }
```

```java
public void setCurrentOp(char op) {
    switch (op) {
        case CalculatorModel.ADD:
        case CalculatorModel.SUBTRACT:
        case CalculatorModel.MULTIPLY:
        case CalculatorModel.DIVIDE:
        case CalculatorModel.POW:
        case CalculatorModel.SQRT:
        case CalculatorModel.SIGN:
            currentOp = op;
            break;
        default:
            currentOp = CalculatorModel.NONE;
    }
}


/* Gets the current operator */
public char getCurrentOp() {
    return currentOp;
}


/* Indicates if the current operator is binary or unary.
 * Returns true if the current operator is binary,
 * false if it is unary. */
public boolean isOpBinary() {
    switch(currentOp) {
        case CalculatorModel.ADD:
        case CalculatorModel.SUBTRACT:
        case CalculatorModel.MULTIPLY:
        case CalculatorModel.DIVIDE:
```

```
            case CalculatorModel.POW:
                return true;
            default:
                return false;
        }
    }



    public String toString() {
        String s = "operand1 = " + operand1
                + " operand2 = " + operand2
                + " currentOp = " + currentOp
                + " currentDisplayValue = " +
                        currentDisplayValue
                + " mem = " + mem;
        return s;
    }
}
```

Updating CalculatorHelper

The CalculatorHelper class also gets renovated here. First, the work-horse of the calculator project makes changes to account for the new CalculatorModel class, and it takes on some more responsibility of its own. That responsibility takes the form of setting the operands of the CalculatorModel object. There are two operands in the CalculatorModel class, but there is only one setOperation() method in CalculatorHelper. CalculatorHelper does this so that it can encapsulate all of the logic dealing with setting the operands and hide the complexity of it from the outside world. For example, when you use a calculator, you don't have to explicitly tell the calculator that you're setting the first or second operand.

There is no setoperand1 or setoperand2 button; you just press numbers and operators and the equal key and expect the answer to appear. That's what the `CalculatorHelper` class attempts to simulate. The `CalculatorHelper` just provides a single method to enter a number. The method figures out which operand it should be. For example, if no operator is set, when the `setOperand()` method is called, operand1 is set; but after a binary operator is set, we need a second operand, so a call to `setOperand()` sets the second operand after the first one is already set for a binary operation.

The mathematical methods (`add()`, `subtract()`, and so on) have also changed. They are now `private`, so you can't call them on a `CalculatorHelper` object directly. Instead, `CalculatorHelper` provides one `public` method, `performOperation()`, that figures out what method to call for you. Before you call this method, though, you need to call the `setCurrentOp()` method of the `CalculatorHelper` class. You can set it to any of the `CalculatorModel`'s operator constants, like `CalculatorModel.ADD`. When you call `performOperation()`, `CalculatorHelper` checks this value so that it can determine which mathematical method to call. The `CalculatorHelper` class also makes use of a couple of `Math` methods: `pow()` and `sqrt()`.

Another feature that has been added to `CalculatorHelper` is the audit trail. The audit trail is basically a `StringBuffer` that simulates a calculator register. It's just a `String` representation of all of the operations that the calculator performs. The `auditTrail` variable stores this information, and the `CalculatorHelper` class takes care of all of the logic required to create the audit trail. The updated source code for the `Calculator Helper` class is listed here. If you start asking yourself, "Why did Joey do this?" when you're reading this code, just pick up a calculator, play with it, and know that that's the functionality I'm trying to simulate here.

```
/*
 * CalculatorHelper
 * A class that performs mathematical functions for a
 * Calculator program
 */
```

```java
public class CalculatorHelper {
   private CalculatorModel calcModel;
   private StringBuffer auditTrail;
   private boolean opPerformed;
   private int decimalPos;

   public CalculatorHelper() {
      this(20);
   }

   public CalculatorHelper(int decimalAlignmentPos) {
      calcModel = new CalculatorModel();
      auditTrail = new StringBuffer();
      decimalPos = decimalAlignmentPos;
   }

   public CalculatorModel performOperation() {
      double value;
      if (calcModel.isOpBinary()) {
         auditTrail.append(align(calcModel.getCurrentOp() + " "
                        + calcModel.getOperand2()) + "\n");
      }
      else if (calcModel.getCurrentOp() == CalculatorModel.SQRT){
         auditTrail.append("SQRT\n");
      }
      else if (calcModel.getCurrentOp() == CalculatorModel.SIGN){
         auditTrail.append("+/-\n");
      }
      switch (calcModel.getCurrentOp()) {
```

```
case CalculatorModel.ADD:
    value = add();
    break;
case CalculatorModel.SUBTRACT:
    value = subtract();
    break;
case CalculatorModel.MULTIPLY:
    value = multiply();
    break;
case CalculatorModel.DIVIDE:
    value = divide();
    break;
case CalculatorModel.POW:
    value = pow();
    break;
case CalculatorModel.SQRT:
    value = sqrt();
    break;
case CalculatorModel.SIGN:
    value = sign();
    break;
default:
    value = calcModel.getCurrentDisplayValue();
    calcModel.setOperand1(value);
    calcModel.setOperand2(0.0);
}
calcModel.setCurrentDisplayValue(value);
//makes the currently displayed value ready for another op
calcModel.setOperand1(value);
opPerformed = true;
```

```java
            auditTrail.append("=============================\n"
                            + align(String.valueOf(value)) + "\n");
        return calcModel;
    }


    public CalculatorModel setOperand(double value) {
        if (calcModel.isOpBinary() && !opPerformed) {
            calcModel.setOperand2(value);
        }
        else {
            auditTrail.append("\n" + align(String.valueOf(value))
                    + "\n");
            calcModel.setOperand1(value);
            calcModel.setOperand2(0.0);
            calcModel.setCurrentOp(CalculatorModel.NONE);
        }
        calcModel.setCurrentDisplayValue(value);
        return calcModel;
    }


    public CalculatorModel setOp(char op) {
        if (opPerformed == false
            && calcModel.getCurrentOp() != CalculatorModel.NONE) {
            performOperation();
        }
        opPerformed = false;
        calcModel.setCurrentOp(op);
        //get ready to accept operand2 for binary operations
        if (calcModel.isOpBinary()) {
            calcModel.setOperand2(0.0);
            calcModel.setCurrentDisplayValue(0.0);
```

```
    }
        //automatically perform unary operations
        else {
            performOperation();
        }
        return calcModel;
    }


public CalculatorModel memAdd() {
    calcModel.setMem(calcModel.getMem()
        + calcModel.getCurrentDisplayValue());
    return calcModel;
}


public CalculatorModel memRecall() {
    setOperand(calcModel.getMem());
    return calcModel;
}


public CalculatorModel memSwap() {
    double swapVal = calcModel.getMem();
    calcModel.setMem(calcModel.getCurrentDisplayValue());
    setOperand(swapVal);
    return calcModel;
}


public CalculatorModel memClear() {
    calcModel.setMem(0.0);
    return calcModel;
}
```

```java
public void clear() {
    //clears only second operand if mid-binary operation
    setOperand(0.0);
}


/* Clears everything except the memory value */
public CalculatorModel clearAll() {
    calcModel.setOperand1(0.0);
    calcModel.setOperand2(0.0);
    calcModel.setCurrentDisplayValue(0.0);
    calcModel.setCurrentOp(CalculatorModel.NONE);
    opPerformed = false;
    return calcModel;
}


public String getAuditTrail() {
    return auditTrail.toString();
}


private String align(String decimalString) {
    String aligned = decimalString;
    int currDecPos = aligned.indexOf('.');
    for (int pos = currDecPos; pos < decimalPos; pos++) {
        aligned = " " + aligned;
    }
    return aligned;
}

private double add() {
  return calcModel.getOperand1() + calcModel.getOperand2();
}
```

```
private  double subtract() {
    return calcModel.getOperand1() - calcModel.getOperand2();
}


private double multiply() {
    return calcModel.getOperand1() * calcModel.getOperand2();
}


private double divide() {
    return calcModel.getOperand1() / calcModel.getOperand2();
}


private double pow() {
    return Math.pow(calcModel.getOperand1(),
        calcModel.getOperand2());
}


private double sqrt() {
    return Math.sqrt(calcModel.getOperand1());
}


private double sign() {
    return calcModel.getOperand1() * -1;
}
}
```

Testing It

Now that you've updated the classes, you should test them to make sure they're working properly. The `CalculatorTest` class simulates the use of a calculator by entering numbers and performing operations. Then it prints the audit trail to see what the results were. Here is the source code for the `CalculatorTest` program:

```java
/*
 * CalculatorTest
 * Tests the CalculatorHelper class
 */

import java.text.*;

public class CalculatorTest {

    public static void main(String args[]) {
        CalculatorHelper calcHelper
            = new CalculatorHelper();
        calcHelper.setOperand(100.0);
        calcHelper.setOp(CalculatorModel.ADD);
        calcHelper.setOperand(25.0);
        calcHelper.performOperation();
        calcHelper.performOperation();
        calcHelper.setOp(CalculatorModel.SUBTRACT);
        calcHelper.setOperand(25.0);
        calcHelper.performOperation();
        calcHelper.setOp(CalculatorModel.MULTIPLY);
        calcHelper.setOperand(0.25);
        calcHelper.performOperation();
        calcHelper.setOp(CalculatorModel.DIVIDE);
        calcHelper.setOperand(10.0);
        calcHelper.performOperation();
```

```
                    calcHelper.setOp(CalculatorModel.SIGN);

                    calcHelper.setOperand(9.0);

                    calcHelper.setOp(CalculatorModel.SQRT);

                    calcHelper.setOperand(3.0);

                    calcHelper.setOp(CalculatorModel.POW);

                    calcHelper.setOperand(3.0);

                    calcHelper.performOperation();

                    System.out.println(calcHelper.getAuditTrail());

             }

    }
```

The `CalculatorHelperTest` program is a good test for the calculator project classes. The output illustrated in Figure 3.16 shows the audit trail that was generated by the `CalculatorHelperTest` program.

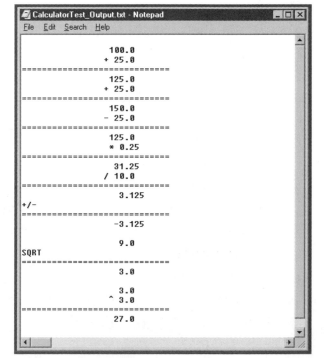

Figure 3.16

As you can see, the Calculator Test run makes sure that the Calculator Helper class is working properly and that the audit trail is being generated correctly.

The `CalculatorModelStateTest` program is more verbose. It's geared more toward testing whether the variables of the `CalculatorModel` class always have the correct values based on the operations that are being performed by the `CalculatorHelper` class. After each `CalculatorHelper` method call, the `CalculatorModel` state is printed so that you can see the values of its variables and make sure that things in the guts of this project are working properly. Since each of `CalculatorHelper`'s methods return the `CalculatorModel` object, printing out the `CalculatorModel`'s state is as easy as putting the method calls within `System.out.println()` methods. Here is the source code listing for the `CalculatorModelStateTest` program:

```
/*
 * CalculatorModelStateTest
 * Tests out how operations affect the state of the
 * CalculatorModel
 */

public class CalculatorModelStateTest {

  public static void main(String args[]) {
    CalculatorHelper calcHelper = new CalculatorHelper();
    System.out.println("New CalculatorModel");
    System.out.println("Set operand to 123.45");
    System.out.println(calcHelper.setOperand(123.45));
    System.out.println("Set operator to CalculatorModel.ADD");
    System.out.println(calcHelper.setOp (CalculatorModel.ADD));
    System.out.println("Set operand to 2000.001");
    System.out.println(calcHelper.setOperand(2000.001));
    System.out.println("Performed the operation");
    System.out.println(calcHelper.performOperation());
    System.out.println("called memAdd()");
    System.out.println(calcHelper.memAdd());
```

```
System.out.println("Set operand to 1000.0");

System.out.println(calcHelper.setOperand(1000.0));

System.out.println("called memRecall()");

System.out.println(calcHelper.memRecall());

System.out.println("set operator to "
    + "CalculatorModel.SUBTRACT");

System.out.println(
    calcHelper.setOp(CalculatorModel.SUBTRACT));

System.out.println("Called memRecall()");

System.out.println(calcHelper.memRecall());

System.out.println("Performed the operation");

System.out.println(calcHelper.performOperation());

System.out.println("Called memSwap()");

System.out.println(calcHelper.memSwap());

System.out.println("Called memClear()");

System.out.println(calcHelper.memClear());

System.out.println(calcHelper.getAuditTrail());
    }
}
```

I redirected the output of this program and the `CalculatorTest` program to a text file because the output wouldn't fit in a standard MS-DOS prompt window (in case you were wondering). The output of the `CalculatorModelStateTest` program can be seen in Figure 3.17. You can see the audit trail listing after the actual `CalculatorModelStateTest` output.

Wrapping Up

This afternoon was packed with information. If you got through it in a single afternoon, congratulations! I know it's no easy task, especially if you're not an experienced programmer.

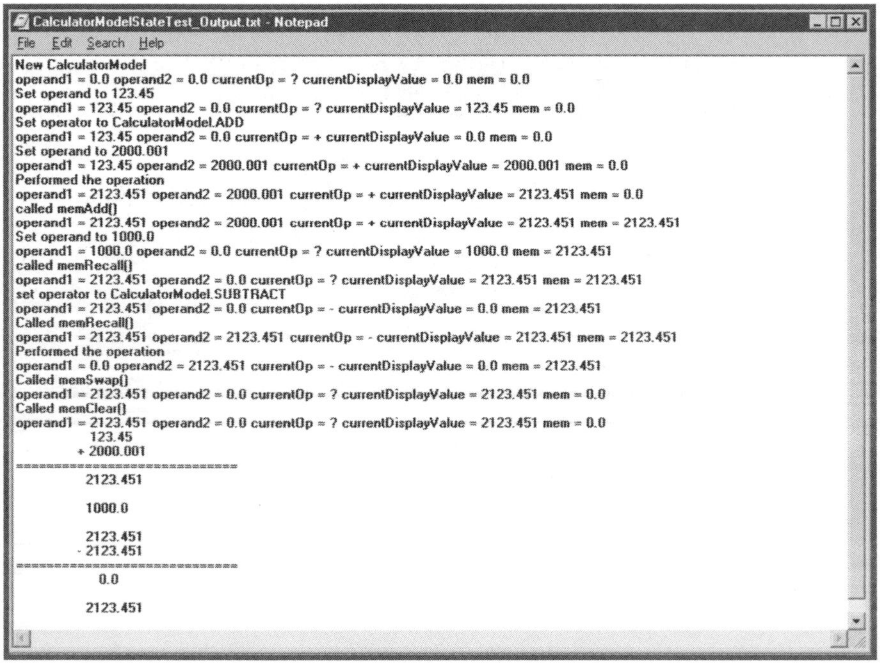

Figure 3.17

The Calculator ModelState Test program makes sure that the Calculator Model class contains the correct information through multiple calculations.

You learned important information about conditional statements and loops, which are fundamental programming concepts that you'll see in almost all Java programs. You also learned about the Math class and about the java.util package. Tonight, you'll learn about Java GUI (*Graphical User Interface*) programming, so you'll be creating windows, buttons, text fields, and so on and using event handling to capture user input. You'll also start to give the calculator project a facelift by creating the CalculatorKeypad class. After this chapter, I'm sure you would like to take a break! Go ahead and relax for a while and grab some dinner, and we'll meet back here this evening.

Graphical User Interface Programming

- ➤ Intro to GUI Programming
- ➤ AWT Components and Event Handling
- ➤ Layout Managers
- ➤ Creating the `CalculatorKeypad` Component

This evening, you'll learn about GUI programming with Java. Up to this point, everything you've been doing has been text-based. That is, all of the programs you've written generate textual output. Starting with this evening's session, your programs will begin to take a different form. All of what you've already learned is still applicable, but now your programs will take on a graphical representation in the form of windows and components such as buttons, check boxes, and drop-down menus—all the stuff that you're so familiar with. Most of the programs you're probably used to dealing with provide some graphical representation with which you must interact in order to accomplish your goals. Now, you'll learn the other side of things. You'll learn how to construct these graphical components as a Java programmer.

Introduction to GUI Programming

Before you start programming GUI applications, I want to get you acclimated. In this section, you'll learn what a GUI is and how Java supports GUI programming. If you've ever done GUI programming with other programming languages, you'll find that doing it in Java is actually quite easy in comparison. In other programming languages, you typically make native calls to the operating system's windowing API. Because Java is platform-independent, you can't do this. Well, actually you can, but don't—it's not considered good practice. Java provides all the classes you need for GUI programming.

After you are introduced to GUI programming, you'll learn the major GUI components and how to handle GUI events (such as a user clicking a button). Next, you'll move on to layout managers, which are used for positioning components within a window. After that, you'll update the calculator project by creating the `CalculatorKeypad` class, which is a set of buttons that will be used like calculator buttons to interface with the calculator program. This afternoon, the calculator project started acting like a calculator. Tonight, the calculator project will start to *look* like a calculator.

What Is a GUI?

A Graphical User Interface, or GUI (pronounced "gooey"), is a graphical representation of windows, buttons, or whatever with which a user can interact in order to interface with your program. In other words, a GUI is the face of your application. It's what the user sees when your program runs, and it provides a way for a user to do useful things with your application. Consider the calculator project. When it's complete, it will have buttons for numbers and operations that you can click, as though pressing a real calculator's buttons. There will also be a digital display that looks like a real calculator's digital display that will show you the results of the calculator's operations.

How Does Java Support GUI Programming?

So, just how does Java support GUI programming? Java does it with the `java.awt` package, or AWT for short. AWT stands for Abstract Windowing Toolkit. Inside this package are classes that represent different components that can be graphically rendered inside windows on your computer screen and added to your GUI. The AWT also defines the GUI containers, like windows, within which you put AWT components. When using the AWT, you need to import the `java.awt` package.

The AWT package components are heavyweight components. The term *heavyweight* in this context refers to the fact that each component, behind the scenes, makes native calls to your operating system's windowing API in order to create the graphics. This means that AWT components will look and behave differently depending on the operating system you're using. The Java code itself doesn't change, which is consistent with Java's platform-independence selling point. It's the Java interpreter that is different. This is one of the reasons why each supported operating system has its own installation files. Different operating systems require different API calls to be able to use windowing tools. So, each Java AWT component has a native peer—that is, an operating system-specific instance of a graphical component, which it uses to do what it needs to do.

Java also has the `java.awt.event` package, which defines classes that are used for capturing and handling user-initiated events. You import this package if you need to make something happen when a user clicks one of your buttons or interacts with other components in your GUI that trigger some action. There are different classes for handling events, and the class needed is determined by the component that corresponds to the event. As you learn each new component, you'll also learn how to handle their events.

There is also another set of classes defined in Java for GUI programming. The collection of these other classes is known as *Swing*. Swing is a set of lightweight components. Unlike heavyweight components, they don't have native peers. They're completely defined in Java and their graphical representation and behavior are consistent across all supported operating systems. Lightweight components perform better than heavyweight components in terms of memory usage. Swing is not covered tonight, and we only touch on it lightly later in the book. However, to make sure that you gain some Swing experience before the weekend ends, the final calculator project will be a Swing application. So, at the very least, the components that the calculator project makes use of will be covered.

AWT Components and Event Handling

In this section, you'll learn the specific AWT component classes and related event-handling classes, as well as their associated interfaces. Each new component you come across is accompanied by an example test program that will give you a good feel for how to use the component and show you what the components look like. To start, take a look at Figure 4.1. It displays some common `java.awt` components. In the subsections that follow, we'll go over them all, one at a time.

NOTE   I am running all of these examples and generating the figure files using Microsoft Windows. If you're using a different operating system, your components will look different than mine. That's okay; it just demonstrates that the AWT makes use of the operating system's underlying GUI API to create its components.

Using Frames and WindowEvents

Your first Java GUI program is simple enough that you can jump right in and program it. All the program does is instantiate a `Frame` (a GUI window) object, set its size, and display it. Here is the source code for the `SimpleFrameTest` program:

```
/*
 * SimpleFrameTest
 * A very simple AWT Frame
 */

import java.awt.Frame;

public class SimpleFrameTest {

    public static void main(String args[]) {
        Frame frame = new Frame("Simple Frame Test");
        frame.setSize(400, 300);
        frame.setVisible(true);
    }
}
```

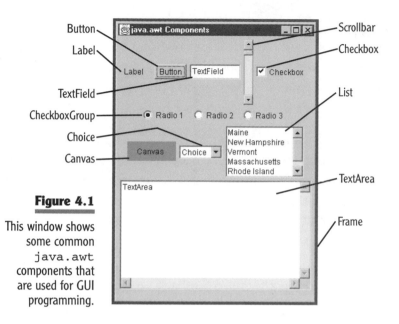

Figure 4.1

This window shows some common java.awt components that are used for GUI programming.

In the SimpleFrameTest program, the first thing you need to do is import the java.awt package. The only class you use from that package is Frame, so you could technically just import that one class. However, most of the other programs tonight use more than one AWT class, so just for the sake of ease, go ahead and import the whole package. Java will only import the classes it actually needs anyway, so there is virtually no difference. The next thing you do should be familiar—just declare the class and open the curly brace for your class definition. The only method needed is the familiar main() method, and it has only three lines of code. It creates a new Frame object by calling the Frame() constructor that accepts a String argument. The String that you pass in is used as the Frame's title. You can see where the Frame's title appears at the top of the window in Figure 4.2. The next line sets the Frame's size to 400 pixels wide by 300 pixels high. The third line of the method makes the Frame appear. The setVisible() method accepts a boolean argument, which indicates whether to show the frame (if it's true), or hide it (if it's false).

Figure 4.2

The `SimpleFrame Test` program creates and displays a `Frame`. You can see the window that it creates, but you can't close it normally!

If you try to run this program, you won't be able to close the window normally. The reason for this is that the `SimpleFrameTest` program doesn't implement any event handling. Yes, you have to explicitly write code to handle what happens when the user tries to close your program by clicking the x. This allows you to perform any cleanup operations or ask the user whether the program should save the user's stuff before exiting, and so on. To exit this program, focus on the command prompt window to make it the active window and press Ctrl+C.

Now, let's create a better `Frame` class that closes when you click the x, that is painted the same color as other windows in your operating system, and that centers itself on the screen when it pops up. The `GUIFrame` class extends the `Frame` class and adds this functionality. Here is the source code:

```
/*
 * GUIFrame
 * An extension of Frame that uses a WindowAdapter to
 * handle the WindowEvents and is centered.
 */

import java.awt.*;
import java.awt.event.*;
```

```java
public class GUIFrame extends Frame implements WindowListener {

   public GUIFrame(String title) {
      super(title);
      setBackground(SystemColor.control);

      addWindowListener(this);
   }

   /* Centers the Frame when setVisible(true) is called */
   public void setVisible(boolean visible) {
      if (visible) {
      Dimension d = Toolkit.getDefaultToolkit().getScreenSize();
      setLocation((d.width - getWidth())/2,
               (d.height - getHeight())/2);
      }
      super.setVisible(visible);
   }

   public void windowClosing(WindowEvent p1) {
      dispose();
      System.exit(0);
   }

   public void windowDeactivated(WindowEvent p1) {}
   public void windowClosed(WindowEvent p1) {}
   public void windowDeiconified(WindowEvent p1) {}
   public void windowOpened(WindowEvent p1) {}
   public void windowIconified(WindowEvent p1) {}
   public void windowActivated(WindowEvent p1) {}

}
```

Because we're doing some event handling in the GUIFrame class, we need to import the java.awt.event package. You should notice something new in the class declaration—it uses the implements keyword. Specifically, it implements the WindowListener interface. You learned a tiny bit about interfaces this afternoon when you learned about the collection API. What you learned still applies here, but keep in mind that interfaces are covered in much more detail tomorrow, so I'm still keeping this subject light here. All you need to know for now is that the Window Listener interface defines seven methods, which are listed in Table 4.1.

Because the GUIFrame class implements the WindowListener interface, it is required to implement all of these methods, even though six of these seven methods are not actually needed by GUIFrame. The required methods that we don't need to use simply have an empty body. That is, they just have opening and closing curly braces with nothing inside of them. The only method that GUIFrame provides a body for is the windowClosing() method. That method is automatically called for us when the user clicks the x to close the window. So, in that method, we just dispose of the window and close the program. The dispose() method de-allocates the memory used for the GUI components and, therefore, makes them unable to display. The System.exit() method stops the program from running. The argument to the System.exit() method is an integer status code. By convention, a nonzero status code indicates some abnormal termination status.

The addWindowListener() method adds a WindowListener to the Frame's list of WindowListeners (which is initially none). In the GUIFrame class, this is passed in as the argument to the addWindowListener() method. Because the GUIFrame class implements the WindowListener interface and, therefore, must have all of its methods, the GUIFrame class qualifies as a WindowListener, and Java lets you refer to a GUIFrame as a WindowListener. Remember that the this keyword signifies the current instance of this class, so we are adding *this* GUIFrame as a WindowListener (it listens for its own window events). The WindowEvent class encapsulates information about window events. When a WindowEvent is triggered, the corresponding WindowListener method is called for all of the GUIFrame's WindowListeners. Because this GUIFrame registered itself as its own Window Listener, any time a WindowEvent is fired (by someone messing around with the Frame—for example, minimizing, maximizing, closing, and so on), the WindowListener methods that are defined within the GUIFrame class will be called.

The GUIFrame() constructor method takes a String argument to use as its title, and makes a call to the super-class's constructor (Frame()), passing the String argument to it. That takes care of constructing the base frame for the GUIFrame class. Next, the method sets the background color using the setBackground() method. SystemColor.control, which is a static Color object that belongs to the java.awt.SystemColor class, is the

TABLE 4.1 WINDOWLISTENER INTERFACE METHODS

Method	Description
void windowActivated(*WindowEvent*)	Called when a window becomes active (able to accept input events).
void windowClosed(*WindowEvent*)	Called when a window is closed (disposed).
void windowClosing(*WindowEvent*)	Called when a user attempts to close a window. (You implement this method to conditionally close the window.)
void windowDeactivated(*WindowEvent*)	Called when a window is deactivated (loses input focus).
void windowDeiconified(*WindowEvent*)	Called when a window is restored from a minimized state.
void windowIconified(*WindowEvent*)	Called when a window becomes minimized.
void windowOpened(*WindowEvent*)	Called when a window initially becomes visible.

color that your operating system uses as the components' background color, so this makes GUIFrame the same color as the other windows in your operating system.

The GUIFrame class also overrides the setVisible() method. Whenever this method is called, the window size and your screen's pixel resolution size are used to center the GUIFrame on your (or any other) screen. The Toolkit class is used to figure out where the center of your screen is. What is the Toolkit class (surely, this is getting confusing)? It's the superclass of all concrete implementations of the AWT, but that's not important right now . . . and stop calling me Shirley! Seriously, though, the details aren't important. If you must know them now, feel free to consult the Java API specification, which you can find on Sun's Java Web site (http://java.sun.com). Actually it's a good idea to bookmark the documentation so that you can refer to it as you progress through this book. The GUIFrame class will make it easier for you to test the other AWT components. We'll define it once here and then use it throughout the rest of tonight's session. The fact that it centers itself on the screen is just a bonus. Feel free to leave that out.

The GUIFrameTest tests out the GUIFrame class. Here is the source code for the GUIFrameTest program:

```
/*
 * GUIFrameTest
 * Demonstrates the GUIFrame Class
 */


public class GUIFrameTest {

  public static void main(String args[]) {
    GUIFrame frame = new GUIFrame("GUIFrame Test");
    frame.setSize(400, 300);
    frame.setVisible(true);
```

```
    }


}
```

The `GUIFrameTest` program is very similar to the `SimpleFrameTest` program. The only difference is that `GUIFrameTest` uses the `GUIFrame` class that you created, instead of using a standard `Frame`. You can see the difference right away in Figure 4.3. The background color is different (well, the figures aren't in color, but you can still tell). Also, it appears in the center of the screen, and you can close it by clicking the x.

The Label Component

Let's start adding components to the `GUIFrame`! The `Label` component is a simple component. It is typically used to label other components or sections of your GUI or to display some short textual information to the

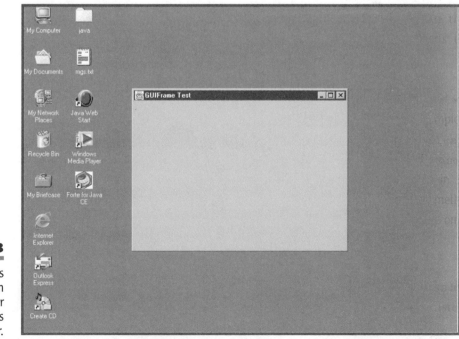

Figure 4.3

The `GUIFrame` is centered onscreen and uses your operating system's GUI color.

user in the Frame. The LabelTest program, like most of the remaining classes in tonight's session, extends the GUIFrame class. Inside of the LabelTest() constructor method, the first line calls the GUIFrame constructor method, passing the title, "Label Test" to it. Next, it creates a new Label component, label. The Label() constructor used here takes a String argument, which is the value of the text that the Label will display. The Label is added to the Frame by calling the add() method, which is inherited from the Container class.

The Container class is the super-class for all GUI components that can contain other components. The add() method accepts a Component argument. The Component class is the super-class for all GUI components. The Label is a Component, and the Frame is a Container (which is actually also a Component), so you can call the Frame's add() method to add the label to the Frame. After the Label is added, the size is set, and the LabelTest Frame is made visible. This all happens within the constructor. So the main() method needs only to instantiate a new Label Test object, which results in a call to the constructor, and thus the Frame appears. Note that you can still close the Frame by clicking the x because the LabelTest inherits all of the functionality we put into the GUIFrame class. Here is the source code listing for the LabelTest program:

```
/*
 * LabelTest
 * Demonstrates the java.awt.Label Component
 */

import java.awt.Label;

public class LabelTest extends GUIFrame {

    public LabelTest() {
        super("Label Test");
```

```
        //create a label and add it to the frame
        Label label = new Label("This is a Label");
        add(label);
        setSize(200, 100);
        setVisible(true);
    }


    public static void main(String args[]) {
        new LabelTest();
    }
}
```

You can see what the label looks like in Figure 4.4.

The Button Component and ActionEvents

Okay, you've got your first component, Label, out of the way, which is good, because you can apply what you know about adding components to Frames and the concept of what a container and a component are to the rest of the AWT components. However, the Label component example didn't make use of any event-handling mechanisms. The next component covered, the Button component, is the perfect component to demonstrate some component event handling. The ButtonTest example program not only shows you how to instantiate a Button and add it to a Frame, but also how to do something when the user clicks the Button. This is accomplished through the AWT's event-handling model. First, take a look at the ButtonTest source code that follows; then I'll explain it:

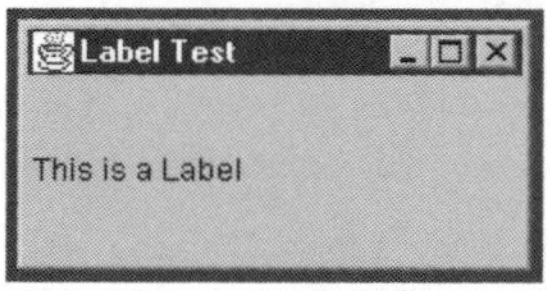

Figure 4.4

This is what a Label looks like.

```
/*
 * ButtonTest
 * Tests out the java.awt.Button Component
 */

import java.awt.Button;
import java.awt.event.*;

public class ButtonTest extends GUIFrame
    implements ActionListener {

    public ButtonTest() {
        super("Button Test");
        Button button = new Button("Click me");
        button.addActionListener(this);
        add(button);
        setSize(200, 100);
        setVisible(true);
    }


    //ActionListener Method
    public void actionPerformed(ActionEvent event) {
        if (event.getSource() instanceof Button) {
            System.out.println("Button was clicked");
        }
    }

    public static void main(String args[]) {
        new ButtonTest();
    }
}
```

Which Constructor?

Even though it uses event handling, it's not much more involved than the `LabelTest` program, is it? The first thing you'll notice is that it implements a new interface, `ActionListener`. The `ActionListener` interface requires that you implement only one method, `actionPerformed()`. When the `Button` is clicked, this method will automatically be called for you, as long as you register with the `Button` as an `ActionListener`, which the `ButtonTest` program does by calling `addActionListener(this)`. Adding an event listener by calling one of the add methods is sometimes referred to as *registering* a listener.

Any code that appears in the `actionPerformed()` method will be executed whenever the `Button` is clicked. All the `ButtonTest` program does in this method is test that the source of the event is a `Button` object and if it is, it prints the message, `Button was clicked`. The argument to the `actionPerformed()` method is an `ActionEvent` object. It tests whether the source of the event is a `Button` by calling the `ActionEvent`'s `get-Source()` method, which it inherits from the `java.util.EventObject` class, as all AWT event classes do. The `getSource()` method returns the `Object` that triggered the event, so if the `Button` object, `button`, triggered the event by someone clicking it, then a reference to `button` is passed as the argument to the `actionPerformed()` method. The `instanceof` operator is used to make sure that the `Object` returned from `getSource()` is an instance of the `Button` class. That's all there is to it. You can see what this should look like in Figure 4.5.

TextFields, TextAreas, and TextEvents

The AWT provides two text components, the `TextField` component and the `TextArea` component. These components enable the user to enter text data into a GUI. The `TextField` component allows a single line to be entered, while the `TextArea` component allows multi-line entry. Both of these classes extend the `TextComponent` class. The `TextListener` and `TextEvent` classes enable you to handle text component-related events. The `TextComponentTest` program demonstrates this. Here is the source code:

Figure 4.5

The
`ButtonTest`
program adds a
`Button` to a
`Frame`. It
implements
`Action`
`Listener` so
that each time you
click it, a message
is printed to
standard output.

```
/*
 * TextComponentTest
 * Tests the java.awt.TextField and java.awt.TextArea
 * Components
 */

import java.awt.*;
import java.awt.event.*;

public class TextComponentTest extends GUIFrame
    implements TextListener {

    public TextComponentTest() {
        super("Text Component Test");
        TextField tf = new TextField();
        tf.addTextListener(this);
        add(tf, BorderLayout.NORTH);

        TextArea ta = new TextArea(10, 50);
        ta.addTextListener(this);
```

```
        add(ta, BorderLayout.CENTER);
        pack();
        setVisible(true);
    }


    public void textValueChanged(TextEvent event) {
        TextComponent src = (TextComponent)event.getSource();
        System.out.println(src.getText());
    }


    public static void main(String args[]) {
        new TextComponentTest();
    }
}
```

The TextComponentTest program instantiates both a TextField and a TextArea component and adds them to the frame. The BorderLayout stuff you see in the add() method just indicates where in the Frame to display the components. BorderLayout is a layout manager. Border Layout.NORTH indicates that the TextField, tf, should appear at the top of the window, while BorderLayout.CENTER indicates that the TextArea, ta, should go in the center. Layout managers are covered in more detail later this evening. The TextField constructor that the TextComponent Test program uses is the no-arg constructor, which initializes the TextField so that it initially has no text in it. There is also another constructor that accepts a String argument that is used to initialize the TextField's text value. The TextArea() constructor is given two integers that represent the number of rows and columns of text, respectively. Text components also have methods for setting and getting their text values. These method are setText() and getText(), respectively. The pack() method, which is inherited from the java.awt.Window class, tells Java to set the size of the Frame to the smallest possible size in which all of its components can still fit.

The `TextListener` interface defines one method, `textValueChanged()`, which is called any time (yup—you guessed it) that the text value within the text component changes. The `TextComponentTest` program implements this method so that the entire text value of the event source component is printed to standard output each time its text value changes. First, the event source is cast to a `TextComponent`; then the `getText()` method is called, and the return value, which is the text value of the event source, is printed. You can see this program in action in Figure 4.6.

To get the output you see in Figure 4.6, first I typed "only a" in the `TextField`; then I typed "test" in the `TextArea`.

Choices, Lists, and ItemEvents

`Choices` and `Lists` are components that allow users to make selections from lists of options. The `Choice` component is a drop-down list that lets you select a single item. The `List` component can display multiple items simultaneously and optionally allows for multiple selections to be made. The interface that allows you to handle `Choice` and `List` events is the `ItemListener` interface. The associated event class is the `ItemEvent` class. The `ChoiceListTest` program demonstrates this:

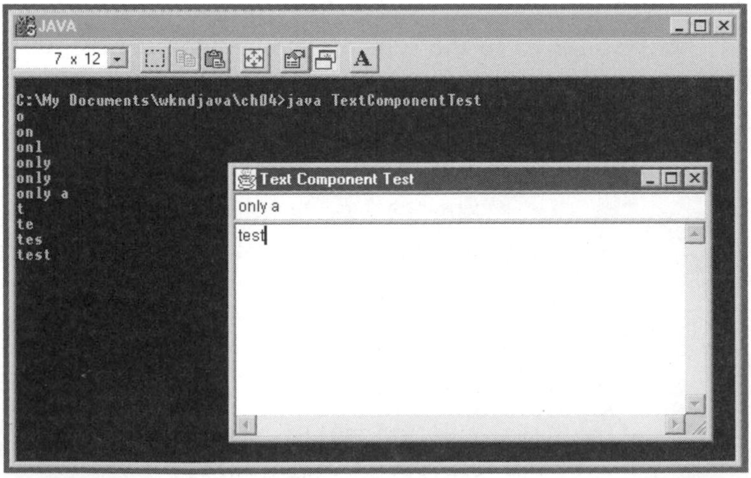

Figure 4.6

The `Text` `Component` `Test` program demonstrates the `TextField` and `TextArea` components. It also uses `Text` `Listener` to print to standard output any time the affected text component's value changes.

```java
/*
 * ChoiceListTest
 * Tests the java.awt.Choice and java.awt.List Components.
 */

import java.awt.*;
import java.awt.event.*;

public class ChoiceListTest extends GUIFrame
        implements ItemListener {

    public ChoiceListTest() {
        super("Choice/List Test");

        Choice choice = new Choice();
        choice.add("Playstation 2");
        choice.add("GameCube");
        choice.add("Dreamcast");
        choice.add("Xbox");
        choice.addItemListener(this);
        add(choice, BorderLayout.WEST);

        List list = new List(4, true);
        list.add("Mustard");
        list.add("Mayo");
        list.add("Lettuce");
        list.add("Tomato");
        list.add("Pickles");
        list.add("Onions");
        list.addItemListener(this);
```

```java
        add(list, BorderLayout.EAST);

        pack();
        setVisible(true);
    }


    public void itemStateChanged(ItemEvent event) {
        //get the object that triggered the event (Choice or List)
        ItemSelectable selectable = event.getItemSelectable();
        //get the selected/deselected item
        Object affectedItem = event.getItem();

        String msg = "itemStateChanged: \"";
        if (selectable instanceof List) {
            //for List, affectedItem is an Integer index value
            int index = ((Integer)affectedItem).intValue();
            msg += ((List)selectable).getItem(index);
        }
        else {
            //for Choice, affectedItem is the actual String item
            msg += event.getItem();
        }

        msg += "\" " + (event.getStateChange()
          == ItemEvent.SELECTED ? " selected" : " deselected");

        System.out.println(msg + " from "
            + selectable.getClass().getName());
    }
```

```
public static void main(String args[]) {
    new ChoiceListTest();
}
}
```

The `ChoiceList` program has a `Choice` object, `choice`, and a `List` object, `list`. The `Choice` is instantiated using the no-arg constructor, which is the only constructor method available in the `Choice` class. It creates an empty `Choice` object. To add selectable options to the `Choice`, you call the `add()` method, which accepts a `String` argument. Each time you call the `add()` method, a new option is added to the `Choice` object. The `ChoiceList` program adds four options to `choice`. `list` is instantiated using the `List()` constructor. The `ChoiceTest` program passes two arguments to it—an `int` and a `boolean`. The `int` argument specifies how many rows are visible simultaneously. This program sets the number of rows to 4. The `boolean` argument specifies whether multiple selections are allowed. Because this program passes in `true` for this argument, you can select multiple items from `list`.

The `TextListener` interface has only one method in it, `itemState Changed()`. This method is called anytime an item is selected or deselected. Like all event classes, `ItemEvent` returns the source of the event as an `Object` when its `getSource()` method is called. `ItemEvent` has another method in it, `getItemSelectable()`, which returns the source of the event as an `ItemSelectable` object. `Choice` and `List` both implement the `ItemSelectable` interface and can both be referred to as `Item Selectable` objects. The first thing this program does in the `itemState Changed()` method is call the `getItemSelectable()` method. Next, it calls `ItemEvent`'s `getItem()` method, which returns the `Object` within the `ItemSelectable` that actually triggered the event. For example, selecting "PlayStation 2" from `choice` will cause the `getItem()` method to return a `String` object (as an `Object` object) having the value "PlayStation 2." `getItem()` returns `Object` instead of `String` because different `ItemEvent` sources can have different types of items in them.

Take `List`, for example. Instead of returning a `String`, `getItem()` returns an `Integer` object that represents the index of the selected item when the source of the `ItemEvent` is a `List` component. This is why the `Item Selectable` object, `selectable`, is checked to see whether it's an instance of `List` or an instance of `Choice`. If it's an instance of `List`, you have to get the `Integer` object returned by `getItem()`, parse it to an `int` primitive, and get the value of the item from the `List` using that `int` value as an index. The `getItem()` method defined in the `List` class (not to be confused with `ItemEvent`'s `getItem()` method), which accepts an `int` argument, returns the `String` value of the item found at the given `int` index.

Yet another method in the `ItemEvent` class is `getStateChange()`, which returns an `int`. You can test the returned `int` against two `ItemEvent` constants, `ItemEvent.SELECTED` and `ItemEvent.DESELECTED`. As you might guess, they are flags that indicate whether this `ItemEvent` was triggered by an item being selected or deselected from the `ItemSelectable` object. In the `ChoiceListTest` program, the `itemStateChanged()` method calls these methods and builds a `String` that describes the event that was triggered and prints that `String` to standard output. You can see the results in Figure 4.7.

Figure 4.7

A `Choice` and a `List` component are shown here, and the events that they trigger show up in the MS-DOS prompt window.

Checkboxes and CheckBoxGroups

Checkboxes, which are also known as radio buttons or toggle buttons, are also available in the AWT. These components have a label associated with them, as well as the actual checkbox with which the user can interact to toggle their true/false state. An example of a possible use of a Checkbox component would be a mute button on an audio player. The audio is either muted or it's not, so it's either true or false. Checkbox Group objects are used to group Checkbox components together so that only one of them can be used at a time. An example of a possible use for a CheckboxGroup is a stereo/mono choice. It must be one or the other; if you select stereo, then mono is automatically deselected and vice versa. The CheckboxTest program tests some Checkbox components without an associated CheckboxGroup and also tests some Checkbox components with an associated Checkbox group. Here is the source code listing for CheckboxTest:

```
/*
 * CheckboxTest
 * Tests the Checkbox Component and CheckboxGroup class
 */


import java.awt.*;
import java.awt.event.*;


public class CheckboxTest extends GUIFrame
    implements ItemListener {

    public CheckboxTest() {
        super("Checkbox Test");
        Panel p = new Panel();
        Checkbox c1 = new Checkbox("shirt");
        c1.addItemListener(this);
```

```java
        Checkbox c2 = new Checkbox("pants");
        c2.addItemListener(this);
        Checkbox c3 = new Checkbox("socks");
        c3.addItemListener(this);

        p.add(c1);
        p.add(c2);
        p.add(c3);

        CheckboxGroup cbg = new CheckboxGroup();
        Checkbox c4 = new Checkbox("sneakers", false, cbg);
        c4.addItemListener(this);
        Checkbox c5 = new Checkbox("shoes", false, cbg);
        c5.addItemListener(this);
        Checkbox c6 = new Checkbox("boots", false, cbg);
        c6.addItemListener(this);

        p.add(c4);
        p.add(c5);
        p.add(c6);

        add(p);
        pack();
        setVisible(true);
    }

    public void itemStateChanged(ItemEvent event) {
        String msg = (String) event.getItem();
        //this is not always intuitive
        msg += event.getStateChange() == ItemEvent.SELECTED
```

```
          ? " selected" : " deselected";
        System.out.println(msg);
    }


    public static void main(String args[]) {
        new CheckboxTest();
    }


}
```

First, three Checkbox components are created that don't belong to a CheckboxGroup: "shirt", "pants", and "socks". This means that each of these components can individually be selected and deselected. The constructor that I used for these accepts a single String argument, which sets the text for the Checkbox labels. Next, three other Checkboxes that do belong to a CheckboxGroup are created: "sneakers", "shoes", and "boots". Because they all belong to the same CheckboxGroup, only one of these three options can be selected at one time. The constructor that I used for these other three Checkbox components accepts three arguments: a String label, a boolean state, and a CheckboxGroup object. The label argument works exactly as before; the boolean argument sets whether or not the Checkbox is initially selected (true) or deselected (false). The Checkbox is associated with the CheckboxGroup object argument. You associate Checkbox components with each other in a CheckboxGroup by passing the same CheckboxGroup object to each of their constructors.

Like Choices and Lists, Checkbox events are handled by the ItemListener interface. The itemStateChanged() method in the CheckboxTest program prints the label of the source of the ItemEvent, and, in much the same way as the ChoiceListTest program handled ItemEvents, it also indicates whether the event was triggered as a result of the Checkbox being selected or deselected. Did you see the in-line comment that the getStateChange() method is not always intuitive? It's not because, if you click a Checkbox that belongs to a CheckboxGroup multiple times successively, even though the Checkbox stays selected, every time after the initial selection will appear to be a deselection. Keep this in mind when you handle ItemEvents for Check boxes. It would be a better idea to check which item is selected using the getSelectedCheckbox() method that is defined in the CheckboxGroup class, instead of checking which Checkbox generated the event and checking whether it was selected or deselected. Figure 4.8 shows the results of the CheckboxTest program.

Canvases and MouseEvents

The Canvas component is basically used for drawing graphics. AWT Graphics programming is covered tomorrow morning, so I'll just intro- duce you to the Canvas component quickly here. It's also a good time to cover MouseEvents. The CanvasMouseTest uses a Canvas and adds a MouseListener to it so that when you click on the Canvas, a dot is painted in the location of the mouse cursor, and the coordinates are printed to the standard output stream. Here is the source code:

```
/*
 * CanvasMouseTest
 * Tests the Canvas component and MouseListener interface.
```

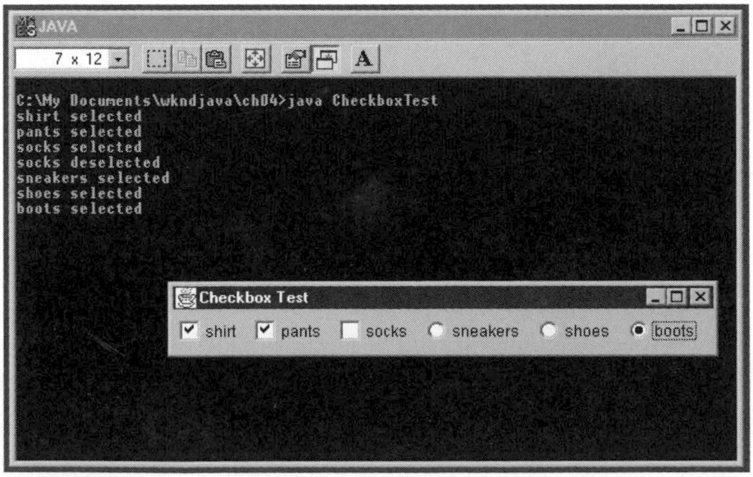

Figure 4.8

Shirt, pants, and socks are individual CheckBoxes, but sneakers, shoes, and boots are part of a CheckBox Group.

```
 */

import java.awt.*;
import java.awt.event.*;


public class CanvasMouseTest extends GUIFrame
    implements MouseListener {

    public CanvasMouseTest() {
        super("Canvas and MouseListener Test");
        Canvas canv = new Canvas();
        canv.setSize(200, 200);
        canv.addMouseListener(this);
        canv.setBackground(Color.red);
        add(canv);
        pack();
        setVisible(true);
    }



    public void mousePressed(MouseEvent event) {
        Point p = event.getPoint();
        System.out.println("Mouse Pressed at: " + p);
        Graphics g = ((Canvas)event.getSource()).getGraphics();
        g.fillOval(p.x, p.y, 10, 10);
    }


    public static void main(String args[]) {
        new CanvasMouseTest();
    }
```

```
public void mouseReleased(MouseEvent event) {}
public void mouseEntered(MouseEvent event) {}
public void mouseClicked(MouseEvent event) {}
public void mouseExited(MouseEvent event) {}


}
```

The `Canvas`, `canv`, is constructed with the no-arg constructor method. Then `canv`'s size is set to 200 pixels by 200 pixels. The `CanvasMouseTest` program implements the `MouseListener` interface and is registered as `canv`'s `MouseListener`. Then `canv`'s background color is set to red and added to the `Frame`. The `mousePressed()` method of the `MouseListener` interface is implemented by `CanvasMouseTest` so that a dot is drawn when you press the mouse button on `canv`. Also, the location of the click, which is determined by calling `MouseEvent`'s `getPoint()` method, which returns a `Point` object, is printed to standard output. The details of how the dot gets there are not important. I put it there for fun and so that you can more easily see the effect of pressing the mouse button directly within the GUI. The `mousePressed()` method is called when you depress the mouse button in the area of the component, in this case `canv`.

The other four `MouseListener` methods work as follows. The `mouseReleased()` method is called when you let go of the button. The `mouseEntered()` and `mouseExited()` methods are called when the mouse pointer enters and exits the area over the component, and the `mouseClicked()` method is called when the mouse button is clicked over the component. The `MouseEvent` class also has a method called `getModifiers()`, which returns an `int` value that can be compared to constants that are defined in the `InputEvent` class to determine which mouse button triggered the `MouseEvent`, if any. For example, `InputEvent.BUTTON1_MASK` indicates that the left mouse button was used, and `InputEvent.BUTTON3_MASK` (yes that's a 3!) indicates that the right mouse button was used. You can see the output of the `Canvas MouseTest` program in Figure 4.9.

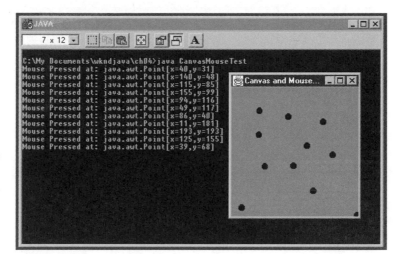

Figure 4.9

A dot appears wherever you click the Canvas, and the coordinates print to standard output.

Menus and Popup Menus

Every Frame object can be associated with a MenuBar object. A frame's menu bar is usually at the top of the frame, underneath the title bar. It contains a set of options, which themselves are Menu objects. A menu appears when an option is selected from the menu bar. The Java classes that build menus are organized as follows. When selected, Menus drop down from the MenuBar. Menu objects contain MenuItem objects. A MenuItem is the option that exists within a Menu. To use MenuItems, you must first create them and add them to Menus, then add the Menus to the MenuBar, and then, finally, associate the MenuBar with the Frame object. Here's a quick example:

```
MenuItem myItem = new MenuItem("Some Option");

Menu myManu = new Menu("Some Menu Title");

myMenu.add(myItem);

MenuBar myBar = new MenuBar();

myBar.add(myMenu);

frame.setMenuBar(myMenuBar);
```

This assumes that `frame` is a valid `Frame` object. The `PopupMenu` component is a subclass of `Menu` that doesn't have to be attached to a `MenuBar`. It can pop up anywhere you want. The `MenuTest` program, listed next, tests the `Menu` and `PopupMenu` components:

```
/*
 * MenuTest
 * Demonstrates how to build a GUI Menu.
 */

import java.awt.*;
import java.awt.event.*;

public class MenuTest extends GUIFrame implements ActionListener,
        MouseListener {

    PopupMenu popup;

    public MenuTest() {
        super("Menu Test");

        //create MenuBar object
        MenuBar menuBar = new MenuBar();

        //create a new Menu object
        Menu fileMenu = new Menu("File");

        //add "New" to the menu (including menu shortcut)
        MenuItem fm_new = new MenuItem("New");
        fm_new.setShortcut(new MenuShortcut(KeyEvent.VK_N));
        fileMenu.add(fm_new);
```

```
//add some more menu items without shortcuts
fileMenu.add(new MenuItem("Open"));
fileMenu.add(new MenuItem("Save"));
fileMenu.add(new MenuItem("Save as..."));

//create a submenu
Menu submenu = new Menu("Sub menu");
submenu.add(new MenuItem("subitem 1"));
submenu.add(new MenuItem("subitem 2"));
submenu.add(new MenuItem("subitem 3"));

//add the submenu to the file menu
fileMenu.add(submenu);
menuBar.add(fileMenu);

//add a separator
fileMenu.addSeparator();

//add a MenuItem that actually does something
MenuItem fm_exit = new MenuItem("Exit");
fm_exit.setShortcut(new MenuShortcut(KeyEvent.VK_X));
fm_exit.addActionListener(this);
fileMenu.add(fm_exit);

setMenuBar(menuBar);

//create the popup menu
popup = new PopupMenu("Popup Menu");
popup.add(new MenuItem("Copy"));
popup.add(new MenuItem("Cut"));
```

```java
        popup.add(new MenuItem("Paste"));
        add(popup);

        addMouseListener(this);

        setSize(300, 200);
        setVisible(true);
    }

    public void actionPerformed(ActionEvent event) {
        dispose();
        System.exit(0);
    }

    public static void main(String args[]) {
        new MenuTest();
    }

    public void mousePressed(MouseEvent event) {
        if (event.getModifiers() == InputEvent.BUTTON3_MASK) {
            popup.show(this, event.getX(), event.getY());
        }
    }

    public void mouseReleased(MouseEvent event) {}
    public void mouseEntered(MouseEvent event) {}
    public void mouseClicked(MouseEvent event) {}
    public void mouseExited(MouseEvent event) {}

}
```

The MenuTest program creates a menu similar to the previous example, but it does some more cool stuff. The first cool thing it does is set a MenuShortcut for the "New" MenuItem. It sets the shortcut to KeyEvent.VK_N, which is a constant that signifies the N key on your computer's keyboard. When you look at Figure 4.10, you can see that the keyboard shortcut is automatically printed in the File menu along with the "New" text that I set.

Next, MenuTest creates a submenu. To do this, it just creates a standard Menu and adds MenuItems to it. But, instead of adding it to a MenuBar, it adds it to the fileMenu object, which is a Menu itself. This is possible because Menu is a subclass of MenuItem. You can also see what the submenu looks like in Figure 4.10. The MenuTest program also adds a separator to fileMenu by calling the addSeparator() method. This draws a line to visually separate MenuItems from each other.

The MenuTest program implements both ActionListener and MouseListener. The actionPerformed() method of the Action Listener interface is used to exit the system. The only component that

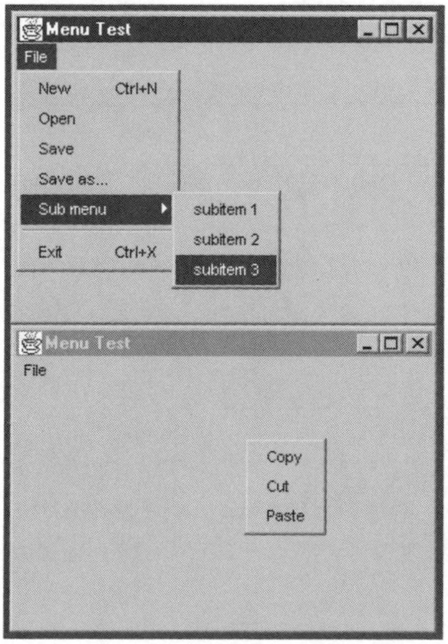

Figure 4.10

Here, you can see the submenu under the File menu. You can also right-click anywhere in the window and see the popup menu appear.

MenuTest listens to is the `fm_exit` MenuItem. An ActionEvent is triggered when you select this item from `fileMenu`. Also, because a shortcut key is set to x, pressing Ctrl+X triggers the action event, and the frame closes. The `MouseListener` interface is used to display the PopupMenu. If you right-click anywhere in the frame, the PopupMenu will appear wherever you clicked.

The Panel Container

The `Panel` Container can be used to hold multiple components, and it can be added to a Container itself. The `Panel` Container gives you a way of nesting components within each other. The PanelTest program demonstrates this fact. Here is the source code for PanelTest:

```
/*
 * PanelTest
 * Demonstrates that you can add other components to the Panel
 * container and add the panel to another container.
 */


import java.awt.*;


public class PanelTest extends Panel {


    public PanelTest() {
        super();


        //add a bunch of buttons
        for (int b = 1; b <= 50; b++) {
            add(new Button(String.valueOf(b)));
        }
        //paint it black
        setBackground(Color.black);
```

```
    }


    public static Panel getMotherOfAllPanels() {
        Panel p = new Panel(new GridLayout(0, 2, 5, 5));
        p.add(new PanelTest());
        p.add(new PanelTest());
        p.add(new PanelTest());
        p.add(new PanelTest());
        return p;
    }



    public Dimension getPreferredSize() {
        return new Dimension (250, 225);
    }


    public static void main(String args[]) {
        GUIFrame frame = new GUIFrame("Panel Test");
        frame.add(PanelTest.getMotherOfAllPanels());
        frame.pack();
        frame.setVisible(true);
    }


}
```

The PanelTest class extends the Panel class. Inside of the constructor, a loop creates 50 buttons and adds them all to the Panel. The constructor also sets the background color to black, so you can see the contrast between the color of the Panel and the color of the GUIFrame that contains the Panel. The getPreferredSize() method returns a Dimension object, which is basically an encapsulation of width and height parameters.

The `PanelTest` overrides this method, which is inherited from the `Component` class. When a `Frame` lays out its component, it calls this method in order to figure out the size the `Component` should be. I just overrode the method to force the size to be 250 x 225. The `setSize()` method won't do here because the `Frame` will turn to the `getPreferred Size()` method in any case. There is also a static method called `get MotherOfAllPanels()`. All it does is create four instances of `PanelTest` and adds them to a new `Panel`, which it returns. The `main()` method creates a `GUIFrame` and then calls `getMotherOfAllPanels()` to get four `PanelTest Panels` inside of another `Panel`. Then it just displays them. You can see what this looks like in Figure 4.11.

Scrollbars and AdjustmentEvents

`Scrollbars` allow users to select from a range of numerical values using a slider that can slide from some minimum value to some maximum value. `Scrollbars` generate `AdjustmentEvents` when their selected

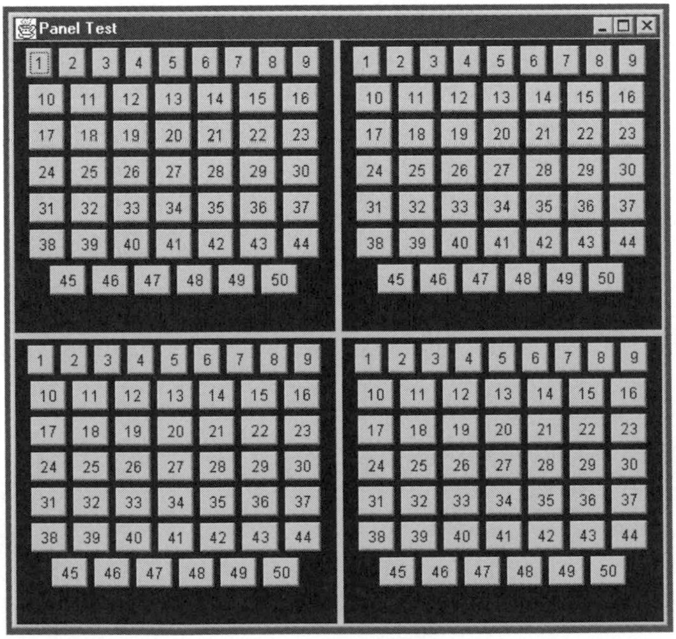

Figure 4.11

Here, four `Panels` are added to another `Panel`, which is added to a `Frame`.

values are modified. The ScrollbarTest program demonstrates the
Scrollbar component and how to handle AdjustmentEvents:

```java
/*
 * ScrollbarTest
 * Tests out the Scrollbar component and AdjustmentListener
 * interface.
 */

import java.awt.*;
import java.awt.event.*;

public class ScrollbarTest extends GUIFrame
    implements AdjustmentListener {

    private Scrollbar scrollbar;
    private Label value;

    public ScrollbarTest() {
        super ("Scrollbar Test");
        //min max value for the scrollbar
        int min = 0, max = 100;

        //construct a new scrollbar (add visible amount to max)
        scrollbar = new Scrollbar(Scrollbar.HORIZONTAL, 0, 1,
            min, max + 1);
        scrollbar.addAdjustmentListener(this);
        add(scrollbar, BorderLayout.CENTER);

        add(new Label(String.valueOf(min)), BorderLayout.WEST);
        add(new Label(String.valueOf(max)), BorderLayout.EAST);
```

```
        value = new Label(String.valueOf(scrollbar.getValue()),
            Label.CENTER);
        add(value, BorderLayout.NORTH);


        setSize(200, 75);
        setVisible(true);
    }


    public void adjustmentValueChanged(AdjustmentEvent event) {
        value.setText(String.valueOf(scrollbar.getValue()));
    }


    public static void main(String args[]) {
        new ScrollbarTest();
    }


}
```

The `ScrollbarTest` program constructs the `Scrollbar` like this:

```
scrollbar = new Scrollbar(Scrollbar.HORIZONTAL, 0, 1, min,
max + 1);
```

All five arguments are `int` values. The first one is the orientation. In this example, the orientation is set to `Scrollbar.HORIZONTAL`. The other option is `Scrollbar.VERTICAL`. The second argument is the initial value, the third is its visible amount, the fourth is its minimum, and the fifth argument is the maximum value. The actual maximum value is the given maximum value minus the visible amount. The visible amount is the size of the slider and the increment amount for the slider as it is moved. So, I set the maximum value in the constructor to `max + 1` (101) because the actual maximum should be 100, for the sake of this example, and the visible amount is 1. If you run this program and slide the slider all the way to the right, you'll see that the value is 100, not 101.

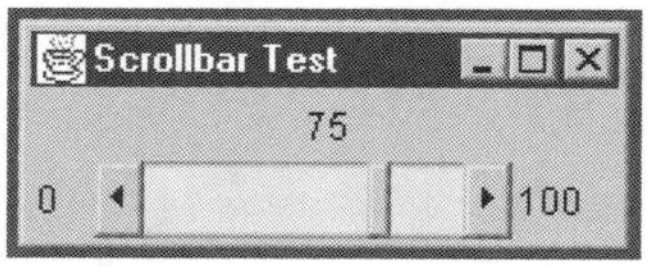

Figure 4.12

The `Scrollbar` `Test` program uses a `Scrollbar` and updates the value of the `Label` above it when an `Adjustment` `Event` is fired. An `Adjustment` `Event` is fired when the `Scrollbar` slider is moved.

The `SliderTest` program uses labels to label the minimum value (left), the maximum value (right), and the current value (top). The `Adjustment` `Listener` interface needs only one method, `adjustmentValue` `Changed()`. All I did for that method was update the `value` label to reflect the current value of the slider. You can see how this should look in Figure 4.12.

ScrollPanes

`ScrollPanes` are `Containers` that can optionally have sliders. This is useful in cases where the contained components don't quite fit within the `Container`. You should be very familiar with the concept of `Scroll` `Panes`. You see them all the time when you're surfing the Web and the whole content of the Web page doesn't fit in the browser's window; you have to scroll down to continue reading. The `ScrollPaneTest` program demonstrates how to do this in Java. Here is the source code:

```
/*
 * ScrollPaneTest
 * Tests out the ScrollPane component.
 */

import java.awt.*;

public class ScrollPaneTest extends GUIFrame {

    public ScrollPaneTest() {
        super ("ScrollPane Test");
        ScrollPane scrollPane
```

```
            = new ScrollPane(ScrollPane.SCROLLBARS_ALWAYS);
        //add a big panel by calling PanelTest's static method
        scrollPane.add(PanelTest.getMotherOfAllPanels());
        scrollPane.setSize(250, 250);
        add(scrollPane);
        pack();
        setVisible(true);
    }


    public static void main(String args[]) {
        new ScrollPaneTest();
    }

}
```

The `ScrollPaneTest` program is actually quite simple. The `ScrollPane()` constructor is passed an `int` flag, `ScrollPane.SCROLLBARS_ALWAYS`, which indicates that the scrollbars (vertical and horizontal) should appear always, no matter if the content fits within the Container or not. There are two other options, `ScrollPane.SCROLLBARS_AS_NEEDED` and `Scroll Pane.SCROLLBARS_NEVER`, which are self-explanatory. The `Scroll PaneTest` program then calls a method you already created, `PanelTest.getMotherOfAllPanels()`, as a quick way to generate an area big enough to test the `ScrollPane Container`. Then the size of the Frame is purposely set to a smaller size than the mother of all panels, so that the scrollbars will actually make a difference. You can see how this looks in Figure 4.13.

Dialog Windows

Dialog windows are popup windows that belong to either a `Frame` or another dialog window. Dialogs can be modal or non-modal. When a modal dialog pops up, it takes focus and won't let go until it's dismissed.

Figure 4.13

The
ScrollPane
Test program
creates a Panel
that is bigger than
its display size.
Scrollbars
enable you to see
what's hidden.

This means that while a modal dialog window is visible, you can't do anything else until the dialog window is no longer visible. A non-modal dialog can coexist with its parent and will share focus with it. This means you can have a non-modal dialog window visible and still do stuff in the parent frame or dialog. The Dialog class is used to create dialog windows. The DialogTest program shows you how to use Dialog objects. The source code is as follows:

```
/*
 * DialogTest
 * Demonstrates Dialog windows
 */


import java.awt.*;
import java.awt.event.*;


public class DialogTest extends GUIFrame implements ActionListener,
        WindowListener {

    Dialog nonModal, modal;


    public DialogTest() {
```

```
    super ("Dialog Test");

    Button fButton = new Button("Open non-modal Dialog");
    fButton.addActionListener(this);
    add(fButton);

    nonModal = new Dialog(this, "Non-modal", false);
    Button dnmButton = new Button("Open modal Dialog");
    dnmButton.addActionListener(this);
    nonModal.add(dnmButton);
    nonModal.setSize(200, 100);
    nonModal.addWindowListener(this);

    modal = new Dialog(nonModal, "Modal", true);
    modal.add(new Label("Modal Dialog"));
    modal.setSize(100, 50);
    modal.addWindowListener(this);

    setSize(300, 200);
    setVisible(true);

    nonModal.setLocation(getLocation());
    modal.setLocation(getLocation());
}

public void actionPerformed(ActionEvent event) {
  Container parent = ((Button)event.getSource()).getParent();
  if (parent == this) {
      nonModal.setVisible(true);
  }
```

```
        else if (parent == nonModal) {
            modal.setVisible(true);
        }
    }


    public void windowClosing(WindowEvent event) {
        if ((Window)event.getSource() == this) {
            super.windowClosing(event);
        }
        else {
            ((Window)event.getSource()).setVisible(false);
        }
    }


    public void windowDeactivated(WindowEvent event) {}
    public void windowClosed(WindowEvent event) {}
    public void windowDeiconified(WindowEvent event) {}
    public void windowOpened(WindowEvent event) {}
    public void windowIconified(WindowEvent event) {}
    public void windowActivated(WindowEvent event) {}


    public static void main(String args[]) {
        new DialogTest();
    }
}
```

The DialogTest program creates two intuitively named Dialog objects:
modal, a modal dialog, and nonModal, a non-modal dialog. The non-
modal dialog has the GUIFrame as its parent and the modal dialog has the
non-modal dialog as its parent. You must specify the parent in the Dialog()
constructor method. I used the three-arg constructor, which is of the form

```
Dialog(parent, title, modal_flag);
```

parent must be of type `Dialog` or `Frame`, *title* is the `String` title of the `Dialog` object window, and *modal_flag* is a `boolean` that indicates if this `Dialog` is modal (`true`) or non-modal (`false`). The `DialogTest` program extends `GUIFrame` and implements `ActionListener` and `Window Listener`. The `actionPerformed()` method gets the source of the `ActionEvent` (a `Button`), which it must explicitly cast as a `Button` object. From there, it figures out who owns the `Button` (either the `GUIFrame` (`this`) or the non-modal `Dialog` object) by calling the `getParent()` method, which can be called on any `Component` to get a reference to its `Container`. If the `Button` is owned by `this` object, it must be in the `GUIFrame` and, therefore, pop up the non-modal dialog. If not, the `Button` must belong to the non-modal `Dialog` object and, therefore, display the modal dialog. That's how the logic for the `action Performed()` method works. The `windowClosing()` method closes the window that corresponds to the x that is clicked. The method figures this out by testing whether the source of the `WindowEvent` is `this` object. If it is `this` object, then we already implemented this method in the super-class (`GUIFrame`) and can pass the buck by calling it like this:

```
super.windowClosing(event);
```

If the source of the `WindowEvent` is not `this`, then it must be one of the two dialogs. Whichever it is, set its visible state to `false` (hide it). You can see the results in Figure 4.14, but you'd actually have to run the program yourself to see the difference between modal and non-modal dialog Windows.

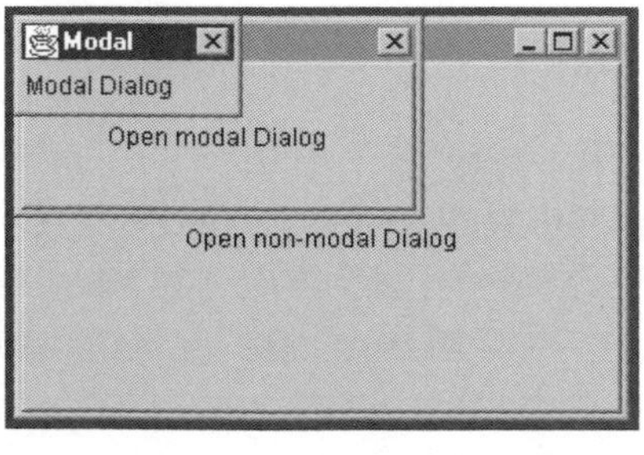

Figure 4.14

The `DialogTest` program demonstrates the use of both modal and non-modal dialog windows.

TIP

■ ■

Don't forget to check out Java's J2SE API documentation for more detailed documentation on the `java.awt` package when you have time. This book covers a lot of stuff in
a relatively short amount of time. I cover everything you need to know to get started
with the AWT, but there's actually a lot more to it. You can find the API documentation
on Sun's Web site at http://java.sun.com.

■ ■

Take a Break

Okay, we've gotten through all the components that this book covers. Now
is a good time for a break. When you're ready to come back, we'll go over
layout managers. Then, finally, we'll get back to the calculator project.

Layout Managers

Containers use layout managers to decide where to place components and
how to organize them. This section covers the five major AWT layout
managers: `FlowLayout`, `BorderLayout`, `GridLayout`, `GridBagLayout`,
and `CardLayout`. They're all quite different from each other, so it's good
to know them all.

FlowLayout

The `FlowLayout` manager is the easiest to use of all of the layout managers. It simply arranges the components from left to right, and when it
runs out of room, it wraps them to a new line. (To visualize this, consider
the way your word processor wraps words within a paragraph.) By default,
each "line" of components is centered, but you can specify left, right, or
center alignment. The `FlowLayoutTest` program demonstrates how to
use the `FlowLayout` layout manager. You set the desired layout manager
for a particular container by calling the `setLayout()` method. `Flow
Layout` is the default layout manager for `Panels`. Here is the source code:

```
/*

 * FlowLayoutTest

 * Demonstrates use of the FlowLayout layout manager.

 */


import java.awt.*;

import java.awt.event.*;


public class FlowLayoutTest extends GUIFrame {


  public FlowLayoutTest() {

    super("FlowLayout Test");

    addWindowListener(this);

    setLayout(new FlowLayout(FlowLayout.RIGHT, 20, 50));


    for (int b=1; b <= 15; b++) {

      add(new Button("Button " + b));

    }

    setSize(575, 300);

    setVisible(true);

  }


  public static void main(String args[]) {

    new FlowLayoutTest();

  }


}
```

I used the `FlowLayout`(*int*, *int*, *int*) constructor method, which sets the alignment and the horizontal and vertical spacing between the components that it lays out. You can see the results in Figure 4.15.

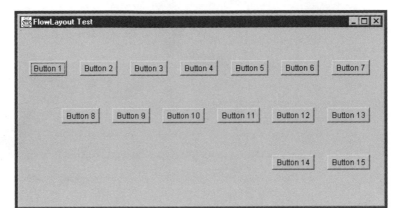

Figure 4.15

In this example, the
`FlowLayout`
manager lays out
15 buttons using
`FlowLayout.`
`RIGHT` alignment.

BorderLayout

The `BorderLayout` layout manager separates a container's area into five sections: north, south, east, west, and center. You will see in the `Border LayoutTest` program that follows that there are five corresponding `Border Layout` constants for each of these sections. `BorderLayout` attempts to resize all of its components so that they completely fill their designated areas. `BorderLayout` is the default layout manager for the `Frame` class (and, thus, for the `GUIFrame` class). The `BorderLayoutTest` program clearly demonstrates how this layout manager works. Here is the source code:

```
/*
 * BorderLayoutTest
 * Demonstrates the BorderLayout layout manager
 */


import java.awt.*;
import java.awt.event.*;


public class BorderLayoutTest extends GUIFrame {
```

```java
public BorderLayoutTest() {
  super("BorderLayout Test");
  addWindowListener(this);
  setLayout(new BorderLayout());

  add(new Button("Center"), BorderLayout.CENTER);
  add(new Button("North"), BorderLayout.NORTH);
  add(new Button("East"), BorderLayout.EAST);
  add(new Button("South"), BorderLayout.SOUTH);
  add(new Button("West"), BorderLayout.WEST);

  pack();
  setSize(400, 300);
  setVisible(true);
}

public static void main(String args[]) {
  BorderLayoutTest blt = new BorderLayoutTest();
}

}
```

The BorderLayout manager's regions are clearly shown by appropriately labeled buttons, as you can see in Figure 4.16.

GridLayout

The GridLayout class lays out its components in a grid of equally sized rectangular cells. You just need to specify the number of rows and columns and then add the components. The GirdLayout layout manager adds the components from left to right in rows, beginning at the top and continuing to the bottom. The GridLayoutTest program demonstrates

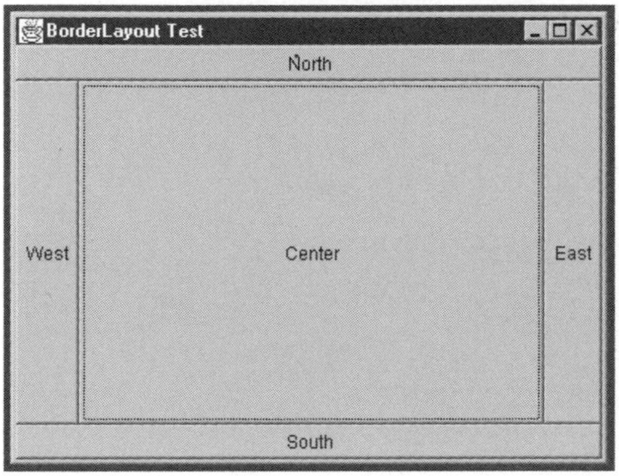

Figure 4.16

The
BorderLayout
manager lays
components out in
five areas: North,
South, East, West,
and Center.

this. Note that when the number of rows or columns is specified as zero, that is an indication that any number of rows or columns can exist. You cannot have both rows and columns specified as zero at the same time. It then bases the layout on the number of components there are to lay out. The GridLayout(*int*, *int*, *int*, *int*) constructor accepts the number of columns, number of rows, horizontal gap between components, and the vertical gap between components. Here is the source code for the GridLayoutTest program. The output is shown in Figure 4.17.

```
/*

 * GridLayoutTest

 * Demonstrates the GridLayout layout manager

 */


import java.awt.*;

import java.awt.event.*;


public class GridLayoutTest extends GUIFrame {


  public GridLayoutTest() {

    super("GridLayout Test");
```

```
        addWindowListener(this);
        setLayout(new GridLayout(0, 3, 5, 10));

        for (int b=1; b <=12; b++) {
            add(new Button("Button " + b));
        }

        pack();
        setVisible(true);
    }

    public static void main(String args[]) {
        GridLayoutTest glt = new GridLayoutTest();
    }

}
```

GridBagLayout and GridBagConstraints

The GridBagLayout layout manager is much more difficult to use than the other layout managers. It's sort of like a loosely defined grid that is less strict than GridLayout. It doesn't have a set number of rows or columns, and it uses a helper class, GridBagConstraints, to set the constraints for each component that it lays out. The GridBagConstraints fields are shown in Table 4.2.

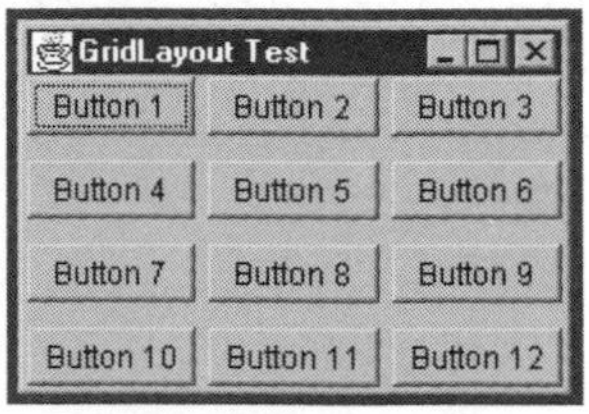

Figure 4.17

In this example, the GridLayout manager lays out 12 buttons in a grid of 4 rows by 3 columns of equal-sized cells.

TABLE 4.2 GRIDBAGCONSTRAINTS FIELDS

Field	Description
`int anchor`	Specifies where to place a component within its cell if the cell area is larger than the component. Possible values are the static constants NORTH, NORTHEAST, EAST, SOUTHEAST, SOUTH, SOUTHWEST, WEST, NORTHWEST, and CENTER.
`int fill`	Specifies how to resize a component to fit its cell if the cell area is larger than the component. Possible values are the static constants HORIZONTAL, VERTICAL, BOTH, or NONE.
`int gridheight`	Specifies how many rows this cell spans.
`int gridwidth`	Specifies how many columns this cell spans.
`int gridx`	Specifies the x-coordinate at the left side of this component, where the leftmost cell has the value `gridx=0`.
`int gridy`	Specifies the y-coordinate at the top of this component, where the topmost cell has the value `gridy=0`.
`Insets insets`	Specifies how much space to allow outside the component (*external padding*).
`int ipadx`	Specifies the *internal horizontal padding*, or how much to add to the horizontal size of the component.
`int ipady`	Specifies the *internal vertical padding*, or how much to add to the vertical size of the component.
`int weightx`	Specifies how much horizontal weight this component has when its container is resized. The greater the number, the larger it will be in comparison to other components when the container is enlarged.
`int weighty`	This is the same as `weightx` except that it specifies vertical weight.

continued

TABLE 4.2 GRIDBAGCONSTRAINTS FIELDS

Field	Description
static int RELATIVE	This value can be set to `gridwidth` or `gridheight`, in which case it signifies that this component is the next-to-last component in that row or column, respectively. It can also be set to `gridx` or `gridy`, in which case it signifies that this component should be placed right next to the previous component (just to the right for `gridx` and just underneath for `gridy`).
static int REMAINDER	This value can be set to `gridwidth` or `gridheight` to specify that it should be the last component in its row or column, respectively.

Let's get a quick example out there. Take a look at the `GridBagLayoutTest` program:

```
/*
 * GridBagLayoutTest
 * Tests out the GridBagLayout layout manager.
 */

import java.awt.*;

public class GridBagLayoutTest extends GUIFrame {

    public GridBagLayoutTest() {
        super("GridBagLayout Test");

        GridBagLayout gbl = new GridBagLayout();
        GridBagConstraints gbc = new GridBagConstraints();
        setLayout(gbl);
```

```
Button b1 = new Button("Button 1");
gbl.setConstraints(b1, gbc);
gbc.anchor = GridBagConstraints.NORTHWEST;
add(b1);


Button b2 = new Button("Button 2");
gbc.gridwidth = GridBagConstraints.REMAINDER;
gbc.anchor = GridBagConstraints.NORTH;
gbc.fill = GridBagConstraints.HORIZONTAL;
gbl.setConstraints(b2, gbc);
add(b2);


Button b3 = new Button("Button 3");
gbc.gridwidth = 1;
gbc.gridheight = 2;
gbc.anchor = GridBagConstraints.WEST;
gbc.fill = GridBagConstraints.VERTICAL;
gbl.setConstraints(b3, gbc);
add(b3);


Button b4 = new Button("Button 4");
gbc.gridheight = 1;
gbc.gridwidth = GridBagConstraints.RELATIVE;
gbc.anchor = GridBagConstraints.CENTER;
gbc.weightx = gbc.weighty = 1.0;
gbc.fill = GridBagConstraints.BOTH;
gbl.setConstraints(b4, gbc);
add(b4);


Button b5 = new Button("Button 5");
```

```java
        gbc.gridwidth = GridBagConstraints.REMAINDER;
        gbc.anchor = GridBagConstraints.EAST;
        gbc.weightx = gbc.weighty = 0.0;
        gbc.fill = GridBagConstraints.NONE;
        gbl.setConstraints(b5, gbc);
        add(b5);

        Button b6 = new Button("Button 6");
        gbc.gridwidth = 1;
        gbc.anchor = GridBagConstraints.SOUTHWEST;
        gbl.setConstraints(b6, gbc);
        add(b6);

        Button b7 = new Button("Button 7");
        gbc.anchor = GridBagConstraints.SOUTH;
        gbl.setConstraints(b7, gbc);
        add(b7);

        Button b8 = new Button("Button 8");
        gbc.anchor = GridBagConstraints.SOUTHEAST;
        gbl.setConstraints(b8, gbc);
        add(b8);

        pack();
        setVisible(true);
    }

    public static void main(String args[]) {
        new GridBagLayoutTest();
    }
}
```

When using GridBagLayout, the first thing you do is instantiate a Grid BagLayout object. Next, you instantiate the GridBagConstraints object that will help the GridBagLayout layout manager to arrange its components. Then you start modifying the GridBagConstraints object to suit the needs of the next component being laid out. The GridBagLayoutTest example just lays out some buttons by applying GridBagConstraints values to the buttons. Some of the GridBagConstraints fields, such as fill and anchor specify how to handle components when their Container is resized. (Refer to Table 4.2 as you look through this example code to get an idea of what's going on.) Figure 4.18 shows what the GridBag LayoutTest looks like at its initial size and after it is enlarged.

CardLayout

The CardLayout class lays out components in separate "cards" that can be displayed one at a time. You can think of each card as belonging to a deck of playing cards, except in this case, each card is a Java Component object. When adding components to a CardLayout, you specify a String, which is used as an identifier so that, when necessary, you can flip directly to that card using its name. The CardLayoutTest example program demonstrates the CardLayout layout manager. Here is the source code:

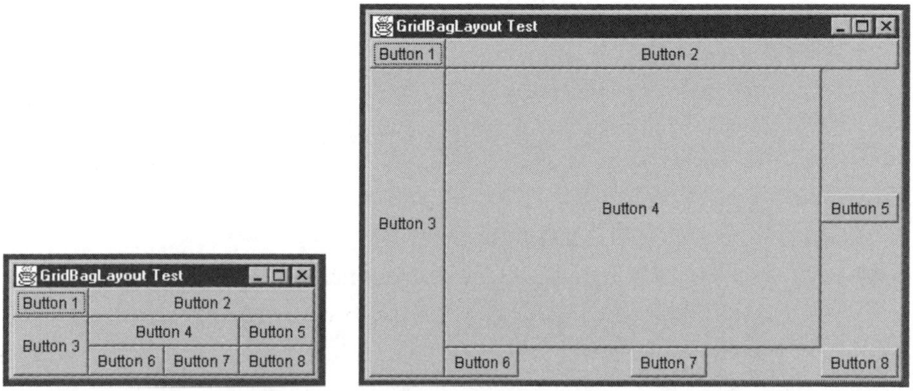

Figure 4.18

The GridBag LayoutTest program demonstrates the Grid BagLayout layout manager. You can see how the window initially appears (left) and what happens when you resize it (right).

```
/*
 * CardLayoutTest
 * Tests the CardLayout manager.
 */

import java.awt.*;
import java.awt.event.*;

public class CardLayoutTest extends GUIFrame
    implements ActionListener {

    private CardLayout layout;
    private Panel cardPanel;

    public CardLayoutTest() {
        super("CardLayout Test");

        cardPanel = new Panel();
        layout = new CardLayout();
        cardPanel.setLayout(layout);
        cardPanel.add("C1", new Label("First", Label.CENTER));
        cardPanel.add("C2", new Label("Second", Label.CENTER));
        cardPanel.add("C3", new Label("Third", Label.CENTER));
        cardPanel.add("C4", new Label("Last", Label.CENTER));

        add(cardPanel, BorderLayout.CENTER);

        Panel buttonPanel = new Panel();
        buttonPanel.setLayout(new GridLayout(1, 0));

        Button prevButton = new Button("<- Previous");
```

```
        prevButton.setActionCommand("PREV");
        prevButton.addActionListener(this);
        buttonPanel.add(prevButton);

        Button nextButton = new Button("Next ->");
        nextButton.setActionCommand("NEXT");
        nextButton.addActionListener(this);
        buttonPanel.add(nextButton);

        add(buttonPanel, BorderLayout.SOUTH);
        setSize(200, 150);
        setVisible(true);
    }


    public void actionPerformed(ActionEvent event) {
        if (event.getActionCommand().equals("NEXT")) {
            layout.next(cardPanel);
        }
        else if (event.getActionCommand().equals("PREV")) {
            layout.previous(cardPanel);
        }
    }


    public static void main(String args[]) {
        new CardLayoutTest();
    }

}
```

You can see the effect that the CardLayout manager has on its components in Figure 4.19.

Figure 4.19

The CardLayout Test program shows how the CardLayout layout manager works. The Next and Previous buttons iterate through the four different Labels.

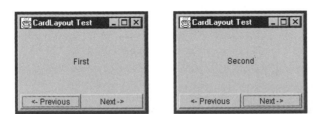

Use Table 4.3 as a CardLayout methods reference.

TABLE 4.3 CARDLAYOUT METHODS	
Method	**Description**
CardLayout()	Constructs a CardLayout object with no horizontal or vertical gaps.
CardLayout(*int, int*)	Constructs a CardLayout object with the given horizontal and vertical gaps.
void first(*Container*)	Displays the first card of the given Container object.
void last(*Container*)	Displays the last card of the given Container object.
void next(*Container*)	Displays the next card of the given Container object.
void previous(*Container*)	Displays the previous card of the given Container object.
void show(*String, Container*)	Displays the card that was added to this Container using the specified String identifier.

Creating the CalculatorKeypad Component

Now that you have some GUI programming skills under your belt, let's go ahead and create the CaclulatorKeypad class. Basically, it's a panel of buttons that can (and will eventually) be used to operate a calculator. There are no new concepts introduced here, so let's get right to the source code listing for CalculatorKeypad, another class for the calculator project:

```
/*
 * CalculatorKeypad
 * A Panel subclass that contains a set of buttons for a calculator
 */

import java.awt.*;
import java.awt.event.*;

public class CalculatorKeypad extends Panel
    implements ActionListener {

    private Button[] buttons;

    public CalculatorKeypad() {
        super();
        GridBagLayout gbl = new GridBagLayout();
        GridBagConstraints gbc = new GridBagConstraints();
        gbc.fill = GridBagConstraints.BOTH;
        gbc.weightx = gbc.weighty = 1.0;
        gbc.ipadx = gbc.ipady = 5;

        // bLabels is an array of button labels in order
        // from left to right; ÷ is #247, ± is #177, _ is #215
        String[] bLabels = { "MR", "MC", "M+", "M-", "MS", "SQ",
```

```
          "C", "AC", "POW", String.valueOf((char)247),
          String.valueOf((char)215), "-", "7", "8", "9",
          String.valueOf((char)177), "4", "5", "6", "+",
          "1", "2", "3", "=", "0", "." };

   //there are four columns of buttons
   int cols = 4;

   //build the Button array and add to Panel
   buttons = new Button[bLabels.length];
   setLayout(gbl);
   for (int b = 0; b < buttons.length; b++) {
       buttons[b] = new Button(bLabels[b]);

       //set different constraints
       if (bLabels[b].equals("=")) {
           // "=" spans two rows
           gbc.gridheight = 2;
           gbc.gridwidth = GridBagConstraints.REMAINDER;
       }
       else if (bLabels[b].equals("0")) {
           // "0" spans two cols
           gbc.gridy = 6;
           gbc.gridx = 0;
           gbc.gridwidth = 2;
           gbc.gridheight = 1;
       }
       else if (bLabels[b].equals("3")) {
           gbc.gridheight = 1;
           gbc.gridwidth = GridBagConstraints.RELATIVE;
       }
```

```
            else if ((b + 1) % cols == 0) {
                gbc.gridheight = 1;
                //end a row
                gbc.gridwidth = GridBagConstraints.REMAINDER;
            }
            else {
                // for the "." button to be next to the "0"
                gbc.gridx = GridBagConstraints.RELATIVE;
                gbc.gridheight = 1;
                gbc.gridwidth = 1;
            }


            //set the constraints and add it to the panel
            buttons[b].setFont(
                new Font("Helvetica", Font.BOLD, 14));
            buttons[b].addActionListener(this);
            gbl.setConstraints(buttons[b], gbc);
            add(buttons[b]);


        }
    }


    public void actionPerformed(ActionEvent event) {
        Button source = event.getSource() instanceof Button
            ? (Button) event.getSource() : null;
        if (source != null) {
            System.out.print(source.getLabel() + " ");
        }
    }


}
```

It's really quite simple. This `Panel` subclass is not yet integrated with any other calculator classes, so for now, it's just a bunch of buttons. I created an array of `Strings` called `bLabels`, which I then looped to create an array of `Button` objects. The `Strings` stored in `bLabels` became the labels for the buttons. I also laid the components into the `Calculator Keypad` panel with an `if-else` statement that changed some `GridBag Constraints` fields based on how each specific button should be laid out. Generally, there are four columns of buttons, so I knew where to end most of the rows. But a couple of the buttons span multiple rows, so I had to use some funky logic—not too funky though. Currently, `Action Events` are used to print the button labels to the standard output stream, but eventually we'll get those buttons to operate the calculator program!

The `CalculatorKeypadTest` program tests the `CalculatorKeypad` component simply by adding it to a `GUIFrame`. Here's the source code for the test program:

```
/*
 * CalculatorKeypadTest
 * Tests out the CalculatorKeypad Component
 */


import java.awt.*;


public class CalculatorKeypadTest extends GUIFrame {

    public CalculatorKeypadTest() {
        super("CalculatorKeypad Test");
        CalculatorKeypad keypad = new CalculatorKeypad();
        add(keypad, BorderLayout.CENTER);
        pack();
        setVisible(true);
    }
```

```
public static void main(String args[]) {
    new CalculatorKeypadTest();
}
}
```

You can see what the `CalculatorKeypad` Component looks like in Figure 4.20.

Wrapping Up

Is it time for bed yet? Tonight's session welcomed you to the world of Java GUI programming and took you away from text-land for a while. There is actually quite a lot of GUI programming that isn't covered in this book—it actually deserves a book of its own. It's definitely good for you to be exposed to GUI programming here, though. After reading tonight's session, you can do all of the basics, and if you move on to more advanced books or projects, you'll have this background on which to build.

Tomorrow morning, we do a bit more GUI programming. You'll learn how to draw shapes and images onto a `Canvas` object, and you'll use that knowledge to program a graphical representation of a digital display for the calculator. You'll also learn about inner classes, and you'll learn more about applets. *Good night!*

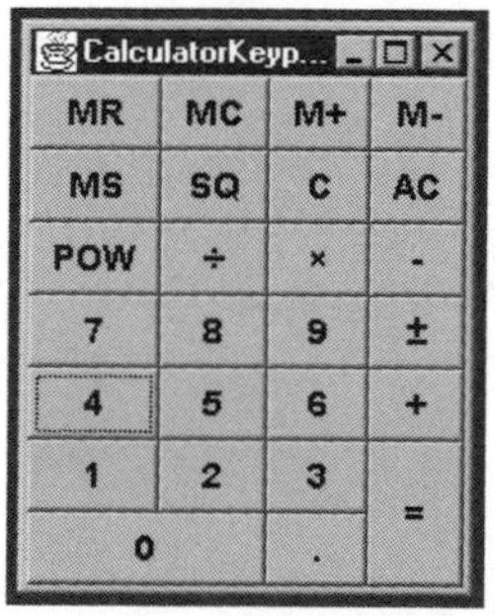

Figure 4.20

The `Calulator KeypadTest` program tests the `Calculator Keypad` component to make sure that it's working properly. Clicking the buttons should generate output to the standard output stream.

More GUI, Graphics, and Exception Handling

➤ **AWT Graphics Programming**

➤ **Creating the `LiquidCrystalDigit` Class**

➤ **Introduction to Swing GUI Programming**

➤ **Converting the `CalculatorKeypad` Class to Swing**

➤ **Inner Classes**

➤ **Abstract Classes**

➤ **Exception Handling**

➤ **Creating the Graphics for the Calculator Project**

This session begins by showing you how to do graphics programming. This session moves beyond the AWT to cover lightweight GUI components. You'll program your own graphics for a lightweight component to create digits that have a liquid crystal appearance for the calculator, like that of a real calculator. Continuing with lightweight components, this session explains the Swing package, which defines a set of lightweight GUI components. Once you learn about Swing, you'll convert the calculator application to Swing. This session gets to more advanced topics—inner classes and exception handling. Finally, you'll update the calculator application by creating a digital display panel using the skills you gain in this session.

AWT Graphics Programming

All of the AWT GUI components are graphically rendered to the screen. The word *render* refers to the fact that Java uses the graphics system to draw buttons, labels, textfields, and so on. For example, a button consists of an outline (made up of different colors to make it appear three-dimensional), a background color, and a text label that indicates the button's function. All of this has to be graphically rendered so that you can see GUI components and interact with them. So far, all of the components, except `Canvas`, that you've used have been rendered behind the scenes. In this section, however, you'll learn how to take control of the graphics system and how to render different colors and shapes so that you can draw some of your own custom components.

Each component has a `paint()` method, which it inherits from the `java.awt.Component` class. To render graphics into a component, all you need to do is override this method and take control of its `Graphics` object. The signature for the `paint()` method is

```
public void paint(Graphics g)
```

The `paint()` method is automatically called each time the component is rendered. The `Graphics` class encapsulates information that is used to render graphics to different devices, such as your computer screen or a printer. You use the `Graphics` object argument, *g*, to render graphics to the component. The `Graphics` class provides different methods for drawing shapes to be rendered. It keeps track of the current color and uses a coordinate system to render graphics. For example, when rendering graphics to a computer screen, the coordinate system specifies pixel locations. *Pixels* are the individual tiny colored dots that make up the graphics of your computer screen. The origin (0, 0), which is in the format (*x, y*) where x=0 and y=0, is at the top-left of the component. The x-coordinate increases as you move horizontally to the right and decreases as you move left. The y-coordinate increases as you move vertically down and decreases as you move up. You use this coordinate system to specify the pixel location for whatever it is you're rendering. Shortly, you'll see the different methods in the `Graphics` class to render lines, ovals, rectangles, and other shapes. The arguments to these methods specify the pixel locations and dimensions for these shapes.

The Color Class

The `Color` class, part of the `java.awt` package, is used to specify colors for graphical rendering. Java AWT components use the `Color` class to define the colors they use to graphically represent themselves in a GUI. Components have background colors and foreground colors. A typical AWT button will use the same background and foreground colors as the underlying operating system's GUI uses. The button is filled with the background color, which makes up most of the button's area, and the button's text will be rendered in the button's foreground color. Buttons and other 3-D-style components frequently have other colors around their edges to create a 3-D appearance. The button looks like it's raised most of the time, but when you click on it, it looks like it's depressed into the window—it looks and feels like a real button. The button uses different colors to render these different appearances. All of the

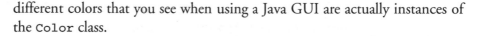

different colors that you see when using a Java GUI are actually instances of the `Color` class.

There are several different ways to create a `Color` object. I won't go into every single `Color` class constructor, but I will cover the most frequently used ones. Computers render colors as RGB values, or combinations of three colors—red, green, and blue. With this in mind, Java provides a `Color` constructor that uses these three values as its parameters:

```
public Color(int r, int g, int b)
```

The three parameters `r`, `g`, and `b` are the red, green, and blue values of the `Color` object, and the resulting color is the combination of these three components. Each one of these color values is an integer between 0 and 255. The intensity of the red, green, and blue color value increases as the integer value increases. So, if all of the parameters are zero, the resulting color is black; if all of the parameters are 255, the resulting color is white. If any one of these parameters is 255 while the other two are both zero, the resulting color will correspond to the parameter with the value of 255. For example, to construct the color red, you would call the constructor as follows:

```
Color red = new Color(255, 0, 0);
```

Green is

```
Color green = new Color(0, 255, 0);
```

Blue is

```
Color blue = new Color(0, 0, 255);
```

There is another constructor that allows you to pass in an alpha value in addition to the red, green, and blue values.

```
public Color(int r, int g, int b, int alpha);
```

A color's *alpha* value is its level of opaqueness. Possible alpha values range from 0 to 255 as well. If the alpha value is zero, then the color is completely transparent, and you won't see it at all. Instead, you'll see whatever may be underneath this color—the component's background, or whatever may have already been rendered. If the alpha value is 255, then the color will be completely opaque, which means that when the color is graphically rendered, you won't see anything that may be underneath it. Values between 0 and 255 are different levels of opaqueness. For example, if the alpha value is 100, then instead of being completely transparent or completely opaque, it will be semi-transparent, so you will see the color rendered to the screen and also whatever is rendered underneath it. As an example, if you constructed a color as

```
Color semiTransparentRed = new Color(255, 0, 0, 100);
```

and you rendered it overlaying something white, the color would look pink, as though you were looking through tinted glass. The Color class also provides some predefined objects for commonly used colors. They are as follows:

```
Color.black
Color.blue
Color.cyan
Color.darkGray
Color.gray
Color.green
Color.lightGray
Color.magenta
Color.orange
Color.pink
Color.red
Color.white
Color.yellow
```

Each of these predefined colors are static members of the Color class and reference Color instances. You use them simply by following the Color class name with a dot and the name of the color that you need to reference. For example, to set the background color of a component to black, you do this:

```
myComponent.setBackground(Color.black);
```

Java provides another useful class in the java.awt package. It encapsulates symbolic colors that your operating system uses to render GUI components. This class is called SystemColor, and it provides static members, which represent these different colors. For example, SystemColor.control, which you used before in the GUIFrame class, is the background color for control objects, such as frames, buttons, and so on. Refer to the JDK API documentation for more information about the `SystemColor` class. You can locate the documentation on Sun's Web site at http://java.sun.com.

Throughout the rest of this section, you'll learn how to use colors to render graphics, so knowing the `Color` class is important. For most of the programs you'll be looking at here, the default foreground color is used to render the graphics. When you write programs for yourself, feel free to play around by setting different colors. Later on, however, you'll be using colors to directly render the `DigitalDisplay` component of the calculator program. The `DigitalDisplay` component will render a graphical display for the calculator that looks like the liquid crystal display found on most calculators and digital watches.

Drawing Lines

The first shape you'll learn to render is the simplest one conceptually. As is the case for the rest of the shapes, to render lines, you override the `paint()` method and make use of the `paint()` method's `Graphics` object. The `paint()` method exists in all components. In this case, you'll be overriding the `GUIFrame`'s `paint()` method. This will allow you to render graphics right inside the `GUIFrame`.

To render a line, use the `Graphics` class's `drawLine()` method. The signature for this method is

```
public void drawLine(int x1, int y1, int x2, int y2)
```

The first two arguments, *x1* and *y1*, are the x- and y-coordinates for the starting point of the line. The second two arguments, *x2* and *y2*, are the coordinates for the ending point of the line. Java will render the line by connecting these two points with a line of pixels, which is one pixel wide. The `LineTest` program demonstrates this. Here is the source code:

```
/*
 * LineTest
 * Uses the Graphics object to draw lines
 */
```

```
import java.awt.Graphics;

public class LineTest extends GUIFrame {

    public LineTest() {
        super("Line Test");
        setSize(275, 175);
    }

    public static void main(String args[]) {
        new LineTest().setVisible(true);
    }

    public void paint(Graphics g) {
        g.drawLine(25, 50, 125, 150);
        g.drawLine(150, 150, 250, 50);
    }

}
```

The LineTest program draws two lines. The first one starts at (25, 50) and ends at (125, 150). The second line starts at the point (150, 150) and ends at the point (250, 50). Note that you have to import the java.awt.Graphics class in order to gain access to it. The LineTest class extends the GUIFrame class, as do the rest of the graphics-rendering programs that follow. Behind the scenes, the Frame's background graphics are rendered prior to the paint() method being called. After these graphics are rendered, the Graphics object's current color is set to the foreground color—which is why you don't have to set it yourself—and then paint() is called. The Graphics object that gets passed into the paint() method is a reference to the GUIFrame's graphics, so any operations you perform using this Graphics object are rendered to the screen inside of the GUIFrame. You can see the results of the LineTest program in Figure 5.1.

Figure 5.1

Use the
Graphics class's
drawLine()
method to
draw lines.

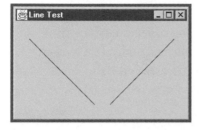

In Figure 5.1, you can see the two lines rendered by the drawLine() methods called on the Graphics object. When looking at the figure, be sure that the coordinates passed into the two drawLine() method calls make sense to you, considering the fact that the coordinate system's origin is the top-left point of the GUIFrame's display area. Once you have a good understanding of how the LineTest program works, it will be easy for you to follow the rest of the graphics-rendering programs because they work similarly.

 TIP

The LineTest program, as well as the other graphics-rendering programs, uses the default foreground color to render the shapes to the screen. If you want to set different colors yourself, you can use the setColor() method of the Graphics class using what you learned about the Color class in the last section. For example, to set the color to red, do this:

```
g.setColor(Color.red);
```

Drawing Rectangles and 3-D Rectangles

Drawing rectangles in Java is as simple as drawing lines. Just like drawing lines, you specify the starting point for the top-left of the rectangle, but instead of specifying the ending point for the bottom-right of the rectangle, you specify the rectangle's width and height. The method you use to draw a rectangular shape is drawRect() and the signature is

```
public void drawRect(int x, int y, int width, int height)
```

This method draws the outline of a rectangle. The x and y parameters are the x- and y-coordinates for the rectangle's starting point and *width* and *height* are the width and height of the rectangle. The `Graphics` class also provides a method to fill the rectangular area with the current color. This method is `fillRect()`, which takes the same parameters that `drawRect()` takes:

```
public void fillRect(int x, int y, int width, int height)
```

The parameters specify the location and dimensions for the rectangle; this method completely fills the area defined by these parameters.

NOTE When I say such things as *the top-left* and *the bottom-right*, I am speaking relatively. When you specify the starting point of a rectangle, it is easier to think of it as the coordinate for the top-left corner of the rectangle, although that may not actually be the case when you see the rectangle rendered. For example, if you specify a negative width and height for the rectangle, the starting point ends up being the bottom-right corner, so the starting point is relative to the width and height of the rectangle. It is easier to think of it this way because it is consistent with Java's graphics coordinate system. Because Java's coordinate system has its origin in the top-left corner and increases as you move right and down, I use this point of reference when specifying points—I am speaking relative to Java's graphics coordinate system, not relative to the shape being rendered.

The `RectTest` program demonstrates both the `drawRect()` and `fillRect()` methods. This program is very similar to the `LineTest` program. The only differences are the methods that are called on the `Graphics` object. Here is the source code:

```
/*
 * RectTest
 * Uses the Graphics object to draw Rects
 */


import java.awt.Graphics;


public class RectTest extends GUIFrame {
```

```java
public RectTest() {
    super("Rect Test");
    setSize(275, 175);
}


public static void main(String args[]) {
    new RectTest().setVisible(true);
}


public void paint(Graphics g) {
    g.drawRect(25, 50, 100, 100);
    g.fillRect(150, 50, 100, 100);
}


}
```

You can see in Figure 5.2 that the drawRect() method draws the outline of a rectangle on the left and the fillRect() method fills the rectangle on the right.

There is another set of methods for rendering rectangles. These next two methods render rectangles that are three-dimensional in appearance. To accomplish this, Java uses different shades of the current color and draws the lines surrounding the rectangle with them. To make the rectangle appear to be raised, it uses a lighter color on the top and left sides of the rectangle and

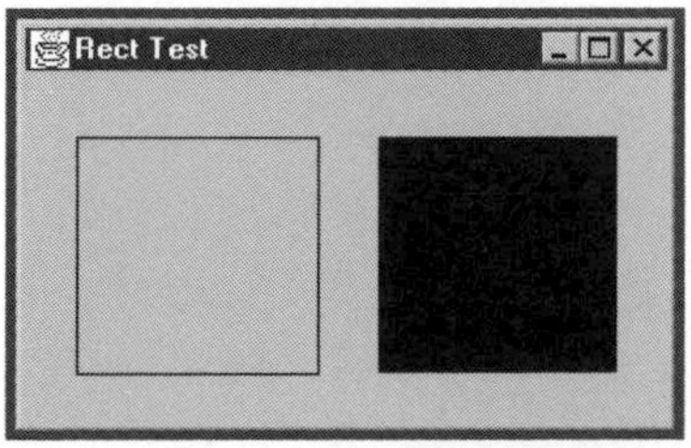

Figure 5.2

The drawRect() method draws the outline of a rectangle, while the fillRect() method completely fills the interior of a rectangle.

a darker color on the right and bottom sides. To make the rectangle appear to be depressed, it uses a darker color on the top and left sides and a brighter color on the right and bottom sides. The methods used for rendering three-dimensional rectangles are draw3DRect() and fill3DRect(). The signature for draw3DRect() is

```
public void draw3DRect(int x, int y, int width, int height,
                       boolean raised)
```

The first four arguments are used in exactly the same way as in the drawRect() method. That is, they specify the location and dimensions of the rectangle. The fourth argument is a boolean value, which specifies whether the rectangle should appear raised or not. If this value is true, the rectangle will be rendered with a raised appearance. If it is false, then the rectangle will be rendered with a depressed appearance. The fill3DRect() method takes the same set of parameters:

```
public void fill3DRect(int x, int y, int width, int height,
                       boolean raised)
```

The Rect3DTest makes use of both of these methods. Here is the source code:

```
/*
 * Rect3DTest
 * Uses the Graphics object to draw 3DRects
 */


import java.awt.Graphics;


public class Rect3DTest extends GUIFrame {

    public Rect3DTest() {
        super("3DRect Test");
        setSize(275, 175);
```

```
    }

    public static void main(String args[]) {
        new Rect3DTest().setVisible(true);
    }

    public void paint(Graphics g) {
        g.setColor(getBackground());
        g.draw3DRect(25, 50, 100, 100, false);
        g.setColor(java.awt.Color.orange);
        g.fill3DRect(150, 50, 100, 100, true);
    }

}
```

Notice that I went ahead and specified the colors for these rectangles. I did this because it is easier to see the three-dimensional effect if the background color is the same as the current graphics color and Java uses different shades of the current color to generate new highlight and shading colors. If these colors appear next to a completely different color, these highlighting and shading effects will lose their usefulness. For the first rectangle, because it is just drawing the outline and not filling the interior, I set the color to be the background color so that it will match the GUIFrame's background. I passed in false as the fourth argument, so the drawn rectangle will appear to be depressed. For the second rectangle, which is filled, I used Color.orange as the Graphics color to demonstrate that Java fills the rectangle with orange (or whatever the current color is). The program then generates two new shades of orange for the outline of the rectangle to make it appear raised. The second rectangle (the one on the right in Figure 5.3) appears raised because I passed in true as the fourth argument.

Figure 5.3

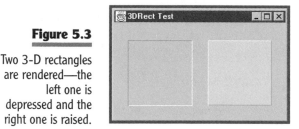

Two 3-D rectangles are rendered—the left one is depressed and the right one is raised.

Drawing Round Rectangles

There are actually two more methods in the `Graphics` class for rendering rectangular shapes. These next two methods render rectangles that have rounded corners. The method names are `drawRoundRect()` and `fill RoundRect()`. The signature for the `drawRoundRect()` method is

```
public void drawRoundRect(int x, int y, int width, int height,
                          int arcWidth, int arcHeight)
```

The first four arguments are the same as all of the other rectangle-rendering methods. The last two arguments specify the dimensions for the rounded corners of the rectangle. The *arcWidth* parameter specifies the horizontal diameter of the arc at each of the four corners, and *arcHeight* specifies the vertical diameter. To better understand how the arced corners work, imagine a smaller rectangle inside the rendered rectangle, sharing a corner. *arcWidth* and *arcHeight* are the dimensions for this inner rectangle. Now picture an oval inside the inner rectangle. The oval is the largest possible oval that can fit within the inner rectangle, such that the top of the oval touches the center of the top of the rectangle, the left side of the oval touches the left side of the rectangle, and so on. The oval is used to round the corner of the rectangle by removing the outer corner and replacing it with the quarter of the oval that is left exposed. This visual is done for you in Figure 5.4. The signature for the `fillRoundRect()` takes the same six parameters, but instead of drawing the outline, it fills the interior of the round rectangle.

```
public void fillRoundRect(int x, int y, int width, int height,
                          int arcWidth, int arcHeight)
```

The RoundRectTest demonstrates how to use these methods. Here is the source code for RoundRectTest.java:

```java
/*
 * RoundRectTest
 * Uses the Graphics object to draw RoundRects
 */

import java.awt.Graphics;

public class RoundRectTest extends GUIFrame {

    public RoundRectTest() {
        super("RoundRect Test");
        setSize(275, 175);
    }

    public static void main(String args[]) {
        new RoundRectTest().setVisible(true);
    }

    public void paint(Graphics g) {
        g.drawRoundRect(25, 50, 100, 100, 25, 50);
        g.fillRoundRect(150, 50, 100, 100, 50, 25);
    }

}
```

The results of the RoundRectTest program are shown in Figure 5.4.

Figure 5.4

The `RoundRect`
`Test` program
renders rectangles
with rounded
corners. One of the
corners of the left
rectangle shows
how the corners are
rounded based on
the arguments that
are passed in.

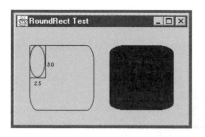

Drawing Ovals and Arcs

The `drawOval()` and `fillOval()` methods of the `Graphics` class are used to render ovular shapes. The signature for the `drawOval()` method is

```
public void drawOval(int x, int y, int width, int height)
```

You should notice that the parameters to this method are the same as the `drawRect()` method. This is because you are, in a way, specifying a rectangle. The parameters to the `drawOval()` method specify the rectangular bounds of the oval. The *x* and *y* arguments specify the coordinates for the top-left corner of the rectangular bounds, not that of the oval. This means that the top-left point is not part of the oval's area. It is outside the oval's area. The `fillOval()` method signature is

```
public void fillOval(int x, int y, int width, int height)
```

As you probably guessed, it fills the oval's interior. The `OvalTest` program demonstrates the use of these two methods:

```
/*
 * OvalTest
 * Uses the Graphics object to draw Ovals
 */


import java.awt.Graphics;
```

```java
public class OvalTest extends GUIFrame {

    public OvalTest() {
        super("Oval Test");
        setSize(275, 175);
    }

    public static void main(String args[]) {
        new OvalTest().setVisible(true);
    }

    public void paint(Graphics g) {
        g.drawOval(25, 50, 100, 100);
        g.fillOval(150, 50, 100, 100);
    }

}
```

The ovals that the OvalTest program renders can be seen in Figure 5.5.

Rendering arcs is very similar to rendering ovals. Actually, you can think of rendering arcs as rendering semi-ovals. In fact, to render an arc, you pass all the same arguments as you do for rendering ovals, plus two more. The two additional arguments are the arc's starting angle and the arc's length. The signature for drawArc() is

```java
public void drawArc(int x, int y, int width, int height, int
startAngle, int arcAngle)
```

Figure 5.5

The OvalTest program renders ovals in an AWT frame.

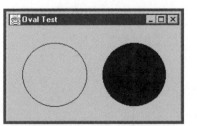

The x and y arguments specify the starting top-left coordinate for the arc's bounding rectangle. The *width* and *height* arguments specify the arc's width and height dimensions. The *startAngle* argument specifies the arc's starting angle, starting at the right side of the bounding area and increasing in a counter-clockwise direction. So zero degrees is at three o'clock, 90 degrees is at twelve o'clock, 180 degrees is at nine o'clock, 270 degrees is at six o'clock, and 360 degrees is back at three o'clock, completing the oval. The last argument, *arcAngle,* is the length of the arc, in degrees. So, an *arcAngle* of 90 degrees always specifies a quarter-oval, no matter where the starting point is. Note that the *arcAngle* also increases in a counter-clockwise direction. In order to draw the angle in a clockwise direction from the *startAngle* point, you must specify a negative number for *arcAngle*.

The fillArc() method fills the area specified by the arguments. To visualize this arc, remember the clock face. Imagine that the minute hand of the clock has paint on it, and as it moves around the clock, it paints the area in its wake, so it resembles a growing piece of pie. The signature for the fillArc() method is

```
public void fillArc(int x, int y, int width, in height,
                    int startAngle, int arcAngle)
```

The ArcTest program uses these two methods to render arcs. Here is the source code:

```
/*
 * ArcTest
 * Uses the Graphics object to draw Arcs
 */


import java.awt.Graphics;


public class ArcTest extends GUIFrame {

    public ArcTest() {
        super("Arc Test");
```

```
        setSize(275, 175);
    }


    public static void main(String args[]) {
        new ArcTest().setVisible(true);
    }


    public void paint(Graphics g) {
        g.drawArc(25, 50, 100, 100, 90, 225);
        g.fillArc(150, 50, 100, 100, 90, 225);
    }


}
```

To see the graphics that this program renders, take a look at Figure 5.6.

Drawing Polygons and Polylines

Polygons are multi-sided, fully-enclosed areas. The `Graphics` class provides methods for rendering these types of shapes. These methods are `draw Polygon()` and `fillPolygon()`. I will cover two different signatures for each of these methods. The signatures differ in the types of arguments that they accept. One of the `drawPolygon()` method signatures is

`public void drawPolygon(int[] xPoints, int[] yPoints, int nPoints)`

The first argument, *xPoints*, is an array of the x-coordinates for all of the points that make up the polygon; the *yPoints* argument is an array of the

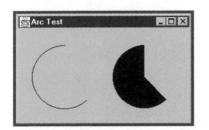

Figure 5.6

Drawing arcs in Java is done by drawing semi-ovals.

corresponding y-coordinates. So, the first coordinates are (*xPoints*[0], *yPoints*[0]), the second coordinates are (*xPoints*[1], *yPoints*[1]), and so on. The *nPoints* argument specifies the number of points for the polygon, so the length of the *xPoints* and *yPoints* arrays do not indicate the number of points. The polygon is rendered by connecting all of these points with lines.

The other signature for the `drawPolygon()` method is

```
public void drawPolygon(Polygon p)
```

The single argument to this method is a `Polygon` object. To construct a `Polygon` object, you pass in the same arguments that the previous `draw Polygon()` method accepts:

```
public Polygon(int[] xPoints, int[] yPoints, int nPoints)
```

The two `fillPolygon()` methods accept the same arguments that the `drawPolygon()` methods accept. One more thing to note about these four methods is that the polygon is automatically closed. The program does this by connecting the starting point and ending point with a line. The `Polygon Test` program demonstrates how to render these polygons. Here is the source code:

```
/*

 * PolygonTest

 * Uses the Graphics object to draw Polygons

 */


import java.awt.Graphics;

import java.awt.Polygon;


public class PolygonTest extends GUIFrame {


    public PolygonTest() {

        super("Polygon Test");

        setSize(275, 175);
```

```
    }


    public static void main(String args[]) {
        new PolygonTest().setVisible(true);
    }


    public void paint(Graphics g) {
        int[] xs = {25, 75, 125, 85, 125, 75, 25, 65};
        int[] ys = {50, 90, 50, 100, 150, 110, 150, 100};
        g.drawPolygon(xs, ys, 8);
        //move it to the right 125 pixels
        for (int i = 0; i < xs.length; i++) {
            xs[i] += 125;
        }
        Polygon poly = new Polygon(xs, ys, 8);
        g.fillPolygon(poly);
    }


}
```

In the paint() method of the PolygonTest program, two arrays are used. The xs[] array specifies all of the x-coordinates for the polygon and the ys[] array specifies all of the y-coordinates for the polygon. These arrays are passed to the drawPolygon() method, along with the number 8, to specify that there are eight points to this polygon. After the polygon is drawn, the xs[] array is run through a loop. Each element of the xs[] array is increased by 125 pixels, effectively moving the entire shape 125 pixels to the right. A new Polygon object is constructed using the changed xs[] array, the same ys[] array, and 8 as the number of points. Then the fillPolygon() method is called. In Figure 5.7, you can see that the same shape appears twice. On the left, it is drawn; and on the right, it is filled.

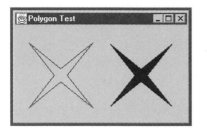

Figure 5.7

Polygons are multi-sided and closed.

The `drawPolyline()` method draws a polygonal shape, taking the same arguments as the `drawPolygon()` methods (either two arrays and an `int` or a `Polygon` object). The difference between `drawPolygon()` and `drawPolyline()` is that with the `drawPolygon()` method, the polygon is always automatically closed, while with the `drawPolyline()` method, the polygon is not closed. Also, there is no corresponding `fillPolyline()` method. Because the area is not necessarily completely enclosed, it doesn't make sense to fill it. (If you intend to fill the shape, you call `fillPolygon()`.) The `PolylineTest` program demonstrates the use of the `drawPolyline()` method.

```
/*
 * PolylineTest
 * Uses the Graphics object to draw Polylines
 */


import java.awt.Graphics;
import java.awt.Polygon;


public class PolylineTest extends GUIFrame {


    public PolylineTest() {
        super("Polyline Test");
        setSize(275, 175);
    }
```

```
public static void main(String args[]) {
    new PolylineTest().setVisible(true);
}


public void paint(Graphics g) {
    int[] xs = {25, 75, 125, 85, 125, 75, 25, 65};
    int[] ys = {50, 90, 50, 100, 150, 110, 150, 100};
    g.drawPolyline(xs, ys, 8);
    //move it to the right 125 pixels
    for (int i = 0; i < xs.length; i++) {
        xs[i] += 125;
    }
    Polygon poly = new Polygon(xs, ys, 8);
    g.drawPolyline(poly.xpoints, poly.ypoints, 5);
}


}
```

The PolylineTest program is very similar to the PolygonTest program. The xs[] and ys[] arrays are created in exactly the same way, and the first drawPolyline() call passes 8 as the number of points. Also, the Polyline Test xs[] array elements are incremented by 125 and are used to create a Polygon object, just as in the PolygonTest program. The second invocation of drawPolyline() uses the xpoints() and ypoints() methods of the Polygon class, which return the corresponding x- and y-coordinate arrays. The number 5 is passed as the number of points, so even though the arrays each are of length 8, only 5 points will be used to render the shape. You can see this for yourself in Figure 5.8.

Drawing Strings

The drawString() method draws the given String object at the given x- and y-coordinates. The x- and y-coordinates indicate the position of the

Figure 5.8

Polylines are like polygons except that they don't have to be closed.

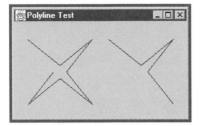

baseline of the left-most character in the string. The string is drawn using the Graphics object's current font and color. The signature for the draw String() method is

```
public void drawstring(String str, int x, int y)
```

The *str* argument is the string value that should be drawn. The *x* and *y* arguments specify the x- and y-coordinates for the starting point of the string. The DrawStringTest program demonstrates how to render strings within a Java GUI component. Here is the source code:

```
/*
 * DrawStringTest
 * Demonstrates how to draw Strings
 */


import java.awt.*;


public class DrawStringTest extends GUIFrame {

    public DrawStringTest() {
        super("drawString Test");
        setSize(275, 175);
    }
```

```
public static void main(String args[]) {
    new DrawStringTest().setVisible(true);
}


public void paint(Graphics g) {
    g.drawString("We are the music makers.", 10, 50);
    Font font = new Font("serif",
        Font.BOLD + Font.ITALIC, 16);
    g.setFont(font);
    g.drawString("We are the dreamers of dreams.", 50, 100);
}


}
```

In the DrawStringTest program, the first call to drawString() renders
the string "We are the music makers." starting at the point (10, 50)
and using the default font. Before calling the drawString() method a
second time, I changed the font by calling the setFont() method of the
Graphics class, passing it a Font object. The constructor for the
java.awt.Font class accepts a String and two integers. The first integer
argument is for specifying the style of the font. The possible values for the
style are Font.PLAIN, Font.BOLD, and Font.ITALIC. You can combine
bold and italic styles, as I did, by adding them together and passing that
value as the second argument to the Font() constructor. The third argument is the point-size for the font. The font that I created is Serif, bold and
italic, size 16. Setting the font on the Graphics object in the paint()
method causes all subsequent calls to drawString() to use the font you set,
until either the paint() method exits, or you set another font. So, when I
draw the string "We are the dreamers of dreams." it is using the font
that I set right above the second call to drawString(). Take a look at Figure
5.9 to see what the rendered strings look like.

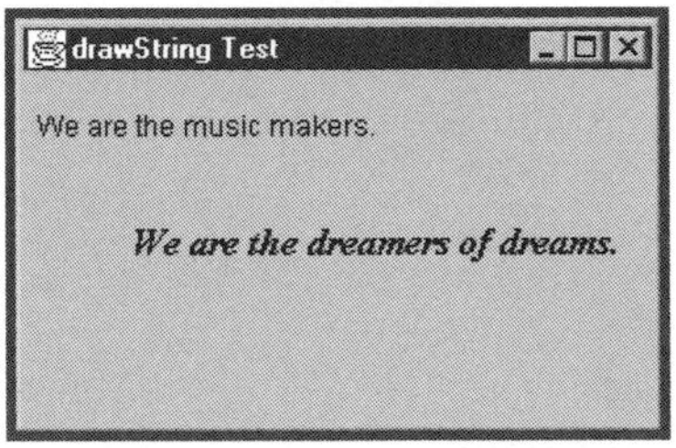

Figure 5.9

The `Graphics` class allows you to draw strings inside GUI components.

TIP

To create a specific font using the `Font` class, you pass in the name of the font as the first argument to the constructor. The name can be a font face name for any font that you have on your system. The name can also be a logical font name. In Java, logical font names are predefined strings that map to common fonts on your system. There are six logical font names: `dialog`, `dialoginput`, `monospaced`, `serif`, `sansserif`, or `symbol`. If you're curious to how this mapping occurs, take a look at the `font.properties` file found in the `<jdk>`/`jre`/`lib` directory, where `<jdk>` is the directory where you installed Java, but be careful not to change this file.

Drawing Images

Java also allows you to render images within its GUI components. To do so, load an image first, then call the `drawImage()` method, passing in that image, its x- and y-coordinates, its width and height (optional), and an image observer. To load an image, you do this:

```
Image img = Toolkit.getDefaultToolkit().getImage(imageName);
```

In this example, `img` is the `Image` object that is used to store the image. To actually get the image, you need to gain access to your operating system's native implementation of the AWT. To do this, you must call the `get DefaultToolkit()` method, which is a static method defined in the `java.awt.Toolkit` class. You pass the image filename as a `String` to the `getImage()` method and the image will be loaded. After you have an `Image` object, you're ready to call the `drawImage()` method. You can draw an image using the image's actual width and height by calling the `drawImage()` method with the following signature:

```
public void drawImage(Image img, int x, int y,
                        ImageObserver observer)
```

The *img* argument is the image to be rendered, the *x* and *y* arguments specify the coordinates of the image, and *observer* is an ImageObserver object. The ImageObserver interface is used to receive notifications about an image as the image is loading. When you load an image using getImage() the way I described it here, the image isn't loaded all at once. The image starts loading, but it might take longer to load the image than it takes to render the GUI. It is possible for the GUI to be displayed before the image is done loading. However, as the image is loading, the GUI is updated with the image data through the ImageObserver interface. This allows the image to be displayed piece by piece as the image is loading. Of course, computers usually work so fast that you will barely notice the image loading, unless the images are loaded over a network. The Component class implements the ImageObserver interface, so any component can be passed in as an ImageObserver. You'll learn more about interfaces this afternoon, which will give you a better understanding of why you can refer to any component as an ImageObserver object.

Another drawImage() signature allows you to scale the size of the image to whatever dimensions you specify:

```
public void drawImage(Image img, int x, int y, int width,
                        int height, ImageObserver observer)
```

The four arguments here that you saw in the previous version of the draw Image() method are exactly the same as in the previous method. The two additional arguments, *width* and *height*, specify the width and the height of the image. The image is scaled to fit these dimensions, so if the values you pass here are different than the image's actual width and height, the image is resized.

There are some other versions of the drawImage() method that I won't go into now. To learn about them, consult the JDK API documentation. The ImageTest program demonstrates how to render images:

```
/*
 * ImageTest
```

```
 * Demonstrates drawing Images.
 */

import java.awt.*;

public class ImageTest extends GUIFrame {

  public ImageTest() {
    super("Image Test");
    setSize(464, 288);
    setBackground(Color.white);
  }


  public static void main(String args[]) {
      new ImageTest().setVisible(true);
  }


  public void paint(Graphics g) {
    Image img = Toolkit.getDefaultToolkit().getImage(
        "brity_xmas01.jpg");
    g.drawImage(img, 0, 0, 464, 288, this);
  }


}
```

The image rendered is named `brity_xmas01.jpg`. I created the `Image` object the same way I did in the example I gave earlier. Then I passed that image to the `drawImage()` method. The starting coordinate is (0, 0). I set the size to 464 by 288. The image is actually four times this size. I did this to demonstrate that the image is resized based on the fourth and fifth arguments. The final argument to the `drawString()` method is `this`, which is a reference to this `ImageTest` object. You can see the image rendered in Figure 5.10.

Figure 5.10

In this example,
an image is
rendered inside
a GUIFrame.

Lightweight Components

The components defined in the java.awt package are heavyweight components. Java makes calls to the underlying native operating system to render
and use these components. Even though you can't see it happening, each
component is rendered in its own window, which takes up a lot of system
resources. Another drawback to using java.awt components is that the
look and feel is not consistent across different operating systems. This means
that a java.awt.Button looks different on Windows than it does on a
UNIX system, as do all other heavyweight components.

Lightweight components, on the other hand, are all graphically rendered in
the same window, provided that they all belong within the same window container. Their graphics are also directly rendered; no calls are made to the
underlying operating system. This means that the look and feel of lightweight
components is controllable and is consistent across all operating systems.

To create a lightweight component, you need to override the Component
class and take control of the Graphics object to draw the component yourself. That's pretty much it. To make it useful, however, you'll need to define
how it handles events and how a user can interact with it. Of course, not all
components need this type of functionality. For instance, a lightweight label
class would need only to render itself graphically.

Creating the LiquidCrystalComponent Class

The `LiquidCrystalComponent` class will be created as a lightweight component. It will be the base class for some components that the calculator application will use to display number values. The `LiquidCrystalComponent` class defines a component that represents a liquid crystal display, like the ones found on most handheld calculators. First, the `LiquidCrystalComponent` class demonstrates how to create a lightweight component. It also demonstrates how to create an abstract class.

An abstract class is a partially defined class that is meant to be extended by a subclass. Because an abstract class is not fully defined, it can never be instantiated, so being extended is actually its sole purpose. To specify that a class is abstract, you use the `abstract` keyword, like this:

```
public abstract class ClassName
```

Inside an abstract class, you are allowed to partially define a class by defining abstract methods, which are methods without bodies. They merely have a method signature, which is followed by a semicolon in place of the method body. The `abstract` keyword is also used to specify that a method is abstract, like this:

```
public abstract returnType methodName(parameterList);
```

So, an abstract method only defines the return type, name, and parameters for a method, not its implementation. Abstract classes are useful because you can have multiple classes inheriting from the same abstract super-class that have identical method signatures but different implementations. For instance, the `Graphics` class is actually an abstract class. Some of its abstract methods are all of the `drawImage()` methods. The `Graphics` class acts as a common super-class for all graphics contexts. Some subclasses of the `Graphics` class are operating system-specific, so the actual implementations of the `drawImage()` method are different, depending on the underlying operating system. In this case, it doesn't make sense to implement these methods within the `Graphics` class. Instead, the `Graphics` class is made abstract and the `drawImage()` methods, as well as most of the others, are made abstract. The `Graphics` class ensures that even though each operating system is different, the method is called in exactly the same way. Note that not all methods in an abstract class must be abstract. Any method that is implemented in an abstract class passes on that implementation to its subclasses.

Conversely, the whole class must be declared abstract if any of its methods are abstract. For example, the `LiquidCrystalComponent` class is abstract because one of its methods is abstract. The abstract method is the `buildLitPattern()` method, which is defined as

```
protected abstract void buildLitPattern();
```

This guarantees that all subclasses of the `LiquidCrystalComponent` class will implement this method, unless they themselves are also abstract. If you look closely at a digital watch or any other object that has a liquid crystal display, you can see that the digits are made up of smaller pieces that light to form the pattern of those digits. If you need a visual of this idea, peek ahead to Figure 5.11 to see the individual pieces of a `LiquidCrystalDigit`, a subclass of `LiquidCrystalComponent` that you'll be creating shortly. Sometimes, you can vaguely see the unlit pieces. That is what the `LiquidCrystalComponent` class simulates. The `buildLitPattern()` method will be implemented by each `LiquidCrystalComponent` subclass to determine which pieces are lit and which are not. Because each `LiquidCrystalComponent` subclass can create its own pattern, such as one for numbers, another for letters, and so on, the implementation does not belong in the super-class. But, because all subclasses will implement this method, it is beneficial to define this abstract method here. Here is the source code for the `LiquidCrystalComponent` class:

```
/*
 * LiquidCrystalComponent
 * An abstract class that defines functionality that is common
 * for all components that use a Liquid Crystal Display look.
 */

import java.awt.*;

public abstract class LiquidCrystalComponent extends Component {
```

```
/* pieces of the pattern that are either on or off */
protected boolean[] litPattern;
/* color for 'off' pieces, (foreground color is 'on') */
protected Color offColor;

protected LiquidCrystalComponent() {
    this(Color.black, new Color(0, 80, 0), Color.green);
}

protected LiquidCrystalComponent(Color bg, Color unlit,
                                     Color lit) {
    super();
    setBackground(bg);
    setUnlitColor(unlit);
    setForeground(lit);
}

/* sets the color used for unlit pieces */
public void setUnlitColor(Color unlit) {
    offColor = unlit;
}

/* returns the color used for unlit pieces */
public Color getUnlitColor() {
    return offColor;
}

/* Sets the lit pattern for this Liquid CrystalComponent
 * by setting the litPattern elements to either true or
 * false. All extending classes must implement this
```

```
 * abstract method */
protected abstract void buildLitPattern();


/* Lights this LiquidCrystalComponent using the given
 * pattern. pattern is an array whose values correspond
 * to litPattern elements that should be lit
 * (set to true). */
protected void lightPattern(int[] pattern) {
    for (int b = 0; b < pattern.length; b++) {
        litPattern[pattern[b]] = true;
    }
}


/* Sets all of this LiquidCrystalComponent's pieces to unlit */
protected void clearPattern() {
    for (int b = 0; b < litPattern.length; b++) {
        litPattern[b] = false;
    }
}


/* Returns the color for the pattern pieces indicated by
 * the given litPattern index. The returned color is either
 * the lit or unlit color. */
protected Color getPieceColor(int patternIndex) {
    if (litPattern[patternIndex]) return getForeground();
    return offColor;
}


public Dimension getMinimumSize() {
    return new Dimension(22, 55);
```

```
    }

    public Dimension getPreferredSize() {
        return getMinimumSize();
    }

}
```

The LiquidCrystalComponent class is abstract, and it acts as a shell for all of its subclasses, which you'll be building shortly. The instance variables and methods are meant to be used to keep track of a pattern of pieces that make up a larger picture. In your case, you'll be creating two subclasses: Liquid CrystalDigit and LiquidCrystalNegative. The LiquidCrystal Digit component will be used to display the digits for our calculator, and the LiquidCrystalNegative component will be used to display a negative symbol (-). Because LiquidCrystalComponent is abstract, it doesn't define an actual pattern of pieces. That's a job for its subclasses. The instance variables and methods defined in LiquidCrystalComponent are common functionality for all of the subclasses of LiquidCrystalComponent.

There are only two instance variables in the LiquidCrystalComponent class. The litPattern[] variable is an array of boolean values. The size of this array is equal to the number of pieces that make up the entire Liquid CrystalComponent pattern. Because each piece is either lit (on) or unlit (off) at any given time, boolean values are the best bet. The values are true for lit and false for unlit.

The other instance variable is offColor. It is used to store the color that graphically renders the unlit pieces. You rely on the foreground color, which is inherited from the Component class, to be the lit color, and the inherited background color to be LiquidCrystalComponent's background color.

As far as constructors go, there are two: one no-argument constructor and one that takes three Color arguments—one for the background color, one for the unlit color, and one for the lit color. Notice that the no-argument constructor calls the three-argument constructor like this:

```
this(Color.black, new Color(0, 80, 0), Color.green);
```

Calling one "worker" constructor from another constructor is a common object-oriented practice. This way, all of the work is done within a single constructor. The no-argument constructor passes default color values to the other constructor rather than repeating the same code by setting the colors itself.

The `LiquidCrystalComponent` class has a getter and setter method for accessing the unlit color: `getUnlitColor()` and `setUnlitColor()`. The background and foreground (lit) colors can be accessed through the corresponding method inherited from the `Component` class: `getBackground()`, `setBackground()`, `getForeground()`, and `setForeground()`. See Table 5.1 for more details about the other `LiquidCrystalComponent` methods.

TABLE 5.1 LIQUIDCRYSTALCOMPONENT METHODS

Method Name	Description
`protected void buildLitPattern()`	An abstract method that `LiquidCrystal Component` subclasses should implement to build the lit pattern by setting the individual pieces to `true` (lit) or `false` (unlit), depending upon which character should be displayed. This character should be stored in an instance variable. For example, to display the number 5, a calculator lights the pattern that represents the number 5.
`protected void lightPattern (int[] pattern)`	Lights the pattern indicated by the `pattern[]` array. The elements of this array are equal to the indices of the `litPattern[]` array that should be set to `true` (should be lit). Note that this method does not turn any pieces of the pattern off, so whatever was lit prior to calling this method will still be lit afterward.

continued

TABLE 5.1 LIQUIDCRYSTALCOMPONENT METHODS	
Method Name	**Description**
`protected void clearPattern()`	Clears the pattern by setting all of the elements of the `litPattern[]` array to `false`.
`protected Color getPieceColor (int pieceIndex)`	Returns the color, which is either the lit color or the unlit color, for the given piece. The `pieceIndex` argument is the index of the piece in the `litPattern[]` array. If the value of `litPattern [pieceIndex]` is true, the lit color is returned, else the unlit color is returned.
`public Dimension getMinimumSize()`	Overrides the `getMinimumSize()` method of the `Component` class. It returns the minimum `LiquidCrystalComponent` size.
`public Dimension getPreferredSize()`	Overrides the `getPreferredSize()` method of the `Component` class. It returns the preferred size, which in this case is the minimum size.

Creating the LiquidCrystalDigit Component

The `LiquidCrystalDigit` component extends the abstract `LiquidCrystal Component` class and, thus, inherits all of its functionality. Because the `LiquidCrystalDigit` component is not abstract, it must provide an implementation of the `buildLitPattern()` method, which it does. This is always the case when extending abstract classes. Any and all abstract methods in the super-class must be implemented, unless the subclass is also abstract. In fact, if you try to compile a concrete class without implementing the super-class's abstract methods, the compiler will tell you that you must declare the subclass to be abstract as well and the class will not compile.

The purpose of the `LiquidCrystalDigit` class is to represent the numbers that the calculator program will display. The `LiquidCrystalDigit` class inherits the two instance variables that are declared in the `LiquidCrystal Component` class and also defines four additional instance variables. The static variable, `EMPTY`, is used as a flag to indicate that the digit to be displayed is empty or blank. It is declared using the `final` keyword, which means that it is a constant, and, therefore, its value never changes. Another static constant declared in the `LiquidCrystalDigit` class is `E`, which is used to indicate that the digit to be displayed is the letter E. Calculators commonly use the letter E to indicate that some error has occurred, such as an overflow error, so we will also use it.

An overflow error occurs when the number to be displayed is too large to display using a set number of digits. The `LiquidCrystalDigit` component can display only a single digit, so the number 10 would be too large to display, and the letter E would be displayed instead. The `digit` variable stores the value of the digit that is to be displayed by an instance of the `LiquidCrystalDigit` class. Because there is room for only one digit, valid values for this range include any number between zero and nine. All other numbers are considered invalid. The final variable is `decimalPoint`, which is a `boolean`, and is `true` if a decimal is to be displayed right after the digit. Here is the source code for `LiquidCrystalDigit`:

```
/*

 * LiquidCrystalDigit

 * A lightweight component that represents an LCD digit.

 */


import java.awt.*;


public class LiquidCrystalDigit extends LiquidCrystalComponent {

    /* the constant that represents the empty display */
    public final static char EMPTY = ' ';
```

```java
/* a constant that represents the error code 'E' */
public final static int E = 99;
/* the currently displayed digit */
protected int digit;
/* indicates whether the decimal point is on or off */
protected boolean decimalPoint;

public LiquidCrystalDigit() {
  this(EMPTY);
 }


public LiquidCrystalDigit(int digitToDisplay) {
    super();
    litPattern = new boolean[8];
    setDigit(digitToDisplay);
 }


public LiquidCrystalDigit(int digitToDisplay,
        Color bg, Color unlit, Color lit) {
    super(bg, unlit, lit);
    litPattern = new boolean[8];
    setDigit(digitToDisplay);
 }


  public void setDigit(int digitToDisplay) {
    digit = isDigitValid(digitToDisplay) ? digitToDisplay : E;
    buildLitPattern();
    repaint();
 }
```

```java
public int getDigit() {
    return digit;
}


public void setDecimalPoint(boolean on) {
    decimalPoint = on;
    buildLitPattern();
    repaint();
}


public boolean hasDecimalPoint() {
    return decimalPoint;
}


public boolean isDigitValid(int digitChar) {
    if ( (digit >= 0 && digit <= 9)
        || (digit == EMPTY)
        || (digit == E)) {
            return true;
    }
    return false;
}


protected void buildLitPattern() {
    clearPattern();
    switch (digit) {
      case 0:
          lightPattern( new int[] { 0, 1, 2, 4, 5, 6 } );
          break;
      case 1:
```

```
                    lightPattern( new int[] { 2, 5 } );
                    break;
        case 2:
                    lightPattern( new int[] { 0, 2, 3, 4, 6 } );
                    break;
        case 3:
                    lightPattern( new int[] { 0, 2, 3, 5, 6 } );
                break;
        case 4:
                lightPattern( new int[] { 1, 2, 3, 5 } );
                break;
         case 5:
                lightPattern( new int[] { 0, 1, 3, 5, 6} );
                break;
         case 6:
                lightPattern( new int[] { 0, 1, 3, 4, 5, 6 } );
                break;
         case 7:
                lightPattern( new int[] { 0, 2, 5 } );
                break;
         case 8:
                lightPattern( new int[] { 0, 1, 2, 3, 4, 5, 6 } );
                break;
         case 9:
                lightPattern( new int[] { 0, 1, 2, 3, 5, 6 } );
                break;
         case E:
                lightPattern( new int[] { 0, 1, 3, 4, 6 } );
                break;
         case EMPTY:
```

```
        default:

            return;

    }

    litPattern[7] = decimalPoint;

}


    public void paint(Graphics g) {

        g.setColor(getBackground());

        g.fillRect(0, 0, getWidth(), getHeight());

        g.setColor(getPieceColor(0));

        g.fillRect(5, 5, 11, 3);

        g.setColor(getPieceColor(1));

        g.fillRect(2, 8, 3, 18);

        g.setColor(getPieceColor(2));

        g.fillRect(16, 8, 3, 18);

        g.setColor(getPieceColor(3));

        g.fillRect(5, 26, 11, 3);

        g.setColor(getPieceColor(4));

        g.fillRect(2, 29, 3, 18);

        g.setColor(getPieceColor(5));

        g.fillRect(16, 29, 3, 18);

        g.setColor(getPieceColor(6));

        g.fillRect(5, 47, 11, 3);

        g.setColor(getPieceColor(7));

        g.fillRect(20, 47, 3, 3);

    }


}
```

The LiquidCrystalDigit class has three constructors. The no-argument constructor constructs an empty LiquidCrystalDigit that has all of the pieces of its pattern unlit, so it displays no digit at all. It calls the `Liquid CrystalDigit(int)` constructor, passing it the `EMPTY` value. Although the `EMPTY` variable is a `char`, it can be assigned to an `int` because the `int` datatype can store all possible `char` values. The `char`s are converted to `int`s when you assign them to `int` variables. The `LiquidCrystalDigit(int)` constructor takes a single argument. The appropriately named `digitTo Display` parameter is used to pass in the digit that is to be initially displayed by the `LiquidCrystalDigit` component. This constructor does not call the third constructor, `LiquidCrystalDigit(int, Color, Color, Color)` to do its work for it.

This example illustrates that you can't always have a single worker constructor do all of the work. The reason here is that the `LiquidCrystalDigit(int)` constructor calls `super()`, which is the no-argument `LiquidCrystal Component()` constructor. If you recall, this super-class's constructor creates a `LiquidCrystalComponent` using the default color scheme. Because the `LiquidCrystalDigit(int)` constructor does not specify any colors, it calls the no-argument superconstructor to do that part of the work. Then the instance variables are initialized. The `litPattern[]` array is initialized to be eight elements long. That's because there are seven pieces that make up the digit and one more that makes up the decimal point. The third constructor, `LiquidCrystalDigit(int, Color, Color, Color)`, accepts the digit to be displayed as well as the three colors that make up the color scheme.

Now, I'll describe the purpose of the other methods. The `setDigit()` method is used to set the display value. This method assigns the given value to the `digit` instance variable, calls `buildLitPattern()`, and then repaints the component so that the lit pattern changes become visible. The `get Digit()` method simply returns the value that is stored in `digit`. The `set DecimalPoint()` method accepts a `boolean` argument. You should pass in `true` if this `LiquidCrystalDigit` should display a decimal point, or `false` if it should not. This method also repaints the component. The `hasDecimal Point()` method returns `true` if the decimal point is set, or else it returns `false`. The `isDigitValid()` method returns `true` if the given digit can be displayed. If the digit's value is `EMPTY`, `E`, or an `int` that inclusively falls within the zero-to-nine range, then it is valid. If not, this method returns `false`.

The buildLitPattern() method provides an implementation for the super-class's abstract method. It builds the lit pattern for the LiquidCrystal Digit. First, it checks the value of the digit instance variable by running it through a switch statement. For each possible value, it lights up the pieces of the pattern in such a way that it visually represents the digit that is to be displayed. To accomplish this, the buildLitPattern() method clears the pattern by calling clearPattern(), which sets all of the lit Pattern[] elements to false. Then the buildLitPattern() method calls the lightPattern() method, passing it a new int array with values that correspond to the indices of the litPattern[] array that need to be lit. For example, to create the pattern for the digit 1, it lights up pieces 2 and 5. Take a look at Figure 5.11 to see how the litPattern[] array elements correspond to the pieces of the LiquidCrystalDigit class. Finally, the build LitPattern() sets the litPattern[7] element, which is the piece for the decimal point. The buildLitPattern() method simply assigns the value of decimalPoint, which is a boolean, to litPattern[7]. It is true if there is a decimal point, or false if there is no decimal point.

The paint() method renders all of the pieces to the LiquidCrystalDigit component. Recall that you have to paint the graphics for custom light-weight components yourself. This is the function of the paint() method.

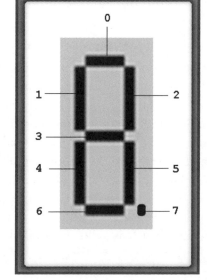

Figure 5.11

The indices of the litPattern[] array correspond to the pieces of the Liquid Crystal Digit's graphical representation.

The first thing the `paint()` method does is fill the entire area with the background color so that the graphics from any previous renderings are cleared. Then it gets the color for each individual piece by calling the `getPiece Color()` method, passing in `litPattern[]` indices. Using the determined color, the `paint()` method then fills a rectangle, which graphically represents one of the lit pattern pieces.

Creating the LiquidCrystalNegative Component

Now that the `LiquidCrystalDigit` lightweight component is out of the way, it should be a breeze to create the `LiquidCrystalNegative` component. The `LiquidCrystalNegative` component is very similar to the `Liquid CrystalDigit` component. The difference is that instead of displaying digits, the `LiquidCrystalNegative` component displays a single negative sign. The negative sign is either lit or unlit, depending on whether the `LiquidCrystalNegative` should indicate a negative number or not. Of course, the `LiquidCrystalNegative` class alone doesn't offer you much, but later the `DigitalDisplay` component will put a `LiquidCrystalNegative` component together with some `LiquidCrystalDigit` components to make the calculators display panel. Here is the source code for `LiquidCrystal Negative`:

```
/*
 * LiquidCrystalNegative
 * A liquidCrystalComponent that represents a negative sign.
 */

import java.awt.*;

public class LiquidCrystalNegative extends LiquidCrystalComponent {

    protected boolean negative;

    /* constructs a new LiquidCrystalNegative that is initially
```

```
    * unlit */
   public LiquidCrystalNegative() {
       this (false);
   }


   /* constructs a new LiquidCrystalNegative that is either
    * lit or unlit */
   public LiquidCrystalNegative(boolean isNegative) {
       super();
       litPattern = new boolean[1];
       negative = isNegative;
       buildLitPattern();
   }


   public LiquidCrystalNegative(boolean isNegative,
           Color bg, Color unlit, Color lit) {
       super(bg, unlit, lit);
       litPattern = new boolean[1];
       negative = isNegative;
       buildLitPattern();
   }


   public void setNegative(boolean isNegative) {
       negative = isNegative;
       buildLitPattern();
       repaint();
   }


   public boolean isNegative() {
       return negative;
```

```
        }

        public void buildLitPattern() {
            clearPattern();
            if (negative) {
                litPattern[0] = true;
            }
        }


        public void paint(Graphics g) {
            g.setColor(getBackground());
            g.fillRect(0, 0, getWidth(), getHeight());
            g.setColor(getPieceColor(0));
            g.fillRect(5, 26, 11, 3);
        }
    }
```

The `negative boolean` instance variable is `true` if the negative sign should be lit, or `false` if it should not be lit. The `litPattern[]` array is only one element long, as there is only one piece to the pattern. The rest of the class works just like the `LiquidCrystalDigit` class.

Testing the LiquidCrystal Components

Just to make sure that our lightweight components are working properly, here is a little test program. It tests all of the possible display values for the `LiquidCrystalDigit` class by constructing a new `LiquidCrystalDigit` object for each of the possible display digits. The first one, which displays the digit 0, is the only instance that displays the decimal point. The `Liquid CrystalDigitTest` also tests the `LiquidCrystalNegative` component.

```
/*
 * LiquidCrystalDigitTest
 * Tests the LiquidCrystalDigit component.
```

```java
    */

import java.awt.FlowLayout;
import java.awt.Color;


public class LiquidCrystalDigitTest extends GUIFrame {

    public LiquidCrystalDigitTest() {
        super("Liquid Crystal Digit Test");

        setLayout(new FlowLayout(FlowLayout.CENTER, 0, 0));
        Color bg = new Color(88, 207, 233);
        Color unlit = new Color(30, 189, 223);
        Color lit = Color.black;
        System.out.println(
            "Constructing new LiquidCrystalDigits...");
        System.out.println(
            "Adding LiquidCrystalDigit 0 with decimal...");
        LiquidCrystalDigit zero
            = new LiquidCrystalDigit(0, bg, unlit, lit);
        zero.setDecimalPoint(true);
        add(zero);

        for (int d = 1; d <= 9; d++) {
            System.out.println(
                "Adding LiquidCrystalDigit " + d + "...");
            add(new LiquidCrystalDigit(d, bg, unlit, lit));
        }

        System.out.println("Adding LiquidCrystalDigit E...");
```

```
        add(new LiquidCrystalDigit(LiquidCrystalDigit.E,
                                bg, unlit, lit));


        System.out.println("Adding empty LiquidCrystalDigit...");
        add(new LiquidCrystalDigit(LiquidCrystalDigit.EMPTY,
                                bg, unlit, lit));


        System.out.println("Adding LiquidCrystalNegative...");
        add(new LiquidCrystalNegative(true, bg, unlit, lit));


        pack();


        setVisible(true);
    }


    public static void main(String args[]) {
        new LiquidCrystalDigitTest();
    }


}
```

If you are coding along with the examples in this book, make sure that you run this test program. If it works properly, it proves that the LiquidCrystal Digit and LiquidCrystalNegative components are working. What's more, it proves that the underlying abstract LiquidCrystalComponent class is valid. It also demonstrates the fact that you can create your own custom lightweight components using Java. Finally, it is important that this test program works properly because these components are part of the calculator project, and you won't be able to move on unless your code is working. If you're stumped or want to save time, visit the companion Web site for this book at http://www.premierpressbooks.com/downloads.asp and download the code. Figure 5.12 shows how the components should look.

Figure 5.12

The displayable values of the `LiquidCrystal Digit` component are shown here along with a `Liquid CrystalNegative` component.

Take a Break

Now is a good time to take a break. Get up and step away from the computer for a while so that you can come back refreshed. After your break, you'll learn about Swing, named inner classes, and anonymous inner classes. You'll learn how to use inner classes and adapter classes for GUI event handling. Exception handling is also covered. You'll learn how to use `try-catch` blocks to handle exceptions; then you'll move on to create a custom exception class. Using just about all of what you learned this morning, you'll create the `DigitalDisplay` component for the calculator project and then write a test program to see how the project is progressing.

Introduction to Swing GUI Programming

You've learned about lightweight components and how to create custom lightweight components. Now is a good time to go over the Java *Swing* API. Java provides a set of ready-made lightweight components that are part of the Swing API. It provides lightweight versions of all of the heavyweight components that you've already learned about. It has buttons, text fields, checkboxes, and so on. In this section, I'll begin by providing an overview of the Swing package components and compare them to the Java AWT components. Then I'll put the Swing package to work by converting the `Calculator Keypad` class from Saturday night's session to Swing.

Overview of the Swing Package

The main set of classes in the Swing API can be found in the `javax.swing` package. In order to make use of Swing components, you need to import this package. The `javax.swing` package provides a set of lightweight components that work the same across all platforms. Within this package, you'll find such lightweight components as `JButton`, `JTextField`, `JPanel`, and so on. For the most part, the Swing components have the same name as that of the AWT, with the exception of a "J" prefix. Table 5.2 lists a subset of these components.

TABLE 5.2 JAVA SWING COMPONENTS

Swing Component Name	Description
JButton	A button
JCheckbox	A checkbox component
JComponent	The abstract super-class for all Swing components
JDialog	A dialog window
JFileChooser	A component that allows you to select a file (for opening/ saving, and so on)
JFrame	A frame that provides the same usefulness as the `java.awt.Frame` class—basically, a window
JLabel	A label component
JPopupMenu	A popup menu
JRadioButton	A radio button whose state can be either selected or deselected
JScrollBar	A scrollbar
JTextArea	A text area that can have multiple lines of text and is typically editable by the user
JTextField	A single-line text entry or display field

While Swing package component use is vastly similar to AWT component use, there are some subtle differences. The first difference you will notice is that when you're adding components to a JFrame, you don't add them *directly* to the JFrame. Instead, you add them to the content pane of the JFrame. This is just the way that the JFrame is implemented. The content pane is where all of the components that the JFrame contains are laid out. A reference to the content pane can be had by calling the getContent Pane() method on the JFrame instance.

Another difference is the way that you can set default closing operations. To exit the application upon a JFrame closing, you can call

```
setDefaultCloseOperation(EXIT_ON_CLOSE);
```

Calling the setDefaultCloseOperation() method in this way relieves you of the responsibility to create a WindowListener object to exit the application when the user closes the window. There are four possible values that can be passed to the setDefaultCloseOperation() method:

➤ WindowConstants.DO_NOTHING_ON_CLOSE: Sets the default close operation to do nothing.

➤ WindowConstants.HIDE_ON_CLOSE: Hides the frame when it is closed.

➤ WindowConstants.DISPOSE_ON_CLOSE: Hides the frame and frees up its resources.

➤ JFrame.EXIT_ON_CLOSE: Exits the application when closed using System.exit(0).

The SwingTest program is a very simple demo of how to use the Swing package. It creates a JFrame and adds a JLabel, JTextField, and JButton to it. Here is the source code:

```
/*
 * SwingTest
 * Demonstrates, very basically, how to use swing
 */


import javax.swing.*;
```

```java
import java.awt.*;
import java.awt.event.*;

public class SwingTest extends JFrame {

  public SwingTest() {
    super("Swing Test");
    JLabel label = new JLabel("JLabel");
    JTextField tfield = new JTextField("JTextField", 15);
    JButton button = new JButton("JButton");
    getContentPane().setLayout(new FlowLayout());
    getContentPane().add(label);
    getContentPane().add(tfield);
    getContentPane().add(button);
    setDefaultCloseOperation(EXIT_ON_CLOSE);
    pack();
    setVisible(true);
  }

  public static void main(String args[]) {
    new SwingTest();
  }

}
```

As you can see, the constructors for the three Swing components correspond to the AWT Label, TextField, and Button component constructors. Also, this program clearly demonstrates that the components are added to the content pane, rather than to the JFrame directly. If you tried to add them directly to the JFrame, you would get a runtime error. Also, this program demonstrates that when you attempt to close the JFrame by clicking on the x, it actually closes, even though it didn't have to register a WindowListener because it set the default close operation to EXIT_ON_CLOSE. This Swing example program is shown in Figure 5.13.

TIP

■ ■

By default, Swing components use the Java look and feel, also known as the *Metal* look and feel. The term *look and feel* refers to the appearance and behavior of Swing components. The Java look and feel is not the only one available. Swing applications can also have a Macintosh, Motif, or Windows look and feel. While I don't describe how to change the look and feel, I will give you a way to check them out. If you're at all interested in Swing or GUI programming in general, you should definitely check out the Swing demo included in your Java SDK. To run the Swing demo, open the command prompt to the following directory (where *<jdk>* is the directory where you installed Java):

`<jdk>\demo\jfc\SwingSet2`

(*Hint:* If you installed the version described on Friday Evening, the directory will be named `jdk1.3.1_01`; if you installed a different version, the directory should at least have either `jdk` or `j2sdk` as part of its name). Once you get to the right directory, use the following command:

`java -jar SwingSet2.jar`

This will start up the very cool Swing demo. This demo lets you play around with all of the different Swing components and lets you change the look and feel on the fly. It even lets you peek at the source code!

■ ■

NOTE

● ●

As far as coding goes, you've already seen that Swing applications are very similar to AWT applications. Because of this similarity, it is pretty easy to convert between the two. Performance-wise, Swing performs a bit better because it is less of a memory hog than the AWT. Unlike AWT, Swing does not render its components in separate windows, giving Swing applications greater memory efficiency and earning them the title of lightweight components. Finally, the fact that Swing components behave the same across all operating systems is also a benefit.

● ●

Figure 5.13

Swing components use the Java look and feel.

Converting CalculatorKeypad to Swing

The final calculator project will be a Swing application. That you've already created the `CalculatorKeypad` component using AWT is actually a plus here because you won't have to start from scratch, and it is fairly easy to convert the AWT `CalculatorKeypad` to a Swing `CalculatorKeypad`. Here is the source code for the Swing version of the `CalculatorKeypad`:

```
/*
 * CalculatorKeypad
 * A Panel subclass that contains a set of buttons for a
 * calculator
 * /

import java.awt.*;
import javax.swing.*;

public class CalculatorKeypad extends JPanel {

    private JButton[] buttons;

    public CalculatorKeypad() {
        super();
        GridBagLayout gbl = new GridBagLayout();
        GridBagConstraints gbc = new GridBagConstraints();
        gbc.fill = GridBagConstraints.BOTH;
        gbc.weightx = gbc.weighty = 1.0;
        gbc.ipadx = gbc.ipady = 5;

        // bLabels is an array of button labels in order
        // from left to right ÷ is #247, ± is #177, _ is #215
        String[] bLabels = { "MR", "MC", "M+", "M-", "MS", "SQ",
```

```
        "C", "AC", "POW", String.valueOf((char)247),
        String.valueOf((char)215), "-", "7", "8", "9",
        String.valueOf((char)177), "4", "5", "6", "+",
        "1", "2", "3", "=", "0", "." };

//there are four columns of buttons
int cols = 4;

//build the Button array and add to Panel
buttons = new JButton[bLabels.length];
setLayout(gbl);
for (int b = 0; b < buttons.length; b++) {
    buttons[b] = new JButton(bLabels[b]);

    //set different constraints
    if (bLabels[b].equals("=")) {
        // "=" spans two rows
        gbc.gridheight = 2;
        gbc.gridwidth = GridBagConstraints.REMAINDER;
    }
    else if (bLabels[b].equals("0")) {
        // "0" spans two cols
        gbc.gridy = 6;
        gbc.gridx = 0;
        gbc.gridwidth = 2;
        gbc.gridheight = 1;
    }
    else if (bLabels[b].equals("3")) {
        gbc.gridheight = 1;
        gbc.gridwidth = GridBagConstraints.RELATIVE;
```

```
        }
        else if ((b + 1) % cols == 0) {
            gbc.gridheight = 1;
            //end a row
            gbc.gridwidth = GridBagConstraints.REMAINDER;
        }
        else {
            // for the "." button to be next to the "0"
            gbc.gridx = GridBagConstraints.RELATIVE;
            gbc.gridheight = 1;
            gbc.gridwidth = 1;
        }


        //set the constraints and add it to the panel
        buttons[b].setFont(
            new Font("Helvetica", Font.BOLD, 14));
        gbl.setConstraints(buttons[b], gbc);
        add(buttons[b]);
    }
}


}
```

Table 5.3 lists the differences between the AWT version of the Calculator Keypad and the new Swing version of the CalculatorKeypad.

There's not much to change, is there? I recommend that if you are coding along with the examples, copy the original AWT CalculatorKeypad source code into a new directory and make these changes. It is the quickest way.

Though the changes are few, there are some similarities and differences you should note. First, the Swing version of CalculatorKeypad still has to import the java.awt package. It does this so that it can access the classes

TABLE 5.3 CALCULATORKEYPAD SWING CONVERSION CHANGES	
AWT CalculatorKeypad	**Swing CalculatorKeypad**
Extends `Panel`	Extends `JPanel`.
Does not import `javax.swing.*`	Imports `javax.swing.*`.
Imports `java.awt.event.*`	Does not import `java.awt.event.*`.
Implements `ActionListener`	Does not use an `ActionListener`.
Lays out an array of `Buttons`	Lays out an array of `JButtons`.

used to lay out the buttons—`GridBagLayout` and `GridBagConstraints`. Second, the new Swing version of `CalculatorKeypad` does not implement the `ActionListener` interface to listen to the button events. The elimination of the `ActionListener` interface is not actually related to the Swing conversion. I've eliminated it because I'm going to create a new event model for the calculator program this afternoon, so I just cut the `ActionListener` loose here with the other changes. The `ActionListener` will return, but in a new form and with a different function. It will be implemented as an inner class. You learn about inner classes next.

Inner Classes

Java allows you to create classes within the definition of another class. These types of classes are called *inner classes*. To define an inner class, all you have to do is declare a class within the opening and closing curly braces of another class, like this:

```
public class OuterClass {

    ...

    public class InnerClass {

        ...
```

```
        }

        ...

}
```

An inner class has access to all of the members and methods of the class in which it's defined—and vice versa. Why would you ever want to create an inner class? Because you might find that you want to define a helper class that could be useful to only one other class, and that helper class needs access to the other class's members and methods (even the private ones). Inner classes are typically specific enough so that they should be members of a parent class. In fact, that's what inner classes are. Inner classes typically encapsulate a related set of functions that are of use only to its outer parent class.

It's good to know the naming scheme that Java uses when compiling inner classes. If you completed and compiled the preceding snippet of code, two class files will be generated. One class will be generated for `OuterClass` and another one for `InnerClass`. The class filename for `OuterClass` will be `OuterClass.class`. The filename for `InnerClass` is a bit different. It starts with the `OuterClass` name, as the inner class belongs to its corresponding outer class. Then a dollar sign ($) is used, followed by the name of the inner class. So, the filename for `InnerClass` becomes `OuterClass$Inner Class.class`. To reference the `InnerClass` class from outside `OuterClass`, you prefix the `InnerClass` name with `OuterClass` and a dot:

```
OuterClass.InnerClass inner;
```

Anonymous Inner Classes

Anonymous inner classes are different from the previous type of inner class in that they are not named. Anonymous inner classes are declared within an expression, such as a method body. For example, you can subclass a class within another class without having to create a new source file. In the following example, I've created an anonymous inner class that is a subclass of the Canvas class:

```
import java.awt.*;


public class SomeClass {
```

```
Canvas canv;

public SomeClass() {
    canv = new Canvas() {
        public void paint(Graphics g) {
            g.fillRect(10, 10, 100, 100);
        }
    };
}

}
```

You can see that the outer class name is SomeClass, and it has a Canvas instance variable called canv. The SomeClass() constructor method creates an anonymous inner class, which is a subclass of Canvas, and assigns it to canv. To do this, it calls the Canvas() constructor method, but instead of ending the line with a semicolon, it opens a block with an opening curly brace. This is how you define the code that belongs in an anonymous inner class. In this example, the anonymous inner class overrides the paint() method and fills a rectangle. If the anonymous Canvas were ever rendered, it would have that rectangle painted inside it. Note that you override and declare methods and instance variables in the usual way. On the line below the closing curly brace, the curly brace that closes the inner class definition appears. You have to put a semicolon after this curly brace because it ends the assignment statement. Because the inner class has no name (it is an anonymous inner class, after all), the compiler creates a special class file for the inner class. Here, the class file-name for the anonymous inner class would be SomeClass$1.class. The compiler uses numbers to name anonymous inner classes.

Using Adapter Classes for Event Handling

One very common use for anonymous inner classes in GUI programming is event handling. You've already done some event handling where you had to implement an interface and include all of the interface's methods in your class file. There is a shortcut for this. The AWT package defines event-handling classes, called adapter classes, that already implement their corresponding interfaces, so you don't have to. These adapter classes implement the interface methods as do-nothing methods that have an opening and closing curly brace but no statements inside. Thus, they do nothing. The adapter classes act as a shortcut as you can extend these classes without having to implement every single interface method. Instead, you only implement the methods that you're interested in.

For example, if you want to add a WindowListener to a JFrame but you're only interested in closing the application when the user closes the window, you can create a subclass of its corresponding adapter class—WindowAdapter. Instead of implementing every single method defined in the WindowListener interface, you only need to override the windowClosing() method and register the WindowAdapter subclass that you created as the WindowListener for the Frame. For such a trivial operation, you wouldn't want to have to create an entirely new source file. Instead, you would create an anonymous inner class that extends WindowAdapter. As an example, here is a rewrite of the GUIFrame class that does just that:

```java
import java.awt.*;
import java.awt.event.*;


public class GUIFrame extends Frame {

    public GUIFrame(String title) {
        super(title);
        setBackground(SystemColor.control);

        addWindowListener(new WindowAdapter() {
            public void windowClosing(WindowEvent e) {
                dispose();
                System.exit(0);
```

```
            }
        });
    }


    /* Centers the Frame when setVisible(true) is called */
    public void setVisible(boolean visible) {
        if (visible) {
        Dimension d =
Toolkit.getDefaultToolkit().getScreenSize();
        setLocation((d.width - getWidth())/2,
                    (d.height - getHeight())/2);
        }
        super.setVisible(visible);
    }


}
```

Notice that this version of GUIFrame no longer implements the Window
Listener interface and doesn't pass itself in to the addWindowListener()
method. Instead, it passes the anonymous inner class. Because the anonymous inner class is a subclass of WindowAdapter and WindowAdapter
implements the WindowListener interface, the anonymous inner class is a
WindowListener, too, which is why you are able to register it as the
GUIFrame's WindowListener. The whole inner class definition resides
within the parentheses of the addWindowListener() method. Note that
the closing parenthesis of the addWindowListener() method appears after
the anonymous inner class definition and is followed by the semicolon that
ends that statement. Also, if you choose to compile this code, take a look at
the class files that are created. For the anonymous inner class, the class filename is GUIFrame$1.class. There are other adapter classes that correspond
to other types of event handlers. Take a look at the Java JDK API documentation to see them. They reside within the java.awt.event package.

Using Exception Handling

Sometimes when a program is running, abnormal conditions may occur. Those conditions are called *exceptions*. For example, you might have a string that you are trying to parse to an int. What if the string is not in the correct format? The program expects a string that represents a valid int value, such as "13354". The static method parseInt() in the Integer class can convert that String into an int without any problems. On the other hand, if the String looks more like "monkey", then there's no way it can be converted into an int because "monkey" is not a valid representation of an int value. So, what happens? Your program crashes! That is, unless you prepare for this type of exception.

What Are Exceptions?

Exceptions are errors that occur even when the code is correct and compiles without any errors. They are abnormal conditions that cause a program to become unable to continue normally. Without exception handling, exceptions cause programs to stop what they're doing and die. When this happens, you should see a stack trace printed to the standard output stream, like Windows' MS-DOS window. A *stack trace* lists the stack of method calls that preceded and led to the exception, making it easier to get to the root of the problem. Java uses specialized classes, called *exception classes,* to encapsulate information about exceptions that occur. The root class for all exceptions is the Exception class, which is found in the java.lang package. The Exception class implements the Throwable interface. (All exceptions must implement the Throwable interface.) Because all standard exceptions are subclasses of the Exception class, they all implement the Throwable interface through inheritance.

NOTE A *stack* is a special kind of list (FILO—First In Last Out). Think of it like stacking pennies one at a time. The first one that you put down will be the last one that you pick up when you are unstacking the pennies. Java maintains a stack of method calls to track the program flow from method to method. As an example, consider three methods, main(), method1(), and method2(), where method1() is called from main() and method2() is called from method1(). The stack starts out with the main() method.

When `method1()` is called from the `main()` method, `method1()` goes to the top of the stack (adding to a stack is called a *push*). When `method2()` is called from `method1()`, `method2()` is pushed onto the stack. When `method2()` completes, it gets removed from the stack (removing from a stack is called a *pop*). At this point, the top of the stack is `method1()` This makes sense. Because `method2()` is called from `method1()`, program control returns to `method1()` when `method2()` returns. When `method1()` returns, it gets popped from the stack, leaving only `main()`.

This is how the stack trace works. If you get a stack trace listing for an exception, the listing will start out with the method in which the exception occurred and continue down the stack to the `main()` method (if the program is an application) so that you can trace all of the method calls leading up to the one that threw an exception.

● ●

Wrapping Exceptions in try-catch Blocks

Java has a built-in way of handling exceptions. Five keywords are used exclusively for exception-handling purposes. The five keywords are `try`, `catch`, `finally`, `throw`, and `throws`. Their names are descriptive of the functions they perform. When you write a line of code that might throw an exception, you use the `try` keyword to indicate that you're trying to execute code. You're "trying" it because there's a chance that it might not work. If it doesn't work, the code throws an exception, which means it creates a new `Exception` object and throws it. This action stops the execution of your code and, normally, crashes your program. To prevent your program from crashing, you "catch" the thrown exception using the `catch` keyword. After you catch the exception, you can write code that handles the abnormal condition associated with the thrown exception. This is the basic idea of exception handling.

For example, consider the situation I mentioned previously in which parsing a `String` to an `int` doesn't work; the `parseInt()` method throws a `Number FormatException`. In this case, you could handle the exception by placing the `parseInt()` method in a `try` block, catching the `NumberFormat Exception` and then assigning some default `int` value instead, like this:

```
int myInt;
```

```
try {

    myInt = Integer.parseInt(myString);

    System.out.println("Parsing was successful");

} catch (NumberFormatException e) {

    myInt = 1;

    System.out.println("Parsing was unsuccessful… using default");

}
```

In this example, myInt is an int and myString is a String object that has its value set elsewhere, which means you do not yet know the value of myString. If the String object's value does not represent a valid int, the parseInt() method throws the NumberFormatException, taking you out of the try block. Java looks for the nearest catch block that catches a NumberFormat Exception and enters it. It's right below the try block, where it should be. Actually, try must always be followed immediately by at least one catch statement, or the program will not compile. So, the NumberFormatException is caught, and the program assigns a valid int, 1, to myInt and prints a message indicating that parsing was not successful. It is important to know that when the exception is thrown, the rest of the try block is ignored. In this case, the message "Parsing was successful" will not be printed. It's important to know that if myString represents a valid int and no NumberFormatException is thrown, all of the code in the catch block is ignored.

It is always the case that when a method that may throw an exception is reached, either the code after the method within the try block is executed, *or* the code in the catch block is executed, but never both in a single run. This presents a slight problem. What if you must do something after an iffy method, regardless of method success or exception? For example, when reading the contents of a file, an exception may occur. Whether or not the exception thrown is meaningless; you still want to close the file when you're done reading it so that you can free up system resources. One solution is to close the file in both the try and the catch blocks. This is inefficient because it forces you to repeat the same code in two places, which is especially bad if there is a lot of code. Another solution is to put the code after the try-catch. It will work, but only in some situations. Sometimes—especially in large applications—a catch block will handle an exception by performing whatever exception-handling responsibilities it has. Then it will either re-throw the exception or throw a new exception. This course of action throws you out of the code (typically a method), and the code after the catch block is ignored. Yet another, better solution is to use the finally keyword to create a finally block. finally blocks are optional, but if you use one, it must immediately follow a catch block. Any code that you want executed regardless of exception occurrence, should be placed in the finally block.

The ExceptionTest program demonstrates what you've learned so far about exception handling. Here is the source code:

```java
/*
 * ExceptionTest.java
 * Demonstrates how to perform exception handling
 */

public class ExceptionTest {

    public static void main(String args[]) {
        String str = null;
        boolean success = false;
        int num;

        try {
            str = args[0];
        } catch (ArrayIndexOutOfBoundsException e) {
            System.out.println(e);
            System.out.println(
                "\nYou forgot to pass an argument!");
            System.out.println("Using default value...");
            str = "1";
        } finally {
```

```
        System.out.println("String value: "
            + "\"" + str + "\"");
    }


    try {
        num = Integer.parseInt(str);
        success = true;
    } catch (NumberFormatException e) {
        success = false;
        throw new NumberFormatException("\n\"" + str + "\""
            + " cannot be parsed to an int!");
    } finally {
        //will get here no matter what
        System.out.println("parsing "
            + (success ? "successful!": "not successful."));
    }


    //won't get here if NumberFormatException occurs
    System.out.println("int value is: " + num);
    }


}
```

The `ExceptionTest` program uses exception handling to handle two exceptions—`ArrayIndexOutOfBoundsException` and `NumberFormatException`. The first handled exception in this demo program is `ArrayIndexOutOf BoundsException`, which is thrown if the program tries to access an array element that is out of bounds. For example, if you have an array of size 1 and you try to access the tenth element, you've exceeded the array's size, causing an `ArrayIndexOutOfBoundsException`. Here, it is used for the `args[]` array. The size is definitely not known at this point in the program because there is no way to predict how many arguments will be passed when the program is invoked. If no arguments are passed, then the array size is zero, and accessing the first element, which is `args[0]`, will cause the `ArrayIndex OutOfBoundsException` to be thrown. `ExceptionTest` handles this exception by printing a message to indicate that the program was run without any arguments and to set up the `str` variable with the default value "1". If no exception occurs here, then the program was run with at least one argument, and the first argument was assigned to `str`. This prevents the program from crashing, and it continues to the second exception-handling code.

The second handled exception is `NumberFormatException`. When `parse Int()` attempts to parse `str` to an `int`, a `NumberFormatException` may occur. `ExceptionTest` handles this exception by first trying to perform the parsing, and then catching the possible `NumberFormatException`. If the parsing is successful, the `success` variable is set to `true`. If the parsing is not successful, `success` is set to `false` and a new `NumberFormatException` is created and thrown. In either case, a message is printed indicating whether or not the parsing worked because the code that prints this message is in the `finally` block. Even though the code following the `finally` block is ignored if the `NumberFormatException` occurs because the `catch` block throws a new `NumberFormatException`, the code in the `finally` block will always be executed. Only if the parsing is successful will this line be executed:

```
System.out.println("int value is: " + num);
```

Figure 5.14 shows a possible output for the `ExceptionTest` program.

Throwing Exceptions

Not only can you handle exceptions that are thrown by Java, but also you can throw exceptions yourself. You throw exceptions using the `throw` keyword. In the previous code example, `ExceptionTest`, a new `Number FormatException` object is created and thrown. Look back at `ExceptionTest` to see how the `throw` keyword is used in a Java program. There is another keyword that you use to indicate that a method may throw an exception. You use the `throws` keyword for this purpose. You must place it after the parameter list in a method signature, like this:

```
public void myMethod(int myInt, String myString) throws Exception {
```

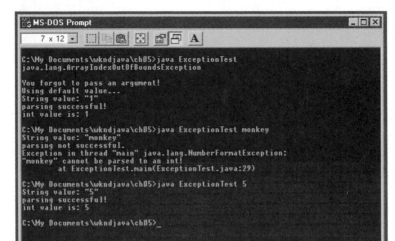

Figure 5.14

The first run of
Exception
Test handles an
ArrayIndex
OutOfBounds
Exception, the
second one throws
a Number
Format
Exception, and
the third one is a
normal run.

Because this method throws an exception, anytime a program calls the method, it must be called within a try-catch. If you fail to handle a required exception in a program, the program won't compile. By not compiling, Java forces you to handle the exception. The ForcedException HandlingTest program demonstrates this. The sleep() method might throw an InterruptedException. It is part of the Thread class, which you'll learn about this afternoon. The sleep() method pauses the program's execution for the given number of milliseconds. If the pause is interrupted, it might throw an InterruptedException. You actually don't need to know exactly what this method does; you need only know that, in some situations, it throws an InterruptedException and that, by not compiling, Java forces you to handle this exception. Figure 5.15 shows you the error message that the compiler will issue. Here is the source code:

```
/*

 * ForcedExceptionHandlingTest.java

 * Demonstrates that Java forces you to handle exceptions

 * This program won't compile!

 */


public class ForcedExceptionHandlingTest {
```

```
public static void main(String args[]) {

    //MUST handle InterruptedException

    System.out.println("sleeping for 2 seconds...");

    Thread.sleep(2000);

    System.out.println("done");

}


}
```

To find out which methods throw exceptions, consult the JDK API documentation. Any method that has a `throws` clause in its signature may throw an exception and must be handled in a `try-catch`, or any method that calls another method that throws an exception can add the same exception to its own `throws` clause. For example, if method `a()` throws exception `e` and method `b()` calls method `a()`, then method `b()` can either use a `try-catch` block or add the `throws e` clause to its own method signature. If method `b()` uses the `throws` clause, method `b()` no longer has to use a `try-catch` block. The `ForcedExceptionHandlingTest2` program adds a `throws` clause to the end of the `main()` method. This is the only difference between `ForcedExceptionHandlingTest` and `ForcedExceptionHandlingTest2`. This change allows the program to compile. So, instead of catching the

Figure 5.15

Java programs won't compile unless you handle your exceptions!

InterruptedException, the main() method throws it. Putting the sleep() method in a try block and catching the InterruptedException would also allow ForcedExceptionHandlingTest2 to compile.

```
/*
 * ForcedExceptionHandlingTest2.java
 * Demonstrates that Java forces you to handle exceptions
 * ... or at least throw them back to the caller
 */

public class ForcedExceptionHandlingTest2 {

    public static void main(String args[])
            throws InterruptedException {
        //MUST handle InterruptedException
        System.out.println("sleeping for 2 seconds...");
        Thread.sleep(2000);
        System.out.println("done");
    }

}
```

Runtime Exceptions versus Exceptions

The main difference between normal exceptions and runtime exceptions is that while Java forces you to handle normal exceptions, it does not force you to handle runtime exceptions. The RuntimeException class is a subclass of the Exception class. All subclasses of RuntimeException are runtime exceptions, so you can perform operations that throw these exceptions without having to place them in a try-catch. Also, Java does not force you to use a throws clause in method signatures for methods that might throw runtime exceptions. Conversely, all subclasses of Exception, excluding RuntimeException and its subclasses, are not runtime exceptions, and you are forced to handle the exceptions.

`RuntimeExceptions` are reserved for exceptions that may occur during normal program operation. You've already seen two examples of `Runtime Exceptions`—`ArrayIndexOutOfBoundsException` and `NumberFormat Exception`. You can take the exception-handling code right out of the `ExceptionTest` program, and it will compile and run fine—unless an exception occurs. If an exception does occur, the program will crash. Runtime exceptions usually occur in the underlying system. For example, `ArrayIndexOutOfBoundsException` occurs when you try to access a piece of memory that doesn't belong to the array. This is a system exception. With this in mind, just about all of the custom exceptions that you may create would not be runtime exceptions. You might be tempted to create runtime exceptions so that you don't have to write exception-handling code, but this is considered bad practice, so don't do it, okay?

NOTE Creating a subclass of `RuntimeException` just so you don't have to write exception-handling code is a bad idea. This completely negates the Java exception framework. If you don't handle your exceptions, then every time an exception occurs, your program will just die. No message to the user—nothing—just a stack trace that a user won't be able to understand. If you want your programs to crash every time it encounters an exception, then by all means, extend `RuntimeException` to your heart's content, but I don't think you do.

Creating DigitalDisplayOverflowException

Now, it's time for you to create a custom exception for your calculator application. This is not hard to do. Application-specific exceptions, such as this one, are called *application exceptions*. The exception class that you are using here is `DigitalDisplayOverflowException`. The calculator application will use this exception to indicate that the yet-to-be-created `Digital Display` class can't display a number because it has too many digits and won't fit in the liquid crystal display. `DigitalDisplayOverflowException` is not a runtime exception. It is a subclass of the `Exception` class. One of the `Exception` class constructors takes a `String` argument that is used as the error message. `DigitalDisplayOverflowException` makes use of that constructor by calling `super()`. Here is the source code for `Digital DisplayOverflowException`:

```
/*
 * DigitalDisplayOverflowException
 * An exception that indicates that a DigitalDisplay cannot
 * display a number due to the size of the number exceeding
 * the display's display capacity.
 */
public class DigitalDisplayOverflowException extends Exception {

    public DigitalDisplayOverflowException() {
        this("DigitalDisplay Overflow");
    }

    public DigitalDisplayOverflowException(String msg) {
        super(msg);
    }
}
```

Creating CalculatorException

There is one more exception class that the calculator application will need. The
`CalculatorException` class defines a generic application exception. This
means that the calculator application should throw a `CalculatorException`
when application-specific exceptions occur that are not specified by any other
exceptions. The calculator application has only one other exception defined
(which you just defined in the previous section) that it throws when the digital
display overflows. Since the calculator application is relatively small, you can
get away with having just one more exception for all other problems that the
calculator application may encounter. Although you're not going to incorporate the `CalculatorException` into the calculator application just yet (that
is, you're not going to throw it from anywhere), since this section is about
exceptions and the source code is pretty short, I'll show you the code here.
We'll use it later on (this afternoon). The source code is listed here:

```
/*
 * CalculatorException
 * A generic Exception for the Calculator application
 */
public class CalculatorException extends Exception {

    public CalculatorException() {
        this("Calculator Exception");
    }

    public CalculatorException(String msg) {
        super(msg);
    }

}
```

One could argue that, because `CalculatorException` is a non-specific exception, other more specific exceptions for the calculator class should extend `CalculatorException`. `DigitalDisplayOverflowException` is a more specific exception, but it does not extend `CalculatorException`. This is because the `DigitalDisplay` class, which throws `DigitalDisplay OverflowException`, should be reusable. You should be able to reuse `Digital Display` anywhere that you want to use a liquid crystal display—in any program. If `DigitalDisplayOverflowException` extended the `Calculator Exception` class, it would become application-specific. Any program that used `DigitalDisplay` would also have to use `CalculatorException`. That wouldn't make much sense if the `DigitalDisplay` component was being used by a game program to display the score.

Creating the DigitalDisplay Panel

Now that the `DigitalDisplayOverflowException` class is done, you can create the `DigitalDisplay` panel for the calculator application. `Digital Display` uses the `DigitalDisplayOverflowException` class, which is why

DigitalDisplayOverflowException was created first. (One of Digital Display's methods throws a DigitalDisplayOverflowException.) Digital Display also uses some of the other components that you created earlier. It uses LiquidCrystalDigit and LiquidCrystalNegative to build the display panel for the calculator. It uses one LiquidCrystalNegative to indicate whether the displayed number is negative and nine LiquidCrystal Digit components to display a nine-digit number that has a liquid crystal appearance. DigitalDisplay also uses an inner class called DigitalDisplay DigitalDisplayFormat to format numbers for displaying. As you'll see, special formatting must take place before displaying the number.

Writing the Code

Here is the code for the DigitalDisplay class. It is a bit long, so feel free to get a copy from the Internet at http://www.premierpressbooks.com/downloads.asp. If you do take the code from the Internet, look it over until it makes sense to you.

```java
/*
 * DigitalDisplay
 * A lightweight component that graphically represents a
 * liquid crystal digital display.
 */

import java.awt.*;
import javax.swing.*;
import java.text.DecimalFormat;
import javax.swing.border.*;

public class DigitalDisplay extends JPanel {

    /* The LiquidCrystalDigit objects */
    protected LiquidCrystalDigit[] lcdDigits;
    /* An optional LiquidCrystalNegative component */
```

```java
protected LiquidCrystalNegative lcdNegative;
/* The color for all of the unlit pieces */
protected Color offColor;
/* The decimal formatter inner helper class */
protected DigitalDisplayFormat digitalFormat;

public DigitalDisplay(int digits) {
    this (digits, 0.0);
}


public DigitalDisplay(int digits,double number) {
    this (digits, number, false);
}


public DigitalDisplay(int digits, double number,
        boolean useNegative) {
    this(digits, number, useNegative,
        Color.black, new Color(0, 80, 0), Color.green);
}


public DigitalDisplay(int digits, double number,
        boolean useNegative, Color bg, Color unlit,
        Color lit) {
    lcdDigits = new LiquidCrystalDigit[digits];
    digitalFormat = new DigitalDisplayFormat();
    setBackground(bg);
    setForeground(lit);
    offColor = unlit;

    setLayout(new GridLayout(1, 0, 0, 0));
```

```java
        if (useNegative) {
            lcdNegative = new LiquidCrystalNegative(false, bg,
                                            unlit, lit);
            add(lcdNegative);
        }

        for (int d = 0; d < lcdDigits.length; d++) {
            lcdDigits[d] = new LiquidCrystalDigit(0, bg,
                                            unlit, lit);
            add(lcdDigits[d]);
        }
        setBorder(BorderFactory.createBevelBorder(
            BevelBorder.LOWERED));

        digitalFormat.parseAndSetValue(number);
        updateDisplay();
    }

    public int getNumDigits() {
        return lcdDigits.length;
    }

    public String getValue() {
        return digitalFormat.value.toString();
    }

    public void setDoubleValue(double dValue) throws
            DigitalDisplayOverflowException {
        DigitalDisplayOverflowException de
                = digitalFormat.parseAndSetValue(dValue);
```

```
        String strValue = digitalFormat.value.toString();
        if (de != null) {
            throw de;
        }
    }


    public double getDoubleValue() {
        return digitalFormat.getDoubleValue();
    }


    protected void updateDisplay() {
        for (int d = 0; d < lcdDigits.length; d++) {
            lcdDigits[d].setDigit(digitalFormat.getIntAt(d));
            lcdDigits[d].setDecimalPoint(
                digitalFormat.decimalIndex == d);
        }
        repaint();
    }


    public void appendDigit(int appendInt) {
        digitalFormat.tryAppend(appendInt);
        updateDisplay();
    }


    public void appendDecimal() {
        if( digitalFormat.decimalIndex
                == DigitalDisplayFormat.NO_DECIMAL) {
            digitalFormat.decimalIndex
                    = lcdDigits.length - 1;
        updateDisplay();
```

```
        }
    }

    /* An inner class that handles the formatting of
     * the numbers for displaying them. */
    private class DigitalDisplayFormat {

      /* The formatter for decimal numbers */
      private DecimalFormat formatter;
      /* The formatted string representation
       * of the displayed number */
      private StringBuffer value;
      /* An instance of the DigitalDisplayFormat inner class */
      private boolean negative;
      /* Indicates the index for the digit that precedes
       * the decimal point */
      private int decimalIndex;
      /* Indicates there is no decimal point */
      private final static int NO_DECIMAL = -2;
      /* Largest possible value that can be displayed */
      private double largestValue;

      private DigitalDisplayFormat() {
          formatter = new DecimalFormat();
          formatter.setMaximumFractionDigits(lcdDigits.length);
              formatter.setMinimumFractionDigits(0);
              formatter.setMinimumIntegerDigits(1);
              formatter.setDecimalSeparatorAlwaysShown(false);
              formatter.setGroupingUsed(false);
          StringBuffer large = new StringBuffer();
```

```java
        for (int d = 0; d < lcdDigits.length; d++) {
            large.append('9');
        }
        largestValue = Double.parseDouble(large.toString());
}


private DigitalDisplayOverflowException parseAndSetValue(
            double number) {
    setNegative(number < 0);
    number = Math.abs(number);
    if (number > largestValue) {
        setNegative(false);
        decimalIndex = NO_DECIMAL;
        value = new StringBuffer(getErrorString());
        return new DigitalDisplayOverflowException(
            "Double value " + number
            + " cannot be displayed with "
            + getNumDigits() + " digits");
    }
    value = new StringBuffer(formatter.format(number));

    //strip decimal point (but remember where it is)
    decimalIndex = value.toString().indexOf('.') - 1;
    if (decimalIndex != NO_DECIMAL) {
        value.deleteCharAt(decimalIndex + 1);
    }

    //ensure length is equal to number of lcd digits
    if (value.length() > lcdDigits.length) {
        while (value.length() > lcdDigits.length + 1) {
```

```
                        value.deleteCharAt(value.length() - 1);
            }
            //round off the extra stuff
            double roundMe =
                Double.parseDouble(value.toString()) / 10.0;
            String rounded = formatter.format(
                Math.rint(roundMe));
            value = new StringBuffer(rounded);
        }
        while (value.length() < lcdDigits.length) {
            value.insert(0, " ");
            if (decimalIndex != NO_DECIMAL) {
                decimalIndex++;
            }
        }
        return null;


    }


    private void tryAppend(int number) {
        if (value.toString() != getErrorString()
                && getDoubleValue() == 0.0
                && decimalIndex == NO_DECIMAL) {
            value.setCharAt(
                value.toString().indexOf('0'), ' ');
        }
        if (value.toString().trim().length()
                < getNumDigits()) {
            value.deleteCharAt(0);
                value.append(number);
```

```java
        if (decimalIndex != NO_DECIMAL) {

            decimalIndex--;

        }

    }

}


private void setNegative(boolean isNegative) {

    negative = isNegative;

    if (lcdNegative != null) {

        lcdNegative.setNegative(isNegative);

    }

}


private String getErrorString() {

    String errorString = "";

    for (int d = 0; d < lcdDigits.length - 1; d++) {

        errorString += " ";

    }

    errorString += "E";

    return errorString;

}


private double getDoubleValue() {

    StringBuffer parseValue

        = new StringBuffer(value.toString());

    if (parseValue.toString().equals(getErrorString()))

        return 0.0;

    if (decimalIndex != NO_DECIMAL) {

        parseValue.insert(decimalIndex + 1, '.');

    }
```

```
            double dValue = Double.parseDouble(
                parseValue.toString().trim());
            if (negative) dValue *= -1;
            return dValue;

        }


        private int getIntAt(int index) {
            String charStrVal = "" + value.charAt(index);
            if (charStrVal.equals(" ")) {
                return LiquidCrystalDigit.EMPTY;
            }
            else if (charStrVal.equals("E")) {
                return LiquidCrystalDigit.E;
            }
            return Integer.parseInt(charStrVal);
        }
    }


}
```

As you can see, this program is rather long and a bit complicated as it uses a lot of the stuff that you've just learned. Tables 5.4 and 5.5 describe all of the methods, so you can refer to them while you look over the source code. You can also refer to the comments in the source code to see what the instance variables are used for. Finally, there is some code in there that creates a border that makes the DigitalDisplay component appear a bit depressed. It's just a graphical effect provided for fun.

Testing It

That's a lot of code! Now you need to make sure that it works properly. The DigitalDisplayTest program tests the DigitalDisplay class. It creates a DigitalDisplay with eight digits, initializes it to display the value

TABLE 5.4 DIGITALDISPLAY METHODS

DigitalDisplay Method	Description
`public void appendDecimal()`	Appends a decimal to the displayed number by turning the decimal point on for the right-most `LiquidCrystalDigit` component.
`public void appendDigit (int appendInt)`	Appends a digit to the end of the currently displayed number.
`public double getDoubleValue()`	Returns the double value of the currently displayed number.
`public int getNumDigits()`	Returns the number of `LiquidCrystalDigit` components and, thus, the maximum number of displayable digits.
`public String getValue()`	Returns the `String` value of the currently displayed number. The decimal point is omitted.
`public void setDoubleValue (double dValue)`	Displays the given `dValue`. If there are too many digits to fit into the display, this method throws a `DigitalDisplayOverflow Exception`.
`public void updateDisplay()`	Updates the display by setting each `LiquidCrystalDigit` to its appropriate value and repainting the graphics.

-123.899, passes true to indicate that the negative sign should be available, and passes some colors for the color scheme. Then it prints some data to make sure that the methods are returning the correct values.

TABLE 5.5   DIGITALDISPLAYFORMAT METHODS

DigitalDisplayFormat Method	Description
`private double getDoubleValue()`	Does the work for the `DigitalDisplay` method of the same name.
`private String getErrorString()`	Returns the displayable error string, right-justified in a field of spaces with a length equal to the number of `LiquidCrystalDigit` components.
`private int getIntAt(int index)`	Returns the `int` value for the digit specified by *index*.
`private DigitalDisplayOverflowException parseAndSetValue(double number)`	Parses the given double value to a format that the `DigitalDisplay` can display. This method returns a `DigitalDisplayOverflowException` to its caller, `setDoubleValue()`, to be thrown by that method.
`private void setNegative (boolean isNegative)`	Sets a flag that turns the `LiquidCrystalNegative` component on and off as determined by the value of *isNegative*.
`private void tryToAppend(int number)`	Simulates the pressing of a numerical calculator button by appending a digit to the end of the display, shifting the preexisting digits to the left. If there is no room for the digit, nothing will happen.

Here is the code for the `DigitaDisplayTest` program:

```
/*
 * DigitalDisplayTest
 * Tests the DigitalDisplay component
 */
```

```java
import javax.swing.*;
import java.awt.*;
import java.awt.event.*;


public class DigitalDisplayTest extends JFrame {

    public DigitalDisplayTest() {
        super("Digital Display Test");
        getContentPane().setLayout(
            new FlowLayout(FlowLayout.CENTER));
        DigitalDisplay display = new DigitalDisplay(
            8, -123.899, true, new Color(88, 207, 233),
            new Color(30, 189, 223), Color.black);
        System.out.println("value: " + display.getValue());
        System.out.println("Length: "
            + display.getValue().length());
        System.out.println("Double: "
            + display.getDoubleValue());
        getContentPane().add(display);

        setDefaultCloseOperation(EXIT_ON_CLOSE);
        pack();
        setVisible(true);
    }


    public static void main(String args[]) {
        new DigitalDisplayTest();
    }
}
```

Figure 5.16 shows what DigitalDisplayTest should look like when it is run.

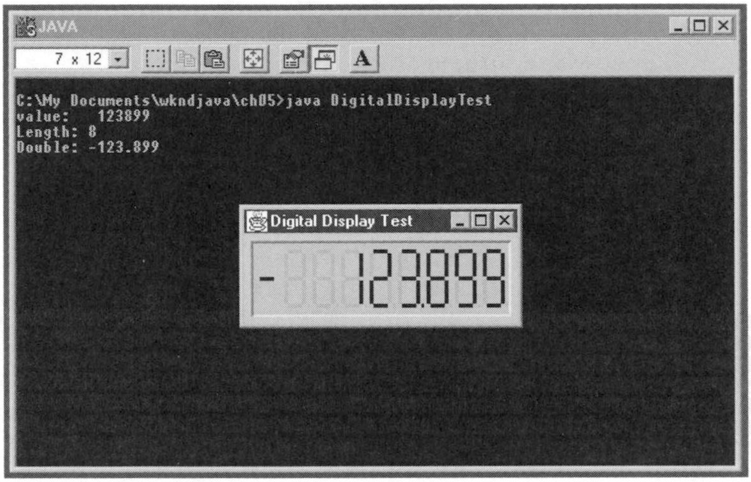

Figure 5.16

This shows you that the `Digital Display` component actually looks like a liquid crystal display!

Combining It with CalculatorKeypad

At this point, you have the `CalculatorKeypad` component and the freshly created `DigitalDisplay` component for the calculator application. Let's see what they look like together. The `CalculatorView` class puts them together in a `JFrame`, nearly finalizing the graphical interface for the calculator. (You'll work on getting the buttons to work this afternoon.) The `CalculatorView` class will be responsible for the view of the calculator application. The calculator application will undergo a few changes, as you learn some new things later today, but the basic look and feel of the calculator is done, with the exception of the menu options you'll be adding tonight. Here is a listing of the source code; it is straightforward enough that it needs no further explanation.

```
/*
 * CalculatorView
 * Encapsulates the Calculator GUI
 */

import java.awt.*;
import java.awt.event.*;
import javax.swing.*;
```

```
public class CalculatorView extends JFrame {
    private DigitalDisplay display;
    private CalculatorKeypad keypad;

    public CalculatorView() {
        super("Java Calculator");
        Container content = getContentPane();

        display = new DigitalDisplay(9, 0.0, true,
            new Color(88, 207, 233), new Color(30, 189, 223),
                Color.black);

        content.add(display, BorderLayout.NORTH);

        keypad = new CalculatorKeypad();
        content.add(keypad, BorderLayout.CENTER);

        setDefaultCloseOperation(EXIT_ON_CLOSE);
        pack();
    }

}
```

The `CalculatorView` class doesn't have a `main()` method, so you can't run it. Because of this, another program needs to create and display it. The `Calculator` program, listed next, does this for you. There isn't much code because the program just creates a new `CalculatorView` and makes it visible. The `Calculator` class is the main class for the calculator project and will start the application when it is run. You'll be adding more to this class later today.

```
/*
 * Calculator
 * The Calculator application
 */
```

```
public class Calculator {

    public static void main(String args[]) {
        CalculatorView calcView = new CalculatorView();
        calcView.setVisible(true);
    }


}
```

Take a look at Figure 5.17 to see the nearly completed graphics for the calculator project.

Wrapping Up

You did a lot this morning. First, you learned about AWT graphics programming. Then you learned about creating lightweight components and using the Swing API. You also learned about named inner classes and anonymous inner classes, abstract classes, and exception handling. Finally, you put all of this together to give the calculator a face and some life. This afternoon, you'll learn about interfaces, applets, threads, and animation. You'll also create a custom-event model for the calculator project and give it some functionality.

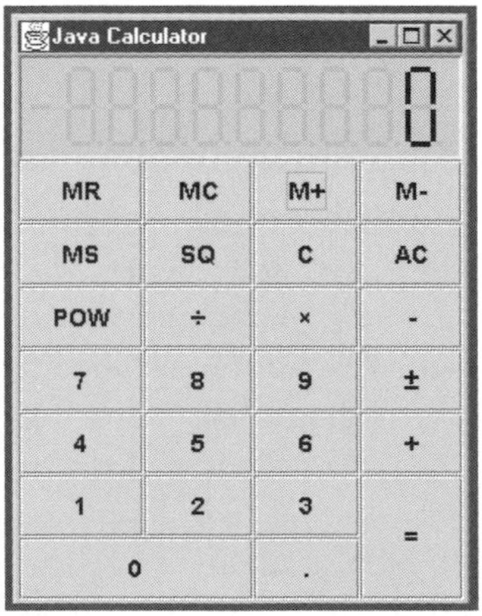

Figure 5.17

Although it's not yet functional, it's starting to look like a calculator!

Interfaces, Applets, and Threads

- ➤ Writing Interfaces
- ➤ Creating an Event Model for the Calculator Project
- ➤ Writing Java Applets
- ➤ Running the Calculator as an Applet
- ➤ Doing Two or More Things Using Threads

his afternoon, you will learn how to create and implement interfaces. You'll create an interface for custom calculator event handling, and then you'll implement it, so the calculator will actually do something useful. Next, you'll update the calculator project source code to make use of the custom event model. You'll also create an interface for the calculator's GUI, making it easier to abstract out the graphical component. Then, you'll learn about applets and how to create and run them. You'll also write an applet for the calculator project so that you can run the calculator as either an applet or an application. You'll see how using an interface for the calculator's view makes it easier to create the calculator applet. Next, you'll learn about threads and how to write thread-safe code. You'll learn how to use threads and double-buffering to perform animation, as well. Finally, you'll learn how to play sounds from applets and applications.

Writing Interfaces

You have already seen interfaces in programs that use AWT event handling. Now, you'll learn more about interfaces and create a couple of custom interfaces for the calculator program. You'll also learn why you'd ever want to use interfaces. Creating interfaces in the calculator program will really help you to understand the purpose of interfaces and the advantages that they provide.

What Is an Interface?

An *interface* is sort of like a contract between an implementing class and the class that makes method calls to the implementing class. When you define an interface, you only define some method signatures; you do not define any of the methods' implementations. A class that implements the interface is responsible for writing the code that goes inside all of the methods that the interface defines. This way, it's guaranteed that a class that implements a certain interface has all of the methods that the interface has. Any other class that calls the implementing class's methods can be sure that it can call any of these methods.

An interface is not a Java class. When you define an interface, you use the `interface` keyword in place of the `class` keyword, like this:

```
public interface MyInterface {
```

All interfaces and the methods they define are implicitly abstract. If you recall, an abstract class provides a partial implementation of a class. An abstract class may provide functionality for some of its methods, but it can also declare abstract methods without implementing them, thus passing that responsibility to its subclasses. Interfaces are a bit different. Interfaces cannot provide functionality for any of its methods, so all of its methods must be abstract. This is why all interfaces and their methods are implicitly abstract. You don't have to use the `abstract` keyword to specify this fact because the interface and its methods cannot be anything but abstract. When you write an interface, all of its methods consist only of their signatures, followed by a semicolon, like this:

```
public interface MyInterface {
    public void myMethod1(int x, int y);
    public String myMethod2();
    public int myMethod3(double d);
}
```

Just like abstract classes, interfaces cannot be directly instantiated. For instance, you can't do this:

```
public MyInterface myObject = new MyInterface();
```

What you can do, however, is assign an object that implements the interface to a variable that is declared to be the interface type, like this:

```
public MyInterface myObject = new
ClassThatImplementsMyInterface();
```

For the previous code to work, `ClassThatImplementsMyInterface` must implement `MyInterface`. To specify that a class implements a certain interface, you must use the `implements` keyword in the class declaration, like this:

```
public class ClassThatImplementsMyInterface implements
MyInterface {
```

You have seen this syntax before in AWT event handling. In this example, `ClassThatImplementsMyInterface` must define the three methods found in `MyInterface`, which are `myMethod1()`, `myMethod2()`, and `myMethod3()`. The method signatures in the implementing class (`ClassThatImplementsMy Interface`) must exactly match the corresponding signatures in `MyInterface`. The `GUIFrame` class extends the `WindowListener` interface in this way; you had to define all of the `WindowListener` methods, even though most of them did nothing.

Defining an Interface

Now, it's time for you to actually write an interface. The `Huggable` interface you'll be creating here is very simple. It only has one method, the `hug()` method. Here is the source code:

```
/*
 * Huggable
 * A simple interface with only one method
 */


public interface Huggable {

    //This method is abstract and can not have a body
    public void hug();

}
```

As it is, the `Huggable` interface can't do anything. An interface is useless by itself. To be of any use, you need at least one class that implements the interface and another class that calls its methods. In the next section, you'll create a class that implements `Huggable`.

Implementing an Interface

Okay, so you have the `Huggable` interface defined and compiled. Now, you need to implement it. The `Puppy` class implements the `Huggable` interface. As you know, the one thing that `Puppy` is required to do when it declares that it implements `Huggable` is to define the `hug()` method. Here is the source code.

```
/*

 * Puppy
 * Implements the Huggable interface
 */


public class Puppy implements Huggable {


    public void hug() {
        System.out.println("You hugged the Puppy!");
    }


}
```

In this example, `Puppy` only defines the one `hug()` method, but it's important to know that you can define as many other methods as you want. Nothing restricts you from creating whatever other methods you need. Also, there is no limit to the number of interfaces you can implement. You can simply list them all in the class declaration, separated by commas, like this:

```
public class Puppy implements Huggable, Lovable, Trainable {
```

When doing this, the only requirement is that you must implement all of the interfaces' methods. For comparison, I've created another class that does not implement the `Huggable` interface. Here is the source code for the `Porcupine` class.

```
/*
 * Porcupine
 * Does not implement the Huggable Interface
 */


public class Porcupine {


    public void avoid() {
        System.out.println("You avoided the Porcupine");
    }


}
```

Notice that there is no `hug()` method defined in `Porcupine`. There is nothing stopping `Porcupine` from defining that method, but because `Porcupine` doesn't implement the `Huggable` interface, the `hug()` method is not required. `HuggableTest` is a program that demonstrates how to handle classes that do or do not implement an interface. It also shows you how to tell the difference between the two. The source code follows.

```
/*
 * HuggableTest
 * Demonstrates a simple interface
 */


public class HuggableTest {

    public static void main(String args[]) {
        Puppy mario = new Puppy();
        Porcupine spike = new Porcupine();
```

```
        System.out.println("Hugging Puppy...");

        tryToHug(mario);

        System.out.println("Hugging Porcupine...");

        tryToHug(spike);

    }


    public static void tryToHug(Object pet) {

        if (pet instanceof Huggable) {

            Huggable hugme = (Huggable) pet;

            //guaranteed to have hug() method

            hugme.hug();

        }

        else {

            System.out.println("Can't hug this pet");

        }

    }


}
```

The first thing that HuggableTest does is to instantiate two objects. One of the objects is a Puppy object, the other is a Porcupine object. Then the program passes the objects to the tryToHug() method. The tryToHug() method checks to see if the given object implements the Huggable interface using the instanceof operator. Even though you cannot directly instantiate a new Huggable object, when you instantiate an object that implements the Huggable interface, you can refer to it as a Huggable object in Java code. If it is a Huggable object, the tryToHug() method calls the hug() method on the object. (All Huggable objects are guaranteed to define that method.) If the object is not an instance of Huggable, tryToHug() doesn't even bother trying to call hug(). There is no guarantee that the method is defined. Because the tryToHug() method accepts an Object parameter, any object can be passed in. But, as you know, not all objects have a hug() method. Figure 6.1 shows the output of the HuggableTest program.

Figure 6.1

You can always
count on an
interface's methods
to be implemented.

Rules for Defining and Implementing Interfaces

The rules for defining an interface are as follows:

➤ An interface must be abstract.

➤ All interface methods must be abstract and, therefore, must not have
a body.

➤ All interface variables must be static constants.

You already learned about the first two rules, but the third is new. Basically, the
third rule means that you can define variables in an interface, but you should
declare them to be `final` and `static`. If you leave these modifiers out, the
compiler will add them for you, so all fields in an interface are static constants
anyway. You can access them using the syntax *InterfaceName.variable
Name*. Anything you define in an interface must be applicable to all objects that
implement the interface, and cannot be specific to one single instance. Interfaces are really not all that complicated because the rules restrict you from
doing anything complicated when defining them.

Interface implementation has its own set of rules: You have to use the
`implements` keyword in the class signature; and you must define all of the
interface's methods, unless the implementing class is abstract. The code listed

here for the BadImplementationTest class shows you what happens when you don't define an interface's methods. It does not implement the hug() method.

```
/*
 * BadImplementationTest
 * Demonstrates that Java forces you to implement all
 * interface methods. NOTE: This will not compile
 */


public class BadImplementationTest implements Huggable {

    public void kiss() {
        System.out.println("I was kissed");
    }


}
```

If you try to compile this as it is, it won't work. The compiler will tell you that you must declare BadImplementationTest to be abstract because it does not define the hug() method. If you don't define this method, you leave an abstract method hanging around. No concrete class can have an abstract method, so the compiler is telling you that you have an abstract class that you didn't declare to be abstract. Figure 6.2 shows you the message that the compiler gives you in this situation.

Advantages of Using Interfaces

Using interfaces gives you certain advantages including a guaranteed set of methods that all of the implementing classes define. This is a benefit because you can define a set of methods that your application requires and let someone else create the implementing class however they want. In this way, interfaces are used like a set of specifications. Because interfaces are used like a set of specification, it is very easy to create multiple implementations of a given set of methods and move between them with very little code modification.

Figure 6.2

If you don't define all of an implemented interface's methods, your code will not compile.

Another interface advantage is *multiple inheritance*. Multiple inheritance refers to a class's ability to inherit from more than one super-class. A common misconception is that Java does not support multiple inheritance. While it is true that a class can inherit from one and only one class (single inheritance), it can implement as many interfaces as it needs to. For instance, you can have one class that extends another class and also implements one or more interfaces. Because a class inherits everything from its super-class and also inherits method signatures and static constants from the interfaces it implements, you can achieve multiple-inheritance functionality. You will really see how this is an advantage when you read the section about threads a bit later.

Creating an Event Model for the Calculator

You've already learned about event handling, and now you know about interfaces, too. Now, it's time to put your knowledge to work and create an event model for the calculator project. First, you'll define the `Calculator KeypadEvent` class and the `CalculatorKeypadListener` interface. Then you'll update the other calculator classes to make use of this event model.

Creating the Event Class and Interface

The `CalculatorKeypadEvent` class is used to encapsulate information about events that are fired by the `CalculatorKeypad` buttons. After all, the `DigitalDisplay` needs to update when you enter numbers, and the mathematical operations have to start somehow. Here is the source code for `CalculatorKeypadEvent`:

```
/*
 * CalculatorKeypadEvent
 */


import java.util.EventObject;
import javax.swing.JButton;


public class CalculatorKeypadEvent extends EventObject {


    public final static String MR = "MR";
    public final static String MC = "MC";
    public final static String MADD = "M+";
    public final static String MSUBTRACT = "M-";
    public final static String MS = "MS";
    public final static String SQRT = "SQRT";
    public final static String C = "C";
    public final static String AC = "AC";
    public final static String POW = "POW";
    public final static String DIVIDE
        = String.valueOf((char)247);
    public final static String MULTIPLY
        = String.valueOf((char)215);
    public final static String SUBTRACT = "-";
    public final static String CK7 = "7";
```

```java
public final static String CK8 = "8";

public final static String CK9 = "9";

public final static String SIGN
   = String.valueOf((char)177);

public final static String CK4 = "4";

public final static String CK5 = "5";

public final static String CK6 = "6";

public final static String ADD = "+";

public final static String CK1 = "1";

public final static String CK2 = "2";

public final static String CK3 = "3";

public final static String EQUALS = "=";

public final static String CK0 = "0";

public final static String DECIMAL = ".";


private String key;


public CalculatorKeypadEvent(Object source, String keyString) {
    super(source);
    key = keyString;
}


public String getKey() {
    return key;
}


public static boolean isNumerical(String keyValue) {
    try {
        Integer.parseInt(keyValue);
        return true;
```

```
        } catch (NumberFormatException nfe) {
            return false;
        }
    }


    public static boolean isOperational(String keyValue) {
        if (keyValue.equals(ADD) || keyValue.equals(SUBTRACT)
            || keyValue.equals(MULTIPLY)
            || keyValue.equals(DIVIDE)
            || keyValue.equals(SQRT) || keyValue.equals(POW)
            || keyValue.equals(SIGN) ) {
                return true;
        }
        return false;
    }


    public static boolean isMemOperational(String keyValue) {
        if (keyValue.equals(MADD) || keyValue.equals(MC)
            || keyValue.equals(MR) || keyValue.equals(MS)
            || keyValue.equals(MSUBTRACT)) {
                return true;
        }
        return false;
    }


    /* Indicates if the current operator is binary or unary.
     * Returns true if the current operator is binary, false
     * if it is unary. */
    public static boolean isOpBinary(String op) {
        return op.equals(ADD) || op.equals(SUBTRACT)
```

```
              || op.equals(MULTIPLY)
              || op.equals(DIVIDE) || op.equals(POW);
    }


}
```

The `CalculatorKeypadEvent` class defines a bunch of static constants. Each of these constants represents a button on the `CalculatorKeypad`. (The constants' names are pretty straightforward.) The `CalculatorKeypadEvent` class uses the constants as flags to indicate which operation should be performed. The `key` instance variable stores a particular key flag value for a particular `CalculatorKeypadEvent` instance. The constructor accepts an Object parameter, `source`, and a `String` value, `keyString`. `source` is used to reference the object (typically a `JButton` object) that fired the `CalculatorKeypadEvent`. The `keyString` argument accepts a `String` value that should equal one of the `CalculatorKeypadEvent` constants. There are also some utility methods that indicate whether the key is numerical, operational, or performs a memory operation. The `isBinary()` method returns `true` if the key represents an binary operator (operates on two operands).

The `CalculatorKeypadListener` interface is meant to be implemented by any class that is interested in listening to `CalculatorKeypadEvents`. That is, if a class wants to be notified whenever a `CalculatorKeypadEvent` is fired, the class should implement `CalculatorKeypadListener`. `CalculatorKeypadListener` declares only one method, the `calculatorKeyPressed()` method. It should be called whenever a button on the `CalculatorKeypad` is used. A `CalculatorKeypadEvent` object gets passed into the `calculatorKeyPressed()` method so that a class that implements the `CalculatorKeypadListener` interface can get the information it needs. Without getting this information, it wouldn't know what it should do about the event. This model is very similar to the AWT `Event` model you should be very familiar with by now. Here is the source code for `CalculatorKeypadListener`.

```
/*
 * CalculatorKeypadListener.java
 */
```

```
public interface CalculatorKeypadListener
    extends java.util.EventListener {


    public void calculatorKeyPressed(CalculatorKeypadEvent event);
}
```

Creating the CalculatorViewer Interface

Later on, you're going to write an applet that runs the calculator program. Once you write the applet, you'll have two ways of running the calculator—as either an applet or an application. To make it easier to switch between the application view and the applet view, abstract out the view by putting a middleman between it and the rest of the application, via an interface. The CalculatorViewer interface defines all of the methods that the class that acts as the view for the calculator program must implement. You need a method to get and set the display value, a method to append digits as numerical keys are pressed, and a method to append a decimal point. You also need a method to add a CalculatorKeypadListener to the view's Calculator Keypad so that you can do something when the buttons are clicked.

A CalculatorViewer class must have a CalculatorKeypad component, but the CalulatorViewer does not do any event handling. The way the calculator application is written, the only way to gain access to the Calculator Keypad is through a CalculatorViewer class, as the Calculator Viewer maintains the only instance of the CalculatorKeypad component. In order for classes that *do* perform event-handling actions to be able to listen to the Calculator Keypad's CalculatorKeypadEvents, the addCalculator KeypadListener() method should register the interested object as a listener to the CalculatorViewer's CalculatorKeypad component. The code for the CalculatorViewer interface follows:

```
/*
 * CalculatorViewer
 * An interface for Calculator Viewers
 */
```

```
import java.awt.event.*;

public interface CalculatorViewer {
    public void setDisplayValue(double value);
    public double getDisplayValue();
    public void appendDisplayDigit(int appendInt);
    public void appendDisplayDecimal();
    public void addCalculatorKeypadListener(
        CalculatorKeypadListener ckl);


}
```

Making Use of the Event Model

Now that you have the event-handling classes built, you need to update the calculator classes so that you can give the calculator program the ability to do what you need it to do. After the calculator classes are updated to use the calculator event model, it will be able to accept user input. Calculator application users will be able to use the calculator to enter numbers and tell the calculator to perform mathematical functions on them.

Writing the CalculatorKeyMap Utility

The calculator will provide two different ways of accepting user input: through the CalculatorKeypad and through the computer's keyboard. The CalculatorKeypadEvent class was created to encapsulate events that are triggered from the CalculatorKeypad, but the calculator will also handle keyboard-initiated events to perform the same actions as the Calculator Keypad. For example, to enter the number 9, the user can either click on the 9 button on the CalculatorKeypad or press 9 on the keyboard. Though there are two different forms of input, the purpose served is the same. For this reason, it would make your programming life much easier to define this relationship. Why trigger two different types of events that do the very same thing? Doing so would mean you would have to handle two different types of events in any calculator class that is interested in handling calculator events. Instead, whenever a user triggers a `KeyEvent` by pressing numbers on the keyboard, that `KeyEvent` will be mapped to its corresponding `Calculator KeypadEvent`, which will be fired. That way, you don't have to propagate the KeyEvent to the rest of the calculator application's classes. The `Calculator Keypad` class is responsible for handling `KeypadEvents`, mapping them to `CalculatorKeypadEvents`, and notifying any `CalculatorKeypad EventListeners`. This way, any of the calculator classes that are interested in calculator events only have to handle `CalculatorKeypadEvents`; they don't have to worry about the keyboard at all!

A new class, `CalculatorKeyMap`, is responsible for defining the mapping of `KeyEvents` to `CalculatorKeypadEvents`. The `CalculatorKeyMap` class's only function is to perform this mapping, which can be done in a single method. The method that performs this mapping is the `map()` method, which accepts a `KeyEvent` and returns the `CalculatorKeypadEvent` key that corresponds to the `KeyEvent`. Here is a listing of the `Calculator KeyMap` class.

```
/*
 * CalculatorKeyMap
 * Maps KeyEvent keys to CalculatorKeypadEvent keys
 */


import java.awt.event.KeyEvent;


public class CalculatorKeyMap {

    public final static String UNKNOWN = "?";

    //cannot be instantiated
    private CalculatorKeyMap() {}
```

```java
public static String map(KeyEvent ke) {
    switch(ke.getKeyCode()) {
        case KeyEvent.VK_0:
        case KeyEvent.VK_NUMPAD0:
            return CalculatorKeypadEvent.CK0;
        case KeyEvent.VK_1:
        case KeyEvent.VK_NUMPAD1:
            return CalculatorKeypadEvent.CK1;
        case KeyEvent.VK_2:
        case KeyEvent.VK_NUMPAD2:
            return CalculatorKeypadEvent.CK2;
        case KeyEvent.VK_3:
        case KeyEvent.VK_NUMPAD3:
            return CalculatorKeypadEvent.CK3;
        case KeyEvent.VK_4:
        case KeyEvent.VK_NUMPAD4:
            return CalculatorKeypadEvent.CK4;
        case KeyEvent.VK_5:
        case KeyEvent.VK_NUMPAD5:
            return CalculatorKeypadEvent.CK5;
        case KeyEvent.VK_6:
        case KeyEvent.VK_NUMPAD6:
            return CalculatorKeypadEvent.CK6;
        case KeyEvent.VK_7:
        case KeyEvent.VK_NUMPAD7:
            return CalculatorKeypadEvent.CK7;
        case KeyEvent.VK_8:
        case KeyEvent.VK_NUMPAD8:
            return CalculatorKeypadEvent.CK8;
        case KeyEvent.VK_9:
```

```
case KeyEvent.VK_NUMPAD9:

    return CalculatorKeypadEvent.CK9;

case KeyEvent.VK_DECIMAL:

case KeyEvent.VK_PERIOD:

    return CalculatorKeypadEvent.DECIMAL;

case KeyEvent.VK_ADD:

    return CalculatorKeypadEvent.ADD;

case KeyEvent.VK_SUBTRACT:

    if (ke.getModifiers() == KeyEvent.ALT_MASK) {

        return CalculatorKeypadEvent.SIGN;

    }

    else {

        return CalculatorKeypadEvent.SUBTRACT;

    }

case KeyEvent.VK_MULTIPLY:

    return CalculatorKeypadEvent.MULTIPLY;

case KeyEvent.VK_DIVIDE:

    return CalculatorKeypadEvent.DIVIDE;

case KeyEvent.VK_ENTER:

case KeyEvent.VK_EQUALS:

    return CalculatorKeypadEvent.EQUALS;

case KeyEvent.VK_DELETE:

    if (ke.getModifiers() == KeyEvent.ALT_MASK) {

        return CalculatorKeypadEvent.AC;

    }

    else {

        return CalculatorKeypadEvent.C;

    }

case KeyEvent.VK_F2:

    return CalculatorKeypadEvent.POW;
```

```
            case KeyEvent.VK_F3:

                return CalculatorKeypadEvent.SQRT;

            case KeyEvent.VK_F4:

                return CalculatorKeypadEvent.MS;

            case KeyEvent.VK_F5:

                return CalculatorKeypadEvent.MR;

            case KeyEvent.VK_F6:

                return CalculatorKeypadEvent.MC;

            case KeyEvent.VK_F7:

                return CalculatorKeypadEvent.MADD;

            case KeyEvent.VK_F8:

                return CalculatorKeypadEvent.MSUBTRACT;

            default:

                return UNKNOWN;

        }

    }


}
```

Because the CalculatorKeyMap class defines only one static method, there is no reason to have a reference to an instance of CacluatorKeyMap. You can call static methods without requiring a reference to an instance of the class. Because you will never need to construct a CalculatorKeyMap object, I made the constructor private, which disallows other classes from constructing a CalculatorKeyMap object.

The map() method gets the key code for the keyboard key that triggered the KeyEvent and puts the key code in a switch statement. The key code, which is equal to one of the KeyEvent key constants, tells you which keyboard key was pressed. The CalculatorKeyMap class is only interested in keyboard keys that correspond to CalculatorKeypad keys and should cause the calculator application to perform some action. The switch statement checks the key code, and if it maps to a CalculatorKeypad key, the map() method returns the `CalculatorKeypadEvent` key constant. For example, the first case in the `switch` statement checks the key code for the 0 keys. If the key code is `KeyEvent.VK_0` (the 0 key) or `KeyEvent.VK_NUMPAD0` (the 0 key on the number pad), the `map()` method returns `CalculatorKeypadEvent.CK0`, which is the flag for the 0 key on the `CalculatorKeypad`. If the `KeyEvent` doesn't map to any `CalculatorKeypadEvent` keys, `Calculator KeyMap.UNKNOWN` is returned. `CalculatorKeyMap.UNKNOWN` is a constant that indicates that the `KeyEvent` doesn't map to a `CalculatorKeypadEvent` key, and is, thus, unknown to the calculator application.

The `CalculatorKeyMap` class goes to work when the user presses a keyboard key, triggering a `KeyEvent`. The `CalculatorKeypad` passes the `KeyEvent` object to the `map()` method, which returns the mapped `Calculator KeypadEvent` key. The `CalculatorKeypad` class uses the `Calculator KeypadEvent` key to construct a `CalculatorKeypadEvent` and fires the event to any registered listeners, causing the calculator application to react in the desired way.

Updating CalculatorKeypad

The `CalculatorKeypad` class needs to be updated so that it can fire `CalculatorKeypadEvents` when the user interacts with either the `CalculatorKeypad` or the keyboard. When a `CalculatorKeypad` button is clicked, an AWT `ActionEvent` is fired. The `CalculatorKeypad` class needs to listen to these `ActionEvents` and fire corresponding `Calculator KeypadEvents`. The `CalculatorKeypad` class also needs to listen for `Key Events` so that it can map `KeyEvents` to `CalculatorKeypadEvents`. Here is the updated source code for `CalculatorKeypad` (note that two lines of code use a continuation tab, ➥; this is not part of the code):

```
/*
 * CalculatorKeypad
 * A Panel subclass that contains a set of buttons for a
 * calculator
 */
```

```java
import java.awt.*;

import java.awt.event.*;

import javax.swing.*;

import java.util.*;


public class CalculatorKeypad extends JPanel {

    private JButton[] buttons;

    private Vector listeners;


    public CalculatorKeypad() {

        super();

        GridBagLayout gbl = new GridBagLayout();

        GridBagConstraints gbc = new GridBagConstraints();

        gbc.fill = GridBagConstraints.BOTH;

        gbc.weightx = gbc.weighty = 1.0;

        gbc.ipadx = gbc.ipady = 5;


        // bLabels is an array of button labels in order

        String[] bLabels = { CalculatorKeypadEvent.MR,

            CalculatorKeypadEvent.MC,

            CalculatorKeypadEvent.MADD,

            CalculatorKeypadEvent.MSUBTRACT,

            CalculatorKeypadEvent.MS,

            CalculatorKeypadEvent.SQRT,

            CalculatorKeypadEvent.C,

            CalculatorKeypadEvent.AC,

            CalculatorKeypadEvent.POW,

            CalculatorKeypadEvent.DIVIDE,

            CalculatorKeypadEvent.MULTIPLY,
```

```
                    CalculatorKeypadEvent.SUBTRACT,

                    CalculatorKeypadEvent.CK7,

                    CalculatorKeypadEvent.CK8,

                    CalculatorKeypadEvent.CK9,

                    CalculatorKeypadEvent.SIGN,

                    CalculatorKeypadEvent.CK4,

                    CalculatorKeypadEvent.CK5,

                    CalculatorKeypadEvent.CK6,

                    CalculatorKeypadEvent.ADD,

                    CalculatorKeypadEvent.CK1,

                    CalculatorKeypadEvent.CK2,

                    CalculatorKeypadEvent.CK3,

                    CalculatorKeypadEvent.EQUALS,

                    CalculatorKeypadEvent.CK0,

                    CalculatorKeypadEvent.DECIMAL };


        //there are four columns of buttons
        int cols = 4;


        //build the Button array and add to Panel
        buttons = new JButton[bLabels.length];
        setLayout(gbl);


        ActionEventHandler actionListener
            = new ActionEventHandler();
        KeyEventListener keyListener = new ➥
        KeyEventListener();
        for (int b = 0; b < buttons.length; b++) {
            buttons[b] = new JButton(bLabels[b]);
```

```
//set different constraints
if (bLabels[b].equals("=")) {
    // "=" spans two rows
    gbc.gridheight = 2;
    gbc.gridwidth = GridBagConstraints.REMAINDER;
}
else if (bLabels[b].equals("0")) {
    // "0" spans two cols
    gbc.gridy = 6;
    gbc.gridx = 0;
    gbc.gridwidth = 2;
    gbc.gridheight = 1;
}
else if (bLabels[b].equals("3")) {
    gbc.gridheight = 1;
    gbc.gridwidth = GridBagConstraints.RELATIVE;
}
else if ((b + 1) % cols == 0) {
    gbc.gridheight = 1;
    //end a row
    gbc.gridwidth = GridBagConstraints.REMAINDER;
}
else {
    // for the "." button to be next to the "0"
    gbc.gridx = GridBagConstraints.RELATIVE;
    gbc.gridheight = 1;
    gbc.gridwidth = 1;
}

//set the constraints and add it to the panel
```

```
        buttons[b].setFont(
            new Font("Helvetica", Font.BOLD, 14));
        gbl.setConstraints(buttons[b], gbc);
        buttons[b].addActionListener(actionListener);
        buttons[b].addKeyListener(keyListener);
        add(buttons[b]);

        listeners = new Vector();
    }
}


    private class ActionEventHandler implements ActionListener {
    public void actionPerformed(ActionEvent event) {
        CalculatorKeypadEvent cke
                = new CalculatorKeypadEvent(event.getSource(),
                    ((JButton)event.getSource()).getText());
        Iterator i = listeners.iterator();
        CalculatorKeypadListener ckl;
        while(i.hasNext()) {
            ckl = (CalculatorKeypadListener)i.next();
            ckl.calculatorKeyPressed(cke);
        }
    }
}


    private class KeyEventListener extends KeyAdapter {
    public void keyPressed(KeyEvent event) {
        String key = CalculatorKeyMap.map(event);
        if (key != CalculatorKeyMap.UNKNOWN) {
            CalculatorKeypadEvent cke
```

```
            = new CalculatorKeypadEvent(
                event.getSource(), key);
            Iterator i = listeners.iterator();
            CalculatorKeypadListener ckl;
            while (i.hasNext()) {
                ckl = (CalculatorKeypadListener)i.next();
                ckl.calculatorKeyPressed(cke);
            }
        }
    }
}


public void addCalculatorKeypadListener(
        CalculatorKeypadListener ckl) {
    if (ckl == null) return;
    listeners.add(ckl);
}


public CalculatorKeypadListener[]➡
getCalculatorKeypadListeners() {
    return (CalculatorKeypadListener[]) listeners.toArray();
}


}
```

The first change is the way the button labels are constructed. Previously, the button labels were hard coded in the CalculatorKeypad class. That is, the button labels were created with actual String values; they did not have to look elsewhere for the label values. Now, the CalculatorKeypadEvent constants are used instead. This change makes the button labels consistent with the CalculatorKeypadEvent constants, which makes it easier to handle the

`ActionEvents`. As you know, you can retrieve the source of an `ActionEvent` by calling the `getSource()` method. In the calculator application, the source of all `ActionEvents` will be one of the `CalculatorKeypad`'s `JButton` objects. When `getSource()` is called, you can get a reference to the `JButton` object that triggered the event. Then you call the `getLabel()` method, which must equal one of the `CalculatorKeypadEvent` constants, which you use to construct and fire a `CalculatorKeypadEvent`. The new `Action EventHandler` inner class is added as an `ActionListener` for all of the calculator buttons and does all of this `ActionEvent` handling processing.

The `CalculatorKeypad` class has a `listeners` `Vector` instance variable that keeps track of all of the registered listeners. Whenever the `addCalculator KeypadListener()` method is called, the given `CalculatorKeypad Listener` object is added to the `listeners` `Vector`. The `listeners` `Vector` is the collection of listeners that are notified of all `CalculatorKeypad Events`. `CalculatorKeypadListeners` are registered by calling the `addCalculatorKeypadListener()` method. Anytime listeners need to be notified of events, the `listeners` `Vector` is iterated over, and its `calculator KeyPressed()` methods are called.

The `KeyEventListener` inner class handles all `KeyEvents`. The `KeyEventListener` is registered as a `KeyListener` of all of the calculator buttons. No matter which button has focus, `KeyEvents` will be captured and processed. `KeyEventListener` maps the `KeyEvent` key to a `Calculator KeypadEvent` by calling the `CalculatorKeyMap.map()` method, and uses the returned `CalculatorKeypadEvent` constant to construct a `Calculator KeypadEvent`. Then `KeyEventListener` notifies the `CalculatorKey padListeners` by calling all of the `listeners`' `calculatorKeyPressed()` methods. With all of these changes, the `CalculatorKeypad` is fitted with the calculator event model.

Updating the CalculatorView Class

The `CalculatorView` class has to be updated to implement the `Calculator Viewer` interface that you created earlier. Doing this will also take care of the event handling, as the interface defines the `addCalculatorKeypad Listener()` method. The `CalculatorKeypad` class generates all `Calculator KeypadEvents`. Because the `CalculatorView` class displays the `Calculator`

Keypad component, but does not handle its events directly, the Calculator View class needs a way to pass the CalculatorKeypadEvents to another class that does handle them. To address this need, the addCalculatorKeypad Listener() method adds the given CalculatorKeypadListener to the CalculatorKeypad by calling the CalculatorKeypad's addCalculator KeypadListener() method.

The CalculatorView class maintains the only instance of the Digital Display component; other classes must access the DigitalDisplay component through the CalculatorView class. The CalculatorView class allows this access by implementing the CalculatorViewer interface methods setDisplayValue(), getDisplayValue(), appendDisplay Digit(), and appendDisplayDecimal(). CalculatorView delegates this work to the Digital Display component. Here is the updated source code for CalculatorView:

```
/*
 * CalculatorView
 * Encapsulates the Calculator GUI
 */

import java.awt.*;
import java.awt.event.*;
import javax.swing.*;

public class CalculatorView extends JFrame
        implements CalculatorViewer {
    private DigitalDisplay display;
    private CalculatorKeypad keypad;

    public CalculatorView() {
        super("Java Calculator");
        Container content = getContentPane();
```

```java
        display = new DigitalDisplay(9, 0.0, true,
                new Color(88, 207, 233), new Color(30, 189, 223),
                Color.black);
    content.add(display, BorderLayout.NORTH);

    keypad = new CalculatorKeypad();

    content.add(keypad, BorderLayout.CENTER);

    setDefaultCloseOperation(EXIT_ON_CLOSE);
    pack();
}

public void setDisplayValue(double value) {
    try {
        display.setDoubleValue(value);
    } catch (DigitalDisplayOverflowException e) {
        System.out.println("DigitalDisplayOverflow: "
            + e.getMessage());
    } finally {
        display.updateDisplay();
    }
}

public double getDisplayValue() {
    return display.getDoubleValue();
}

public void appendDisplayDigit(int appendInt) {
```

```
        display.appendDigit(appendInt);
    }


    public void appendDisplayDecimal() {
        display.appendDecimal();
    }


    public void addCalculatorKeypadListener(
        CalculatorKeypadListener ckl) {
        keypad.addCalculatorKeypadListener(ckl);
    }


}
```

Updating CalculatorModel

Because the calculator application now has the ability to accept user input, you can reintroduce the CalculatorModel class, with some updates, to keep track of that input. To refresh your memory, the CalculatorModel class's function is to keep track of the calculator's operands and operator keys as they are entered. It acts as the calculator's memory. The only update it needs allows it to make use of the CalculatorKeypadEvent constants. The one method that is changed is the setCurrentOp() method. It uses the CalculatorKeypadEvent constants to make sure that the operator being set is a valid one. If the given String, op, is equal to one of the operator keys defined in CalculatorKeypadEvent, the operator is valid. If not, the operation is not valid, and it is set to NONE. Because you are now using CalculatorKeyEvent constants and the isOpBinary() method, the CalulatorModel class no longer needs to define its own constants, and the isOpBinary() method that was taken over by CalculatorKeypadEvent has been removed from CalculatorModel. Here is the updated source code listing, in full, for your convenience.

```
/*
 * CalculatorModel
 * Encapsulates the data model used by the Calculator
 * Application
 */

public class CalculatorModel {

    private double operand1;
    private double operand2;
    /* Stores the value associated with a calculator's memory */
    private double mem;
    /* The current operand that appears in the display */
    private double currentDisplayValue;
    /* Represents operation to be performed on the operands */
    private String currentOp;
    public final static String NONE = "?";

    /*
     * Constructs a new CalculatorModel object.
     * maxDigits - The maximum number of displayable digits
     */
    public CalculatorModel() {
        currentOp = CalculatorModel.NONE;
    }

    public void setOperand1(double value) {
        operand1 = value;
        currentDisplayValue = operand1;
    }
```

```
public double getOperand1() {

    return operand1;

}


public void setOperand2(double value) {

    operand2 = value;

    currentDisplayValue = operand2;

}


public double getOperand2() {

    return operand2;

}


public void setMem(double value) {

    mem = value;

}


public double getMem() {

    return mem;

}


public void setCurrentDisplayValue(double value) {

    currentDisplayValue = value;

}


public double getCurrentDisplayValue() {

    return currentDisplayValue;

}
```

```java
public void setCurrentOp(String op) {
    if (op.equals(CalculatorKeypadEvent.ADD)
        || op.equals(CalculatorKeypadEvent.SUBTRACT)
        || op.equals(CalculatorKeypadEvent.MULTIPLY)
        || op.equals(CalculatorKeypadEvent.DIVIDE)
        || op.equals(CalculatorKeypadEvent.POW)) {
            currentOp = op;
    }
    else {
        currentOp = CalculatorModel.NONE;
    }
}


/* Gets the current operator */
public String getCurrentOp() {
    return currentOp;
}


public String toString() {
    String s = "operand1 = " + operand1
            + " operand2 = " + operand2
            + " currentOp = " + currentOp
            + " currentDisplayValue = "
            + currentDisplayValue
            + " mem = " + mem;
    return s;
}
}
```

Updating CalculatorHelper

Previously, the `CalculatorHelper` class referenced `CalculatorModel`'s operator constants and called the `CalculatorModel`'s `isOpBinary()` method. Since this stuff has been moved over to `CalculatorKeypadEvent`, you need to change all of these references to reflect that fact. Any instance in which the `CalculatorModel` constants appeared, excepting the `CalculatorModel.NONE` constant (which is still used), needs to be changed to use `CalculatorKeypadEvent`'s constants. Also, anywhere that the `CalculatorModel`'s `isOpBinary()` method was previously called needs to be updated to call this method from `CalculatorModel`. These are the only updates that `CalculatorHelper` require. Here is the updated source code:

```
/*
 * CalculatorHelper
 * A class that performs mathematical functions for a
 * Calculator program
 */


public class CalculatorHelper {
    private CalculatorModel calcModel;
    private StringBuffer auditTrail;
    private boolean opPerformed;
    private int decimalPos;

    public CalculatorHelper() {
        this(20);
    }

    public CalculatorHelper(int decimalAlignmentPos) {
        calcModel = new CalculatorModel();
        auditTrail = new StringBuffer();
        decimalPos = decimalAlignmentPos;
```

```java
        }

        private CalculatorModel performUnaryOperation(String op) {
            double value;
            if (op.equals(CalculatorKeypadEvent.SIGN)) {
                value = sign();
            }
            else if (op.equals(CalculatorKeypadEvent.SQRT)) {
                value = sqrt();
            }
            else {
                return calcModel;
            }
            auditTrail.append(align("[" + op
                    + " " + calcModel.getCurrentDisplayValue() + "]")
                    + "\n");
            calcModel.setCurrentDisplayValue(value);
            setOperand(value);
            return calcModel;
        }



        public CalculatorModel performOperation() {
            double value;
            if (CalculatorKeypadEvent.isOpBinary(
                    calcModel.getCurrentOp())) {
              auditTrail.append(align(calcModel.getCurrentOp() + " "
                            + calcModel.getOperand2()) + "\n");
            }
```

```
else if (!calcModel.getCurrentOp().equals(
        CalculatorModel.NONE)) {
    auditTrail.append(calcModel.getCurrentOp() + "\n");
}

String op = calcModel.getCurrentOp();

if (op.equals(CalculatorKeypadEvent.ADD)) {
    value = add();
}
else if (op.equals(CalculatorKeypadEvent.SUBTRACT)) {
    value = subtract();
}
else if (op.equals(CalculatorKeypadEvent.MULTIPLY)) {
    value = multiply();
}
else if (op.equals(CalculatorKeypadEvent.DIVIDE)) {
    value = divide();
}
else if (op.equals(CalculatorKeypadEvent.POW)) {
    value = pow();
}
else if (op.equals(CalculatorKeypadEvent.SQRT)) {
    value = sqrt();
}
else if (op.equals(CalculatorKeypadEvent.SIGN)) {
    value = sign();
}
else {
    value = calcModel.getCurrentDisplayValue();
```

```
                calcModel.setOperand1(value);

                calcModel.setOperand2(0.0);

            }


        calcModel.setCurrentDisplayValue(value);

        //makes the currently displayed value ready for another op

        calcModel.setOperand1(value);

        opPerformed = true;

        auditTrail.append(

            "=============================================\n"

            + align(String.valueOf(value)) + "\n");

        return calcModel;

    }


    public CalculatorModel getCalculatorModel() {

        return calcModel;

    }


    public CalculatorModel setOperand(double value) {

        if (CalculatorKeypadEvent.isOpBinary(

                calcModel.getCurrentOp())

                && !opPerformed) {

            calcModel.setOperand2(value);

        }

        else {

            auditTrail.append("\n" + align(String.valueOf(value))

                    + "\n");

            calcModel.setOperand1(value);

            calcModel.setOperand2(0.0);

            calcModel.setCurrentOp(CalculatorModel.NONE);
```

```java
        }
        calcModel.setCurrentDisplayValue(value);
        return calcModel;
    }


    public CalculatorModel setOp(String op) {
        //automatically perform unary operations
        if (!CalculatorKeypadEvent.isOpBinary(op)) {
            return performUnaryOperation(op);
        }
        if (opPerformed == false
                && !calcModel.getCurrentOp().equals(
                CalculatorModel.NONE)) {
            performOperation();
        }
        opPerformed = false;
        calcModel.setCurrentOp(op);
        return calcModel;
    }


    public CalculatorModel memAdd() {
        calcModel.setMem(calcModel.getMem()
            + calcModel.getCurrentDisplayValue());
        return calcModel;
    }


    public CalculatorModel memSubtract() {
        calcModel.setMem(calcModel.getMem()
            - calcModel.getCurrentDisplayValue());
        return calcModel;
```

```java
    }

    public CalculatorModel memRecall() {
        setOperand(calcModel.getMem());
        return calcModel;
    }

    public CalculatorModel memSwap() {
        double swapVal = calcModel.getMem();
        calcModel.setMem(calcModel.getCurrentDisplayValue());
        setOperand(swapVal);
        return calcModel;
    }

    public CalculatorModel memClear() {
        calcModel.setMem(0.0);
        return calcModel;
    }

    public CalculatorModel clear() {
      //clears second operand if binary operation in progress
      setOperand(0.0);
      return calcModel;
    }

    /* Clears everything except the memory value */
    public CalculatorModel clearAll() {
        calcModel.setOperand1(0.0);
        calcModel.setOperand2(0.0);
        calcModel.setCurrentDisplayValue(0.0);
```

```
        calcModel.setCurrentOp(CalculatorModel.NONE);
        opPerformed = false;
        return calcModel;
    }


    public String getAuditTrail() {
        return auditTrail.toString();
    }


    private String align(String decimalString) {
        String aligned = decimalString;
        int currDecPos = aligned.lastIndexOf('.');
        for (int pos = currDecPos; pos < decimalPos; pos++) {
            aligned = " " + aligned;
        }
        return aligned;
    }


private double add() {
    return calcModel.getOperand1() + calcModel.getOperand2();
}


private  double subtract() {
   return calcModel.getOperand1() - calcModel.getOperand2();
}


private double multiply() {
  return calcModel.getOperand1() * calcModel.getOperand2();
}
```

```
private double divide() {
  return calcModel.getOperand1() / calcModel.getOperand2();
}

private double pow() {
    return Math.pow(calcModel.getOperand1(),
       calcModel.getOperand2());
}

private double sqrt() {
    return Math.sqrt(calcModel.getCurrentDisplayValue());
}

private double sign() {
    return  calcModel.getCurrentDisplayValue() * -1;
}
}
```

Updating and Testing Calculator

Finally, the Calculator class has to be updated to handle calculator events. The Calculator class does all of the CalculatorKeypadEvent handling. Now that CalculatorModel and CalculatorHelper have reappeared, the Calculator class needs to be updated as well. Previously, Calculator's only function was to display the CalculatorView. Now, the Calculator class is required to do much more, so there is a lot to add to the Calculator class. Here is the updated source code for Calculator:

```
/*
 * Calculator
 * The Calculator application
 */
```

```java
import java.awt.*;
import java.awt.event.*;
import java.applet.Applet;


public class Calculator implements CalculatorKeypadListener {
    private CalculatorViewer view;
    private CalculatorHelper helper;
    private boolean needNewNumber = false;
    private int mode;
    public final static int APPLICATION = 1;
    public final static int APPLET = 2;


    public Calculator(CalculatorViewer ui)
            throws CalculatorException {
        view = ui;
        helper = new CalculatorHelper();
        view.addCalculatorKeypadListener(this);
        if (view instanceof Frame) {
            ((Frame)view).setVisible(true);
            mode = APPLICATION;
        }
        else if (view instanceof Applet) {
            mode = APPLET;
        }
        else throw new CalculatorException(
            "CalculatorViewer must be an "
            + "instance of either Frame or Applet");

        System.out.println("The calculator is being started in "
            + (mode == APPLET ? "applet" : "application")
```

```java
                                + " mode");
        }


        public static void main(String args[]) {
            try {
                new Calculator(new CalculatorView());
            } catch (CalculatorException e) {
                System.out.println("CalculatorException: "
                    + e.getMessage());
            }
        }


        public void calculatorKeyPressed(CalculatorKeypadEvent event) {
            CalculatorModel model;
            String key = event.getKey();

            if (CalculatorKeypadEvent.isNumerical(key)) {
                if (needNewNumber) {
                    view.setDisplayValue(0.0);
                    needNewNumber = false;
                }
                view.appendDisplayDigit(Integer.parseInt(key));
            }
            else if (key.equals(CalculatorKeypadEvent.DECIMAL)) {
                view.appendDisplayDecimal();
            }
            else if (CalculatorKeypadEvent.isOperational(key)) {
                helper.setOperand(view.getDisplayValue());
                helper.setOp(key);
                model = helper.getCalculatorModel();
```

```
        view.setDisplayValue(model.getCurrentDisplayValue());
        needNewNumber = !key.equals(
            CalculatorKeypadEvent.SIGN);
    }
    else if (key.equals(CalculatorKeypadEvent.EQUALS)) {
        if (!needNewNumber) {
            helper.setOperand(view.getDisplayValue());
        }
        model = helper.performOperation();
        view.setDisplayValue(model.getCurrentDisplayValue());
        needNewNumber = true;
    }
    else if (key.equals(CalculatorKeypadEvent.C)) {
        model = helper.clear();
        view.setDisplayValue(model.getCurrentDisplayValue());
    }
    else if (key.equals(CalculatorKeypadEvent.AC)) {
            model = helper.clearAll();
        view.setDisplayValue(model.getCurrentDisplayValue());
    }
    else if (key.equals(CalculatorKeypadEvent.MS)) {
        helper.setOperand(view.getDisplayValue());
        model = helper.memSwap();
        view.setDisplayValue(model.getCurrentDisplayValue());
    }
    else if (key.equals(CalculatorKeypadEvent.MR)) {
        helper.setOperand(view.getDisplayValue());
        model = helper.memRecall();
        view.setDisplayValue(model.getCurrentDisplayValue());
    }
```

```
        else if (key.equals(CalculatorKeypadEvent.MC)) {
            helper.setOperand(view.getDisplayValue());
            model = helper.memClear();
            view.setDisplayValue(model.getCurrentDisplayValue());
        }
        else if (key.equals(CalculatorKeypadEvent.MADD)) {
            helper.setOperand(view.getDisplayValue());
            model = helper.memAdd();
            view.setDisplayValue(model.getCurrentDisplayValue());
        }
        else if (key.equals(CalculatorKeypadEvent.MSUBTRACT)) {
            helper.setOperand(view.getDisplayValue());
            model = helper.memSubtract();
            view.setDisplayValue(model.getCurrentDisplayValue());
        }
    }

}
```

Note that some instance variables were added. The `view` variable keeps track of the `CalculatorViewer` component that displays the calculator. `helper` is for the `CalculatorHelper` object. The `boolean` variable, `needNewNumber`, is used as a flag indicating that when a user presses a numerical key, the act should start a new number, rather than append a number to the currently displayed value. The `mode` keeps track of whether the calculator is being run as an applet or an application. The `APPLICATION` and `APPLET` constants are used as flags that indicate the calculator mode.

The `Calculator()` constructor accepts a `CalculatorViewer` object. It stores this object in the `view` instance variable. The constructor also creates a new `CalculatorHelper` instance and assigns it to the `helper` instance variable. The `Calculator` class now implements the `CalculatorKeypad Listener` interface, so it adds itself as a listener to the `CalculatorViewer` by calling the `addCalculatorKeypadListener()` method. Next, the constructor determines whether the calculator is running as an application or an applet. If the given `CalculatorViewer` object is an instance of a `Frame`, then the calculator is running in application mode. If the object is an instance of an `Applet`, the calculator is running in applet mode. The constructor assigns the appropriate value to the `mode` instance variable and prints a message indicating in which mode the calculator is running. If the given `CalculatorViewer` is not a `Frame` or an `Applet` object, the constructor throws a generic `Calculator Exception` because it cannot determine in the calculator's mode.

When the `Calculator` class is run directly, it should run as an application. (The calculator must be started differently if it is to be run in applet mode, which you'll see a bit later.) The `main()` method creates a new `Calculator View` object, which is a `JFrame`, and, thus, also an instance of `Frame`. The `main()` method passes the `CalculatorView` object to the `Calculator` constructor, which starts the calculator in application mode.

Because the `Calculator` class implements the `CalculatorKeypad Listener` interface, it must implement the `calculatorKeyPressed()` method. The `calculatorKeyPressed()` method is responsible for handling all `CalculatorKeypadEvents`. The `calculatorKeyPressed()` method works as follows:

➤ If a numerical key is pressed, the corresponding number is appended to the display unless a new number is needed. If a new number is needed, the display is cleared before appending the number.

➤ If the key is the decimal point, the decimal point is appended to the display.

➤ If the key is an operational key (for example, +, -, and so on), then the currently displayed number is entered as an operand and the operator key is set. In this case, you need a new number as long as the operator key pressed was not `CalculatorKeypadEvent.SIGN`. The `needNewNumber` variable is set accordingly.

➤ If the key is the equal key (=), you need to perform the current operation on the previously set operands by calling `helper.perform Operation()`. First, check the `needNewNumber` variable. If it is false, the currently displayed number is still being constructed (because you only need a new number *after* an operand is previously set). Because the number is still being constructed, it is not yet set as an operand.

➤ The `calculatorKeyPressed()` method continues to check which key is pressed, calls the corresponding `helper` methods, and updates the display as appropriate for the clear and memory functions.

Figure 6.3 shows the most recent version of the calculator application. Of course, you'll need to run it yourself to experience the event handling. At this point, the calculator project is nearly complete and acts just like a calculator.

Writing Java Applets

Java applets are Java programs that run within the context of another application, usually a Web browser. Web browsers interpret the Java code and act as the JVM for Java programs. Applets are very useful in providing GUIs for user input. They're also good for creating games that can be played online. Believe it or not, you already know a good deal of what you need to know to create applets. The `java.applet.Applet` class, which you extend to create applets, extends the `Panel` class. You already learned that the Panel class is a container that you can add AWT components to. You can add AWT components to an applet in the same way. The difference is that the applet panel is displayed directly inside a Web page. There are other differences

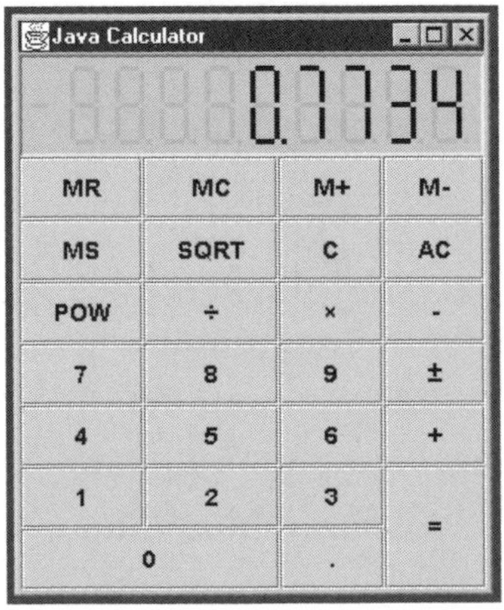

Figure 6.3

The event model gives life to the calculator.

between applets and panels, and you'll need to learn these differences before programming applets. You'll also need to know a bit of HTML (*HyperText Markup Language*). All Web pages on the Internet are defined in HTML, and because an applet runs inside a Web page, you'll need to know some of the language. Don't worry, you need to learn only a small amount, and I'll cover it in this section.

Applet Programming

When you write a Java applet, you need to extend the `Applet` class, which is defined in the `java.applet` package. Table 6.1 lists the methods that you'll find in the `Applet` class.

TABLE 6.1 APPLET METHODS	
Method	**Description**
`destroy()`	Called by the browser to indicate that the applet is being unloaded from memory and that you should perform any clean up.
`String getAppletInfo()`	Returns a `String` object that represents information about the applet. It is meant to be overridden by subclasses to provide information such as author, version, and so on.
`AudioClip getAudioClip(URL)`	Returns the `AudioClip` object at the specified URL.
`AudioClip getAudioClip(URL, String)`	Returns the `AudioClip` object at the specified base URL, having the name specified by the second parameter.
`URL getCodeBase()`	Returns the `URL` object that represents the applet's base URL.

continued

TABLE 6.1 APPLET METHODS

Method	Description
`URL getDocumentBase()`	Returns the absolute (complete, not relative) `URL` object that represents the directory that contains the applet.
`Image getImage(URL)`	Returns the `Image` at the given URL.
`Image getImage(URL, String)`	Returns the `Image` at the given URL, with the specified name.
`String getParameter(String)`	Returns the `String` value of the parameter having the given name or `null`, if the parameter isn't set.
`String[][] getParameterInfo()`	Returns a `String[][]` that represents the parameter information of the applet. This method is intended to be overridden by subclasses of `Applet`.
`void showStatus(String)`	Displays the given string in the browser's status area (for example, in Internet Explorer, it is at the bottom of the browser's window).
`void init()`	Called by the browser to indicate that the applet has been loaded.
`void start()`	Called by the browser to indicate that the applet should begin execution.
`void stop()`	Called by the browser to indicate that the applet should stop execution.

The URL class in the `java.net` package, which appears in some of the methods you saw in Table 6.1, represents a *Universal Resource Locator*. A URL specifies the location of files. Anytime you type a Web page address into your browser (for example, http://www.premierpressbooks.com), you are specifying the URL for that Web page. An applet uses the URL class to locate files that it needs.

One of the big differences between an applet and a panel is the way they are constructed. Anything that you would typically put in a `Panel`'s constructor method is placed instead in the `init()` method. This change is important because the `init()` method is called when the applet is loaded, and you can't start adding stuff to an applet until after it is loaded.

HTML and the Applet Tag

In this section, I'll go over the bare bones of HTML—just the stuff you need to get your applets up and running. First, I'll talk about basic HTML tags and then the `<applet>` tag.

HTML is used to develop Web documents. HTML *tags* are formatting instructions that surround text, giving the text certain attributes that affect the way your browser displays it. Tags are specified within angle brackets (< and >), and typically there is a start tag, an end tag, and some text between. Here is an example.

```
<tag>Here is some text that the tag affects</tag>
```

In this example, *tag* is the name of the tag. An open tag goes at the beginning of the text you are formatting, and a closing tag goes after the text. An example is `<b>bold text</b>`. The bold tags (`<b>` and `</b>`) surround text to make it appear bold when displayed within your browser. An opening tag can also specify certain *attributes*, or parameters that tweak the tag's effect. The attributes are listed and separated by spaces, and their values are usually put within quotation marks (single or double quotation marks will do), but sometimes the quotes are omitted.

```
<tag attribute1='value1' attribute2='value2'>Formatted
text</tag>
```

An ending tag is also the name of the tag within angle brackets, but the name is prefaced with a forward slash (/) to indicate that it is an ending tag. Some tags do not require ending tags. Table 6.2 lists the tags that I use in this book and what they do. HTML is much more robust than explained in this book, but that's why there are entire series of books dedicated to HTML and Web development. Not every attribute of every tag is covered here, just the ones you'll see in the HMTL files you are going to create.

TABLE 6.2   HTML TAGS USED IN THIS BOOK

HTML Tags	Description
`<HTML></HTML>`	Top-level tags that indicate this is an HTML file.
`<HEAD></HEAD>`	Surrounds information about the HTML document, such as the title.
`<TITLE></TITLE>`	Specifies the title that appears in the title bar of the browser window.
`<BODY></BODY>`	Surrounds the main body of the HTML document.
`<H1></H1>`	Specifies header text that is used as titles for document sections.
`<CENTER></CENTER>`	Centers the content that it surrounds.
`<APPLET></APPLET>`	Embeds an applet in the HTML document.

The `<applet>` tag is used to embed a Java applet within a browser window. It is used to specify the class file of the applet as well as its width, height, and other attributes. When a Java-enabled browser encounters a set of `<applet></applet>` tags, it invokes the applet at the location the tags appear. It does not display any text that it finds within the opening and closing tags, but browsers that do not understand Java will, so you could write a message for browsers that do not support Java, like this:

```
<APPLET code='MyApplet.class' width=200 height=100>

Your browser does not support Java.

</applet>
```

If you then open the document with a browser that either does not support Java or has Java disabled, instead of seeing the applet, you would see "Your browser does not support Java."

The `<applet>` tag has a set of attributes. Table 6.3 lists some of them.

TABLE 6.3 <APPLET> ATTRIBUTES	
Attributes	**Description**
`code`	Specifies the class file that defines the applet.
`width`	Specifies the width within the browser window reserved for the applet.
`height`	Specifies the height within the browser window reserved for the applet.
`codebase`	Specifies the location URL of the applet required, if the applet resides in a different directory.
`mayscript`	Indicates that the applet may access JavaScript functionality within the page.
`name`	Specifies the name of the applet used to differentiate it from other applets on the same document.

Passing Parameters to Applets

You already know that when you start a Java application you can pass parameters to it at the command prompt. There is actually a way to do this for Java applets. Because the Web browser starts the applet, passing arguments at the command prompt isn't an option, so there needs to be another way of passing arguments. That's where the <PARAM> tag comes in. The <PARAM> tag is used to pass parameters to an applet. <PARAM> tags must appear inside the opening and closing <APPLET> tags. The syntax for the <PARAM> tag is

```
<PARAM name='paramName' value='paramValue'>
```

There is no closing </PARAM> tag. Here, *paramName* is the name you give to the parameter and *paramValue* is the value you assign to it. Using the <PARAM> tag is only half the work. You also need to retrieve these parameters so the applet can see them. For this purpose, you use the `getParameter()` method. When you use this method, you pass in the parameter name and the method returns its value. For example, to get the parameter specified in the previous HTML example, use this code:

```
String paramValue = getParameter("paramName");
```

The value of the paramValue variable after this call would be *paramValue*, or whatever you specify in the value attribute of the <PARAM> tag. The Simple Applet applet is a simple example of how to create an applet.

```java
/*
 * SimpleApplet
 * Demonstrates how to build a simple applet
 */


import java.applet.Applet;
import java.awt.*;
import java.awt.event.*;


public class SimpleApplet extends Applet {

    public void init() {
        setLayout(new FlowLayout(FlowLayout.CENTER, 3, 10));
        add(new Label("Text:"));
        add(new TextField(getParameter("initialtext"), 25));
        Button b = new Button("OK");
        b.addActionListener(new ActionListener() {
            public void actionPerformed(ActionEvent e) {
                System.out.println("Button Clicked");
            }
        });
        add(b);
    }

}
```

The corresponding HTML for SimpleApplet, simpleapplet.html, looks like this.

```
<HTML>

    <HEAD>

        <TITLE>Simple Applet</TITLE>

    </HEAD>


<BODY>

<H1 align=CENTER>SimpleApplet</H1>

<CENTER>

<APPLET code='SimpleApplet.class' width='300' height='100'>

    <PARAM name='initialtext' value='Hello There'>

    Your browser does not support Java applets!

</APPLET>

</HTML>
```

SimpleApplet adds a Label, a TextField, and a Button. The applet initializes the TextField's text value by getting the value of the initialtext parameter. The <PARAM> tag in simpleapplet.html sets the value of this parameter to 'Hello There'. So, when you start the applet, you should see this value inside of the TextField, as seen in Figure 6.4. The Button has an ActionListener that just prints out the message Button Clicked when the Button gets clicked. A browser usually provides a Java console that accepts System.out.println() messages.

Using the appletviewer Tool

The Java SDK includes a tool called appletviewer. The appletviewer tool is used to run applets from the command line for testing purposes. This way, you can test applets outside of the constraints of a Web browser. It's quite simple to use the appletviewer tool. At the command prompt, simply type **appletviewer**, followed by the name of the HTML file that contains the

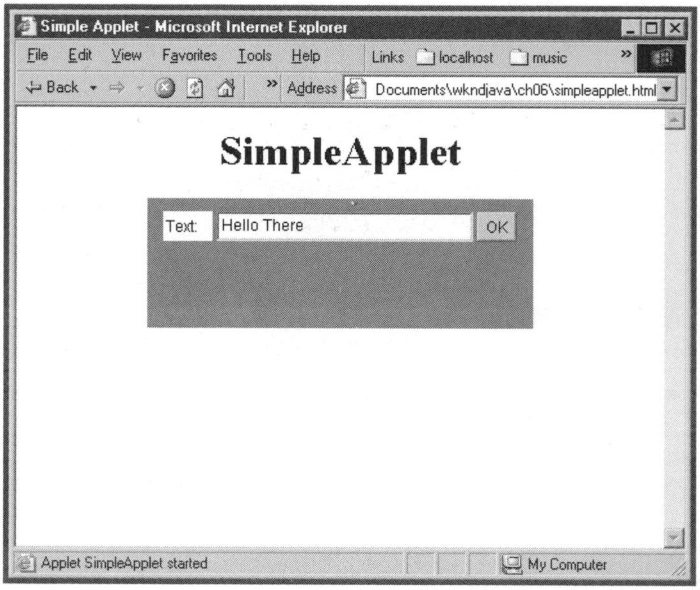

Figure 6.4

Applets can run inside Web pages.

<APPLET> tag for the applet to be run. For example, to run SimpleApplet from the command prompt, type the following command:

```
appletviewer simpleapplet.html
```

Figure 6.5 shows how the applet looks when it's run using the applet viewer utility.

Running the Calculator as an Applet

In this section, I'll show you how to run the calculator as a Java applet. There really isn't much to it. All you need to do is write the CalculatorApplet class to display the calculator and then write the HTML to include the applet in a Web page.

Writing CalculatorApplet

The CalculatorApplet class is the class that runs the calculator as an applet. The difference between this applet and what you've already learned about applets is that this is a Swing applet. It extends the JApplet class

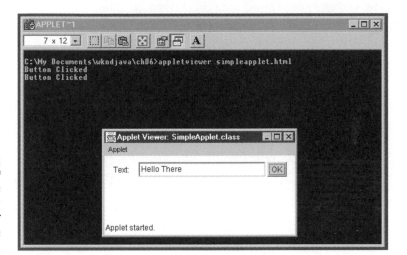

Figure 6.5

You can use
`appletviewer`
to test your
applets outside
of a Web browser.

instead of the `Applet` class. The `JApplet` class is found in the `javax.swing` package. The only difference between `Applet` and `JApplet` is that `JApplet` provides support for adding Swing components to an applet. Because the calculator is a Swing GUI, you should use the `JApplet` instead of the standard `Applet`.

The `CalculatorApplet` implements the `CalculatorViewer` interface. Here you can really see the benefit of abstracting out the calculator's view through the `CalculatorViewer` interface. `CalculatorApplet` is only a bit different from `CalculatorView`, which is the other `CalcluatorViewer` for the calculator. When the calculator is run in application mode, the `Calculator` class is the initiator. Because the `CalculatorApplet` class is the applet, it must act as the initiating class, as the browser starts `CalculatorApplet` first.

Although this is true, the `Calculator` class already has code in it for controlling the calculator's actions and for listening to `CalculatorKeypadEvents`. That's why the `CalculatorApplet` class constructs a new `Calculator` object, passing itself as the `CalculatorViewer`, and registers the `Calculator` as a `CalculatorKeypadListener`. It displays the `CalculatorException`, if there is one, in the status area. Other than that, the `CalculatorViewer` methods are implemented in exactly the same way that the `Calculator View` class implements them. Here is the source code for the `Calculator Applet` class:

```java
/*
 * CalculatorApplet.java
 * Runs the Calculator as an applet
 */

import javax.swing.*;
import java.awt.*;
import java.awt.event.*;

public class CalculatorApplet extends JApplet
    implements CalculatorViewer {

    private DigitalDisplay display;
    private CalculatorKeypad keypad;

    public void init() {
        Container content = getContentPane();

        display = new DigitalDisplay(9, 0.0, true,
            new Color(88, 207, 233), new Color(30, 189, 223),
            Color.black);
        content.add(display, BorderLayout.NORTH);

        keypad = new CalculatorKeypad();

        content.add(keypad, BorderLayout.CENTER);
        try {
            Calculator controller = new Calculator(this);
        } catch (CalculatorException e) {
            e.printStackTrace();
```

```java
            System.out.println("CalculatorException: "
            + e.getMessage());
            showStatus(e.getMessage());
        }

    }


    public void setDisplayValue(double value) {
        try {
            display.setDoubleValue(value);
        } catch (DigitalDisplayOverflowException e) {
            System.out.println("DigitalDisplayOverflow: "
                + e.getMessage());
        } finally {
            display.updateDisplay();
        }
    }


    public double getDisplayValue() {
        return display.getDoubleValue();
    }


    public void appendDisplayDigit(int appendInt) {
        display.appendDigit(appendInt);
    }


    public void appendDisplayDecimal() {
        display.appendDecimal();
    }
```

```
public void addCalculatorKeypadListener➡
(CalculatorKeypadListener ckl) {

    keypad.addCalculatorKeypadListener(ckl);

}


}
```

Writing the HTML

Now, you need to write the HTML that includes the calculator applet. It's actually quite simple. Here is the source code for `calculator.htm`:

```html
<HTML>

    <HEAD>

        <TITLE>Calculator Applet</TITLE>

    </HEAD>


    <APPLET code='CalculatorApplet.class' width=268 height=334>

        Your browser does not support applets

    </APPLET>


</HTML>
```

Figure 6.6 shows how the calculator looks as an applet.

Using Threads

Threads are independently running "jobs" that execute code. Up front, I'll just let you know that you won't be writing threads in the calculator application. Although this is true, threads are extremely important to know about. Anytime you write some code that takes a long time to run, you might consider putting it in a thread and running the greedy code in the background so that it doesn't tie up the rest of your program.

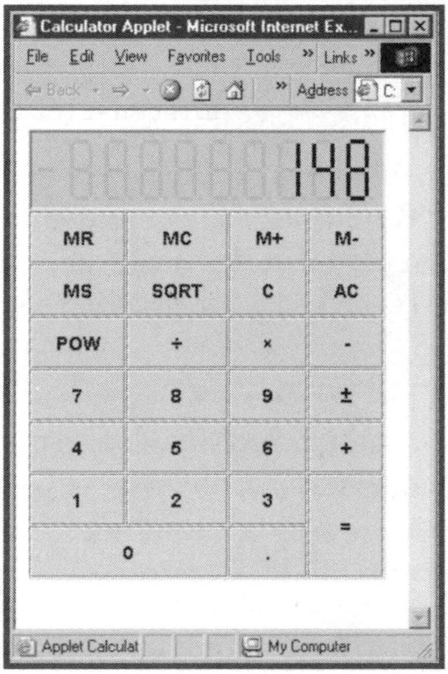

Figure 6.6

The calculator runs as an applet now, so you can actually include it on a Web page on the Internet!

Running multiple threads at a time is called *multithreading*, or *multitasking*. Multiple threads appear to run simultaneously, but that's not exactly how it works. Your computer's single processor runs threads concurrently by switching between the threads to make them appear to run simultaneously. The amount of processor time that a thread gets before the processor moves on to another thread is dependent upon the way your system implements multithreading, and is, therefore, indeterminable from inside your Java code. This idea is important when you're trying to write thread-safe code, which I will touch on in a bit. Threads are useful for running long jobs and in computer terms, even a few seconds can be a long time! For example, in AWT programming, if you have a button to save your work, when you click on this button, it will start working to save your work. After you click on it, no other AWT events can be handled until the saving is complete. If the save takes a long time, you can be stuck for a while and get frustrated. If, instead, you created a new thread to do the saving, that task can get done in the background, while you start doing other stuff.

Extending the Thread Class

One way to write code that can be executed in a new thread is by extending the `Thread` class. The `Thread` class is defined in the `java.lang` package, so you don't need to import it. When you extend the `Thread` class, you override the `run()` method and add code there to be executed in a separate thread. To start the thread, call the `start()` method. Calling the `start()` method will eventually result in the `run()` method getting called behind the scenes.

CAUTION

◆ ◆
You should never call the `run()` method directly. If you do that, the code will not start in a new thread, but in the current thread instead.
◆ ◆

The `ThreadTest` class is a simple example of how to extend the `Thread` class and get the thread running. All applications have a thread, called the *main* thread, which executes Java programs. In the `ThreadTest` program, a new thread is created and its `start()` method is called, causing the code in the `run()` method to be executed in the new thread, not the main thread. While the new thread is moving on to the `run()` method, the main thread moves to print the message, `Thread started`. If, instead, the `main()` method called the `run()` method, the main thread would execute the `run()` method, then move on to print the `Thread started` message. Here is the source code:

```
/*
 * ThreadTest
 * Demonstrates how to create a thread by extending the
 * Thread class
 */


public class ThreadTest extends Thread {

    //override the run method
    public void run() {
        for (int i=1; i <=10; i++) {
```

```
                    System.out.println(i);

            }

    }


    public static void main(String args[]) {

        ThreadTest test = new ThreadTest();

        //start the thread

        test.start();

        System.out.println("Thread started");

    }


}
```

This simple example prints the numbers 1 through 10 in a new thread. Figure 6.7 shows the output. Notice that the `Thread started` message gets printed before the `run()` method prints its output, even though the `run()` method was called first. This is not guaranteed to happen every time. It just means that the main thread got to its `System.out.println()` method before the new thread got to print anything. If a new thread had not been created, the numbers definitely would have preceded the `Thread started` message.

Figure 6.7

A new thread is created to run `ThreadTest`, which counts to 10.

Implementing the Runnable Interface

There is another way to define a thread's execution. Instead of extending the `Thread` class, you can implement the `Runnable` interface. The `Runnable` interface defines only one method, `run()`, which must be implemented. When you implement the `Runnable` interface, all you have to do is provide a body for the `run()` method to define code that runs in a separate thread.

To start the thread, you still need an instance of the `Thread` class because one of the `Thread` constructors accepts a `Runnable` object. When you construct a `Thread` object this way, you are telling the thread to run the `Runnable` object's `run()` method instead of the `run()` method defined in the `Thread` class. When you call the thread's `start()` method, the `Runnable`'s `run()` method is started in a new thread. `RunnableTest` demonstrates how to implement the `Runnable` interface and start it in a new thread. This example does the same thing as the `ThreadTest` program. Here is the source code:

```
/*
 * RunnableTest
 * Demonstrates how to implement the Runnable interface
 */


public class RunnableTest implements Runnable {

    //must implement the run method
    public void run() {
        for (int i=1; i <= 10; i++) {
            System.out.println(i);
        }
    }


    public static void main(String args[]) {
        RunnableTest test = new RunnableTest();
        //Construct a thread with this Runnable
```

```
Thread t = new Thread(test);
//start the thread
t.start();
System.out.println("Thread started");
    }


}
```

You can see the `RunnableTest` output in Figure 6.8.

Why are there two ways of programming threads? Well, for simple threads, extending the `Thread` class is fine because all it needs to do is define code that executes in a separate thread. For more complicated programs, however, the preferred way to create a thread is by extending the `Runnable` interface. For example, say that you have a subclass of `Canvas`, called `Animation Canvas` and you want to define a `run()` method to allow for animation to take place in a separate thread. Because `AnimationCanvas` already extends `Canvas`, it cannot extend another class. Remember, a class can be a direct subclass of only one super-class. This means that `AnimationCanvas` can't extend `Thread`, too. Instead, `AnimationCanvas` should implement the `Runnable` interface so that it can extend `Canvas` *and* be run in a new thread.

Figure 6.8

The `Runnable` Test class implements the `Runnable` interface. Here, a new thread runs the `Runnable` Test.

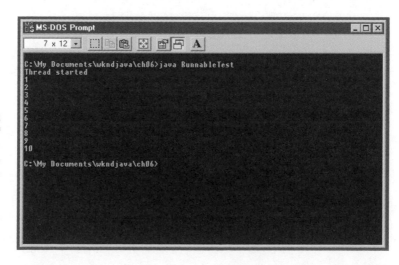

The Thread.sleep() Method

The `Thread.sleep()` method is a static method that is defined in the `Thread` class. The method pauses the currently running thread for a specified number of milliseconds. When you call the `Thread.sleep()` method, you have to handle the `InterruptedException` exception that it throws. You need to do this because the thread can be interrupted by another thread calling the `interrupt()` method and stop `Thread.sleep()` from sleeping; you have to handle this situation. A sleeping thread might be interrupted if the application is closing. If, for example, you have a thread that updates a file every hour for as long as the application is running, you will want to stop the thread when the application exits. When the application is terminated, you call the `interrupt()` method on the thread, so it stops sleeping. Then the code that handles the `InterruptedException` can check for the flag that is set when the application is shutting down and close the file that is being updated. The `SleepTest` example program demonstrates a simpler use of the `Thread.sleep()` method:

```
/*
 * SleepTest
 * Demonstrates how to make a Thread sleep
 */

public class SleepTest extends Thread {

  public void run() {
    for (int i=0; i < 10; i++) {
      if (i % 2 == 0) System.out.println("Tic");
      else System.out.println("Toc");
      try {
        Thread.sleep(1000);
      } catch (InterruptedException e) {}
    }
  }
```

```
public static void main(String args[]) {
    SleepTest t = new SleepTest();
    t.start();
}

}
```

The `SleepTest` program alternately prints `tic` and `toc` and sleeps for one second (1,000 milliseconds) between each, simulating the ticking of a clock. It doesn't handle the `InterruptedException` because I never interrupt the thread. Figure 6.9 shows the output. Of course, you'll want to run this program for yourself so you can see the pause between each printing.

Writing Thread-Safe Java Programs

When you write a program that uses multiple threads that execute concurrently, you need to be careful because you can't predict the order in which things happen. The `ConcurrentThreadTest` uses multiple threads to print a sequence of numbers. It uses the `Thread(Runnable, String)` constructor to construct its threads. The second argument in this constructor is a `String`, which is used as the name of the constructed thread. You'll print this along with each number to tell you which thread is printing the number.

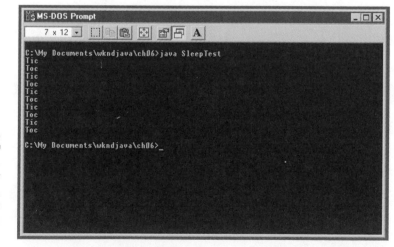

Figure 6.9

The `SleepTest` program alternately prints tic and toc, sleeping one second between each.

The n variable is an `int`. The `run()` method runs while n is less than 20 and calls the `add()` method. The `add()` method increments the n variable and assigns the value to m, a variable that is local to the `add()` method. Then the `add()` method puts the currently executing thread to sleep for a random amount of time to simulate some other processing that can take an indeterminable amount of time.

When the thread wakes up, it prints the value of m. The program prints the name of the current thread after first getting a reference to the current thread by calling `Thread.currentThread()` and then calling `getName()` on that thread reference. The `main()` method sends three different threads to execute the `ConcurrentThreadTest`'s `run()` method. The first two are "`Thread 1`" and "`Thread 2`". After these threads are started by calling their respective `start()` methods, the main thread executes the `run()` method by calling it directly. Here is the source code for `ConcurrentThreadTest.java`:

```
/*
 * ConcurrentThreadTest
 * Demonstrates that you can do multiple things at the same
 * time using Threads
 */

import java.util.Random;

public class ConcurrentThreadTest implements Runnable {
    int n = 0;
    Random rand = new Random();

    public void run() {
        while (n < 20) {
            add();
        }
    }
```

```java
public void add() {
    //check the thread termination condition here too
    if (n < 20) {
        int m = ++n;
        try {
            //sleep a random number of time
            int sleepTime = rand.nextInt(1000) + 1;
            Thread.sleep(sleepTime);
        } catch (InterruptedException e) {
        }
        Thread curr = Thread.currentThread();
        System.out.println("m=" + m + " ("
            + curr.getName() + ")");
    }    }


public static void main(String args[]) {
    Runnable runnable = new ConcurrentThreadTest();
    Thread thread1 = new Thread(runnable, "Thread 1");
    Thread thread2 = new Thread(runnable, "Thread 2");

    System.out.println("Starting Thread 1...");
    thread1.start();
    System.out.println("Starting Thread 2...");
    thread2.start();
    System.out.println("Running Runnable from main...");
    runnable.run();
}


}
```

You can see the output for two separate runs of this program in Figure 6.10. They are different. The difference between the runs demonstrates the unpredictability of multithreaded programs. As you can see, the numbers aren't even printed in order. If the add() method didn't have to be processed in some order, this would not be a problem at all. But what if you required this method to be executed in numerical order? There are instances in which you have to do something like this. For example, what if you are reading a file that needs to be processed sequentially? You might have multiple threads working for other purposes, but that one file reader method needs to be handled carefully. In that case, the type of multithreading solution used in the ConcurrentThreadTest program will not work.

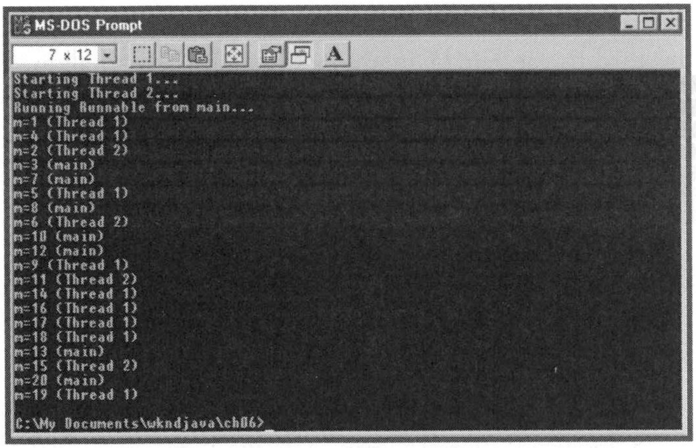

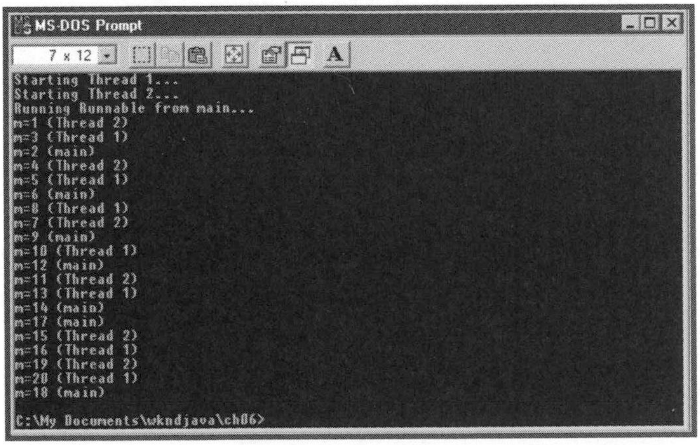

Figure 6.10

Multiple threads running simultaneously produce unpredictable results.

The output of the `ConcurrentThreadTest` was out of order and unpredictable because multiple threads executed the `add()` method concurrently. For example, the first thread incremented n and assigned the value 1 to m. The m variable is local to the `add()` method and is specific to each thread. While the first thread was sleeping, the second thread could come in and get the value 2 assigned to its version of the m variable. The second thread could be faster and print out the number 2 before the first thread even wakes up. When the first thread finally does wake up, it will print the number 1 and cause the numbers to be out of order. To avoid multithreading problems, you can use the `synchronized` keyword. The `synchronized` keyword is used to specify a block of code that can have only one thread executing in it at any given time.

The `ConcurrentSynchronizedThreadTest` program is different from the `ConcurrentThreadTest` program only in that it adds the `synchronized` keyword to the `add()` method. This tells Java to allow only one thread at a time in that method. When a thread enters the `add()` method, the `add()` method is locked; no other threads can get in. When the original thread exits the `add()` method, the `add()` method is unlocked and another thread is allowed to enter. Because only one thread can be in the `add()` method at a time, the numbers are guaranteed to be in order. Here is the source code for `ConcurrentSynchronizedThreadTest.java`.

```
/*

 * ConcurrentSynchronizedThreadTest

 * Demonstrates that you can do multiple things at the same

 * time using Threads

 */


import java.util.Random;


public class ConcurrentSynchronizedThreadTest implements Runnable {

    int n = 0;

    Random rand = new Random();
```

```java
public void run() {
    while (n < 20) {
        add();
    }
}


/* the synchronized keyword makes a big difference */
public synchronized void add() {
    //check the thread termination condition here too
    if (n < 20) {
        int m = ++n;
        try {
            //sleep a random number of time
            int sleepTime = rand.nextInt(1000) + 1;
            Thread.sleep(sleepTime);
        } catch (InterruptedException e) {
        }
        Thread curr = Thread.currentThread();
        System.out.println("m=" + m + " ("
            + curr.getName() + ")");
    }
}



public static void main(String args[]) {
    Runnable runnable = new ➥
    ConcurrentSynchronizedThreadTest();
    Thread thread1 = new Thread(runnable, "Thread 1");
    Thread thread2 = new Thread(runnable, "Thread 2");
```

```
        System.out.println("Starting Thread 1...");

        thread1.start();

        System.out.println("Starting Thread 2...");

        thread2.start();

        System.out.println("Running Runnable from main...");

        runnable.run();

    }


}
```

Figure 6.11 shows that the numbers are printed in order.

Wrapping Up

This afternoon you learned how to write and implement an interface. You applied this knowledge to create an event model for the calculator program and also to abstract the calculator's view by creating the `CalculatorViewer` interface. Then you updated the calculator program to make use of the custom event model that you created.

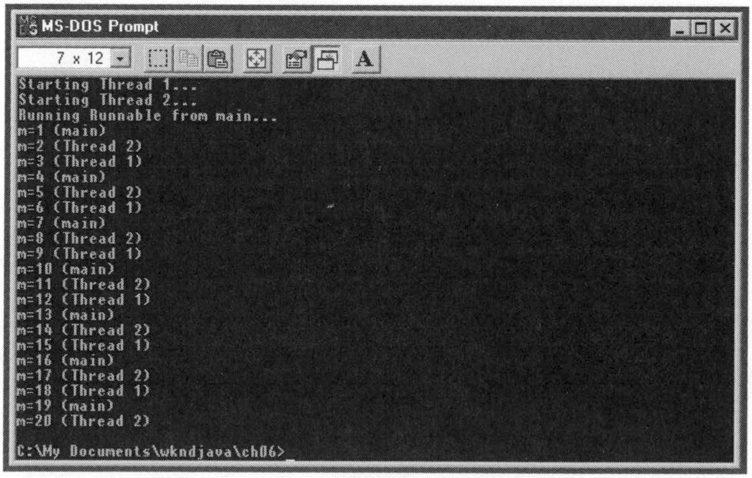

Figure 6.11

No matter how many times you run this program, the output will be in numerical order.

You also learned about Java applets. You learned how to extend the `Applet` class, write the HTML, and pass parameters to an applet. You used this knowledge to write the `CalcluatorApplet` program, which runs the calculator as an applet. Finally, you learned how to do thread programming and how to write thread-safe multithreaded code.

Tonight, you'll finish up the weekend by learning some more advanced Java. You'll learn how to read and write files, how to create your own packages, and how to use the `javadoc` tool to generate API documentation. You'll also learn about the `jar` utility, which you can use to compress files into jars. And, of course, you'll finish the calculator project!

Packages, File I/O, JARs, and Javadocs

- ➤ Creating Packages
- ➤ File Input and Output
- ➤ Using the `JColorChooser` Component
- ➤ Saving Calculator Stuff
- ➤ The `jar` Tool
- ➤ The `javadoc` Tool

This evening, you will learn about Java packages and how to create packages of classes. You will apply this to the calculator project by packaging it into four different packages. You'll also learn how to read and write to the local file system using classes in the `java.io` package. As an enhancement to the calculator application, you'll learn how to use the `JColorChooser` component to allow someone to change the colors of the `DigitalDisplay` component while the calculator application is running. Next, you'll apply what you learned about the `JColor Chooser` component and the `java.io` package to save the calculator's colors and audit trail. This session also introduces two new tools that are widely used by Java developers. The `jar` tool zips (compresses) multiple files into a single file, and the `javadoc` tool generates HTML documentation for your code.

What Are Packages?

Packages are the primary means of organizing Java code. A package contains classes that are related in some way. For example, the `java.lang` package contains a number of classes that are fundamental to the Java programming language. The `java.lang` package contains such widely used classes as `Object`, `String`, `System`, `Thread`, `Math`, and many others. These classes are related in that they define the Java programming language. The `java.lang` package is automatically imported into Java programs by default. Another example of a package is the `java.awt` package, which you already used, that contains classes for building graphical user interfaces and rendering graphics and images. You've been importing packages in almost all of the programs in this book. Now, you'll learn more about packages and how to create them yourself.

Why are packages useful? Looking at very small applications, such as the single-class examples in this book, you would not really see a need for packaging. Single test classes could only benefit from packages if they were part of something bigger. Larger programs, such as a retail store's point-of-sale system or even a computer game, can be made up of a vast amount of classes. If they were not organized in some way, the code would be pure chaos! Think of it this way: You probably have a lot of files on your computer, right? I hope that they're not all in the same folder! You more than likely have a nice directory structure in which you have many different folders that separate all of your files into smaller groups of related files. That is really the idea behind packaging. Packaging allows you to organize your code, making individual classes easier to find by functionality.

Another package benefit is that they reduce problems associated with duplicate class names. You can't have two classes with the same name in the same package. As a rule of thumb, it is not a good idea to duplicate class names, but it sometimes makes sense to do so. For example, there are two `Date` classes in Java. You played around with the `java.util.Date` class Saturday afternoon, so you know that class is for representing a specific instance of time. The other `Date` class is `java.sql.Date`. The `java.sql` package, which is not covered in this book, allows you to access and process data in a database. At the `java.sql` core is Structured Query Language, or SQL (pronounced *sequel*) for short. Very basically put, SQL is used to ask a database to do something with some data (for example, select, insert, delete, update). The `DATE` data type is used in SQL to use dates in databases. The `java.sql.Date` class represents the SQL `DATE` data type. You can see why both of these classes are named `Date`. Providing they are in different packages, you can have multiple classes with the same name.

Packaging is also used to identify the individual, company, or organization that owns the classes, as packages conform to naming conventions. A package name should be lowercase and should be prefixed with a top-level domain name (for example, com, edu, mil, net, org, or a two-letter ISO country code). The second level of a package name is typically an identifier, such as a company name. For example, Sun uses the `com.sun` package name for its products that are written in the Java programming language.

Yet another benefit of packages is that they allow you to provide another level of protection for classes, variables, and methods. Package-level protection differs from class-level protection. In the next section, you will see how access modifiers affect packages.

Access Modifier Effects on Packages

A class uses access modifiers to define which other classes may access its variables, its methods, and the class itself. The access modifiers are as follows:

➤ `public`

➤ `protected`

➤ `private`

➤ friendly

NOTE You already learned about `public`, `protected`, and `private` on Saturday morning. A new one, *friendly*, sometimes also called *package*, is introduced here; "friendly" is not a keyword, so don't do this:

```
friendly int myFriendlyInt = 2;
```

The word "friendly" is used to describe the access that is granted to other classes when none of the other three access modifiers are specified. To give `myFriendlyInt` friendly access, do it without specifying the access modifier, like this:

```
int myFriendlyInt = 2;
```

The `public` access modifier is the most generous one. A public class, variable, or method may be accessed from any other class without restriction. Even classes in other packages are not restricted from accessing public features. Public methods are visible to other classes to provide access to its features. As you know, variables are typically never public, but are accessed through public methods that protect the variables from corruption.

The `private` access modifier is the least generous one. A private variable or method may only be accessed by an instance of the class that declares the variable or method. No other class, whether it is in the same package or in a different package, may access private features. Not even a subclass may access its super-class's private features. No classes, except for inner classes, may be declared to be private. Private methods do specific work for the class that declares them, and it typically would be useless and/or dangerous to give other classes access to these methods. Most instance variables are private or at least protected. Giving other classes direct access to instance variables increases the possibility of corruption.

The `protected` access modifier is less generous than `public`, but more generous than `private`. A top-level class may not have protected access. Only variables, methods, and inner-classes may be protected. Protected features are accessible to all classes within the package that declares the protected features. In addition, a subclass that resides in a different package than its super-class can access the protected features of its super-class. No non-subclass may access protected features of another class in a different package. Always consider inheritance and package structure when deciding which access modifier to use.

The *friendly* access modifier is actually more restrictive than `protected`, which makes the *friendly* moniker a bit unintuitive. However, it is less restrictive than `private`. Friendly protection is friendly only to other classes that share the same package. Friendly protection is very similar to protected protection. Friendly features are accessible to all classes within the same package as the class that declares the friendly features. Also, subclasses can access the friendly features of their super-class. Friendly access is different than protected access in that a subclass does not have access to friendly features of its super-class if the super-class is in a different package. Another difference is that while classes cannot be protected, they can be friendly. Table 7.1 summarizes how access modifiers affect the way classes can access other classes' features.

Including a Class in a Package

You already learned how to import classes from other packages, but how do you declare a class to be part of a specific package? First things first. You have to create a directory structure for your package. For example, if you create a package named `com.mycorp.mypackage`, you must first create a directory (folder) called `com`. Under `com`, you must create a directory called `mycorp`; then under `mycorp`, you have to create a directory called `mypackage`. Once you create the directory structure, you add source files (`*.java`) to the `mypackage` directory. Just having the directory structure in place does not provide Java enough information to know what package your class belongs to. For example, your `com` folder can be located in a folder named `myjava`. Who's to say that `myjava` isn't part of the package structure? You have to provide the package information for a class so that Java will know what directory structure is part of your package, and what part of the directory structure is not part of the

TABLE 7.1 ACCESS MODIFIER PROTECTION

Class Accessibility	public	protected	*friendly*	private
Same class	yes	yes	yes	yes
Same package subclass	yes	yes	yes	no
Same package non-subclass	yes	yes	yes	no
Other package subclass	yes	yes	no	no
Other package non-subclass	yes	no	no	no

package. This is where the `package` keyword comes in. For example, to add a class, `MyClass`, to the package structure just described, its package declaration statement looks like this:

```
package com.mycorp.mypackage;
```

The name of the package follows the `package` keyword. As usual, a semicolon ends the statement. The package statement must be the first statement in a Java source file. It comes before the `import` statements. To access `MyClass` from a class that is in a different package, you have to import `MyClass` with the familiar `import` statement, like this:

```
import com.mycorp.mypackage.MyClass;
```

Or, if you are importing multiple classes of the package, use the asterisk:

```
import com.mycorp.mypackage.*;
```

That's not all, though. Java needs to know where to find your package. When you import classes that are provided in the Java SDK, Java knows where to find them because they're all in the same place—the location of the SDK itself. Your packages can be anywhere, though. Staying with the same example, say that you do have the `com` directory in a directory called `myjava` and you're trying to access `MyClass` from another class called `MyOtherClass`. If `MyOtherClass` is in the `myjava` directory or in a different package that has `myjava` as its root directory, Java will not have any problem finding `MyClass`. That's because, by default, Java searches the current directory (`myjava`, in this case) when looking for classes and source files. When you compile `MyClass` or `MyOtherClass`, you have to do it while working in the `myjava` directory, not the `mypackage` directory. There is a way to specify other locations for your packages and classes, so you don't have to share a directory. You must set the classpath to accomplish this.

In Java, the classpath is the location where Java can find the classes that it needs. There are two ways to set the classpath. You can use it as an option to Java commands, or you can set the `CLASSPATH` environment variable. Say that you are compiling `MyOtherClass` from a directory called `test`, and you make references to `MyClass`. You must set the classpath in order for Java to be able to find it. Here is how it would look if you were to use the -classpath option in the javac command.

```
javac -classpath C:\myjava;. MyOtherClass.java
```

Place the -classpath option after the javac command, followed by the directories that you are adding to the classpath. A semicolon separates each path. The dot (.) signifies the current directory. In this case, you add the test directory to the classpath so that Java can find any other classes in that directory that MyOtherClass may need. I should emphasize here that when adding directories to your classpath, you add the directory that is underneath your package structure, not the directories that are part of your package structure.

Alternatively, you can set the CLASSPATH environment variable. Java checks for the existence of this environment variable. If it does exist, it adds the paths that it defines to the classpath. Here is how you would set this up at the MS-DOS Prompt.

```
set CLASSPATH=C:\myjava;.
```

Setting the CLASSPATH variable in this way saves you from having to reenter the -classpath option each time you compile or run Java programs. Note that an environment variable is specific to the MS-DOS Prompt session in which you created it. To make the CLASSPATH more permanent, add the preceding code to your autoexec.bat file for Windows 95, 98, and ME, or add it to your environment variables in Windows NT, 2000, or XP similar to how you set up the PATH variable Friday night. Just so you know, you don't need to bother with the class path for the calculator application.

CAUTION Be careful that you don't want to screw up your autoexec.bat file because doing so can adversely affect your computer. If you're unsure of yourself, don't bother with the permanent setting and just use either the -classpath option or set the CLASSPATH variable per session. Also, it is very important that you make a backup of your autoexec.bat file when you edit it so that you can always restore it if you make a mistake!

Packaging the Calculator Application

Now that you know about packages and how to create packages and add classes to them, you can apply this knowledge to the calculator application. First, create the `src` directory—put it wherever you want. You're going to copy all of the source code into `src`, in the appropriate package directories. The base package for the calculator application is going to be `com.wknd java.calculator`. (`wkndjava` is just an abbreviation for this book's title. I'm using it to represent a fictional company identifier.) There are three sub-packages, called `event`, `exception`, and `gui`. Their names are descriptive of the functions of the classes that these packages will contain. Here is the directory structure that you need to build your packages:

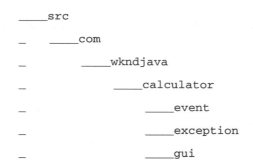

```
_____src
_       _____com
_              _____wkndjava
_                     _____calculator
_                             _____event
_                             _____exception
_                             _____gui
```

Now, you're going to copy the source files into these directories. Because the classes will no longer be in the same package, you'll need to import from other packages those classes on which you're dependent. Tables 7.2 through 7.5 list the classes by their new packages. Copy all of the calculator application's source files into their appropriate packages, as the tables list them. Do not copy the class files; after you build the package structure, you'll have to recompile everything anyway.

The `com.wkndjava.calculator` package is the base package for the calculator application. It contains only one class. The main `Calculator` class that controls the calculator application is the only class needed here. Copy the `Calculator.java` file into the `calculator` directory. Add the `import` statements listed in Table 7.2 to the top of the `Calculator.java` source file. If you have trouble adding the import statements, take a peek at Appendix B (which you can find on the Web at http://www.premier pressbooks.com/downloads.asp). It lists all of the source files, in their entirety. At this point, you only need to look at the `import` and `package` statements. The `package` statement at the top of the `Calculator.java` source code file must look like this:

```
package com.wkndjava.calculator;
```

There are some other changes in those files that you'll be making later tonight.

The `com.wkndjava.calculator.event` package is for your custom event classes. The `CalculatorKeypadEvent` class goes there, along with the listener for the events, `CalculatorKeypadListener`. The `Calculator KeyMap` class goes there, too. Copy the source files for these three classes into the `event` package. As you can see in Table 7.3, there are no import statements to add because these classes are not dependent on any other classes in the calculator application.

TABLE 7.2 THE COM.WKNDJAVA.CALCULATOR PACKAGE

Classes	Imports
Calculator	com.wkndjava.calculator.event.*; com.wkndjava.calculator.exception.*; com.wkndjava.calculator.gui.*;

TABLE 7.3 THE COM.WKNDJAVA.CALCULATOR.EVENT PACKAGE

Classes	Imports
CalculatorKeyMap	(None)
CalculatorKeypadEvent	(None)
CalculatorKeypadListener	(None)

The `com.wkndjava.calculator.exception` package is for the calculator application's two exception classes, `CalculatorException` and `Digital DisplayOverflowException`. Copy their source files into the `exception` directory and add the `package` statement to them. Table 7.4 lists these classes. No imports are necessary.

The `com.wkndjava.calculator.gui` package is for all of the interface stuff, which is all of the rest of the classes. Not all of the classes are GUI components. Some of the classes are here just because the GUI Components depend on them. `CalculatorApplet` goes here because it is a `Calculator Viewer`. I'll come back to the way this package structure affects how to run the applet. (At this point, it's broken.)

Table 7.5 lists the classes that should be added to the `com.wkndjava. calculator.gui` package and the import statements that have to be included. Copy all of their source files to the `gui` folder and add the import statements as they are listed in Table 7.5. Don't forget to add this statement to all of the source files:

```
package com.wkndjava.calculator.gui;
```

Recompiling the Calculator Application

Okay, so you shuffled the source files around. Your're still not done. Now, you have to compile all of the source files (because you moved them around, added `package` statements, and added some new `import` statements). First, create a new directory named `classes`. Make sure that you put the `classes` directory into the same directory as the `src` directory (not in the `src` directory, but at the same level). Open your command prompt and get into the `src` directory (you must be in the `src` directory for this to work). Now, at the command prompt, type the following command (the slashes go the other way if you're using Unix (/)):

```
javac -d ..\classes com\wkndjava\calculator\➡
gui\CalculatorApplet.java
```

TABLE 7.4 THE COM.WKNDJAVA.CALCULATOR.EXCEPTION PACKAGE

Classes	Imports
CalculatorException	*(None)*
DigitalDisplayOverflowException	*(None)*

TABLE 7.5 THE COM.WKNDJAVA.CALCULATOR.GUI PACKAGE

Classes	Imports
CalculatorApplet	com.wkndjava.calculator.Calculator; com.wkndjava.calculator.event.*; com.wkndjava.calculator.exception.*;
CalculatorHelper	com.wkndjava.calculator.event.*;
CalculatorKeypad	com.wkndjava.calculator.event.*;
CalculatorModel	com.wkndjava.calculator.event.*;
CalculatorView	com.wkndjava.calculator.Calculator; com.wkndjava.calculator.event.*; com.wkndjava.calculator.exception.*;
CalculatorViewer	com.wkndjava.calculator.event.*;
DigitalDisplay	com.wkndjava.calculator.exception.*;
LiquidCrystalComponent	*(None)*
LiquidCrystalDigit	*(None)*
LiquidCrystalNegative	*(None)*

The -d option of the javac command lets you specify where the class files will go. This command adds all of the class files to the classes directory. At this point, you are separating the class files from the source files. First off, I wanted to show you that Java programs can be run without the .java files. Also, I wanted to show you how to use the -d option. Lastly, this prepares you for jarring the classes later on. Did you notice that the only file that the command specifies is CalculatorApplet.java? Actually, that's all you needed to specify. Because CalculatorApplet.java is dependent on other classes, and those other classes are dependent on other classes, this works. Java compiles all of the other files that Calculator Applet.java relies on and, due to the fact that this touches all of the source files, everything gets compiled! You could also have compiled all of the files directly, but that would have taken a bit of time. Or you could have specified all of the source files in a particular directory, like this:

```
javac -d ..\classes com\wkndjava\calculator\gui\*.java
```

Now that everything's compiled, look in the classes directory, where all of the class files were sent. You should see a directory structure like this:

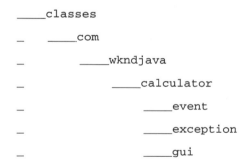

```
_____classes
_        _____com
_            _____wkndjava
_                _____calculator
_                    _____event
_                    _____exception
_                    _____gui
```

It looks just like the directory structure that you created in the src directory, doesn't it? The difference is that the folders contain .class files instead of .java files.

Now that you have packaged the calculator application, you have to run it a bit differently. From your command prompt, get into the classes directory. You're going to run the Calculator class file. You have to specify the package from here for it to work. To run the calculator application, type the following command:

```
java com.wkndjava.calculator.Calculator
```

Use the dot as the separator, not the slash. Make sure everything is working properly. Once you're all set, move ahead to learn about file input and output.

TIP

To list all of the options for the `java` and `javac` commands, simply type **java** or **javac** at the command prompt with no other arguments. This will list the options, along with their brief descriptions.

File Input and Output

The `java.io` package provides for reading and writing to the file system. It provides classes that allow you to read and write files to your computer. Up to this point, all of the programs in this book temporarily stored data only while the programs were running. Using the `java.io` package, you'll learn how to save data for later retrieval. Why is this useful? Take bank software, for example. What good would it be if the software didn't save your account balance somewhere? It would be useless. Another example is word-processing software. It wouldn't be so great if you couldn't save your documents, would it? Most large software packages have to access the file system to be useful. Java provides this function for you behind the scenes with the classes in the `java.io` package. These classes provide an abstraction for you, so you don't have to have intimate knowledge of your operating system's specific file system. The `java.io` package allows you to write code that will port to any operating system without making you rewrite anything. Good news! This package is fairly straightforward and easy to use. First, I'll go over the basics and show you a couple of sample programs that use the `java.io` package; then you'll see how to get the calculator application to save stuff for you.

Overview of the java.io Package

The `java.io` package contains classes for I/O, that is, input and output. The term I/O is not exclusive to files. In fact, the `System.out.println()` method that you're so familiar with is defined in this package. `System.out` is actually a `PrintStream` object, which is found in the `java.io` package. The `System.out` object is open to the standard output stream, so you can write messages to wherever standard output goes, such as the MS-DOS Prompt, for example. An *output stream* is just something that accepts output bytes. The `PrintStream` class defines the `println()` method. This method prints a string to an output stream and terminates the string with the line separator string. The line separator string is not necessarily the newline character (\n). The line separator string varies among operating systems. The `java.io` package also contains the `Serializable` interface, which is implemented by any class to indicate that its state can be serialized, basically allowing it to be read and written across a network or to the file system, for example.

In this section, you'll learn about streams, readers, and writers. You'll learn how to read standard input from the command prompt. To perform I/O operations in Java, you have to import the `java.io` package classes that you need. Before you start looking at actual code, take a look at Table 7.6, which summarizes some of the `java.io` classes, to get an overview of the package you'll be working with.

TABLE 7.6 THE JAVA.IO PACKAGE CLASSES

Class	Description
Serializable	Allows you to read/write object states. (This interface has no methods in it. Simply specifying that a class implements this interface makes it serializable.)
BufferedInputStream	Adds the ability to buffer input from input streams.
BufferedOutputStream	Adds the ability to buffer output from output streams.

TABLE 7.6 THE JAVA.IO PACKAGE CLASSES

Class	Description
BufferedReader	Buffers character input streams.
BufferedWriter	Buffers character output streams.
File	Represents a file on the file system.
FileInputStream	Reads bytes from a file.
FileOutputStream	Writes bytes to a file.
FileReader	Reads a character file.
FileWriter	Writes characters to a file.
InputStream	Abstract super-class for byte input streams.
InputStreamReader	Reads bytes and translates them into characters
ObjectInputStream	Reads objects from an input stream.
ObjectOutputStream	Writes objects to an output stream.
OutputStream	Abstract super-class for byte output streams.
PrintStream	Allows you to conveniently print string representations of Java data types.
Reader	Abstract super-class for character input streams.
Writer	Abstract super-class for character output streams.
EOFException	Indicates that EOF (end-of-file) has been reached unexpectedly.
IOException	Indicates that an I/O exception occurred.

Streams, Readers, and Writers

Streams are open to a source of information (data) and allow for the passage of data to and from the data source. To read input, you need to open an input stream to the data source, read the information, and then close the input stream. Similarly, to write output, you need to open an output stream to the data source, write the information, and then close the output stream. A common programming error is forgetting to close I/O streams after I/O operations are complete. Keeping streams open uses system resources, so try to remember to always close your streams when you're done with them.

Character streams are for reading and writing 16-bit character data. The `java.io` package's `Reader` and `Writer` class are the abstract super-classes for other classes that represent character streams. You should use character streams for reading and writing textual data. Java character streams have the ability to understand characters in the Unicode character set, which is the specification for Java characters.

Byte streams are for reading and writing bytes. Bytes are only 8-bits and, therefore, are not sufficient for reading 16-bit characters. The `java.io` package's `InputStream` and `OuputStream` are the abstract super-classes for byte streams. You should use their subclasses for reading binary data. *Binary* data is usually used to store non-textual information such as images and sounds.

Reading Standard Input

You have already learned how to accept command-line arguments. Now, you'll learn how to accept user input whenever you need it. Earlier, you learned about the `System.out` object, which is used for writing to the standard output stream. `System.out`'s counterpart, the `System.in` object, is used for reading from the standard input stream. `System.in` is an `InputStream` object, which means that it reads bytes from an input stream. Specifically, `System.out` reads from the standard input stream. Because you want to read character data from the standard input stream, you need to convert the bytes into characters. For that function, you'll use the `InputStreamReader` class. The constructor for the `InputStream Reader` class accepts an `InputStream` object as a parameter. To read standard input, you need to pass `System.in` as the `InputStream` argument to this constructor so that the `InputStreamReader` will convert the bytes read in by `System.in` into characters.

To enhance performance, you'll also use a `BufferedReader`. The constructor for the `BufferedReader` class takes a `Reader` object as an argument. You'll pass in the `InputStreamReader` so that the `BufferedReader` will buffer input from the `InputStreamReader`. A *buffer* is a temporary storage area for large amounts of data. `BufferedReader` reads a large amount of data ahead of time to limit the number of times the underlying data is accessed. Without buffering, each method call made to retrieve data would cause bytes to be read from the input stream. This is costly and adversely affects performance. Reading data using `InputStreamReaders` is especially costly, so it is a good idea to buffer these types of streams using `BufferedReader`.

The `StandardInputTest` sample program demonstrates how to use these classes to read input from the standard input stream. Here is the source code:

```
/*
 * StandardInputTest
 * Demonstrates how to accept standard input
 */

import java.io.*;

public class StandardInputTest {

    public static void main(String args[]) {
        BufferedReader reader;
```

```
        String name;
        reader = new BufferedReader(
            new InputStreamReader(System.in));

        System.out.print("What's your name: ");

        try {
            name = reader.readLine();
            reader.close();

            System.out.println("Hello, " + name + "!");
        } catch (IOException e) {
            System.out.println("Could not read input");
            System.out.println(e.getMessage());
        }

    }


}
```

The `StandardInputTest` program declares a `BufferedReader` object called `reader`. Then it instantiates `reader`, passing a new `InputStream` `Reader` object to the `BufferedReader` constructor. The `InputStream` `Reader` constructor gets `System.in` as its `InputStream` parameter. At this point, `reader` is ready to read from the standard input stream. The program then prints a message to prompt for a name. The `System.out.print()` method is used here, which allows for typing the input on the same line as the prompt. The `reader.readLine()` method causes the program to read a line of input.

At this point, you can start typing input into the command prompt. The program will block until it reaches a line separator. When you press Enter, the `readLine()` method will pick up the resulting line separator and return a `String` object that represents the input typed at the command prompt. The `name` variable accepts the value returned from `readLine()`, which should be a person's name. After the program reads the input, it closes the input stream by calling `reader.close()`.

Both the `readLine()` and the `close()` methods throw an `IOException` if an unexpected I/O exception occurs, so you need to wrap these method calls in a `try-catch` block and handle the `IOException` (or declare `main()` to throw `IOException`). To demonstrate that the input was read in properly, the program prints a message, "Hello, *name*!" where *name* is the string that `readLine()` reads. Figure 7.1 shows what a typical run of `StandardInputTest` should look like.

Reading and Writing Files

Reading and writing files is similar to reading and writing standard input and output. The difference is that you need to open the streams to files instead of using the standard input and output streams. The `FileCopy Test` program demonstrates how to read and write files by copying data from a source file to a newly created destination file. To read and write files, you need to instantiate a `File` object. The `File()` constructor you're using here accepts a single `String` object, which represents the filename.

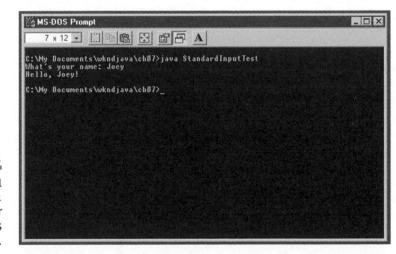

Figure 7.1

`Standard InputTest` reads in your name, and says "hi" to you.

If the file is in the same directory as the program, you can just pass in the filename. If the file is in a different location, you pass in the full path.

TIP

File paths differ among operating systems. For example, Windows uses the backslash (\) as the path separator, but Unix uses the forward slash (/). To keep your programs platform-independent, you should make use of the `pathSeparator` and `pathSeparator Char` static fields of the `File` class, instead of hard-coding the path separators. These two static fields contain the system-dependent path separator regardless of the system your code is running on, making your code portable among different operating systems.

Here is the source code for `FileCopyTest`:

```
/*
 * FileCopyTest
 * Demonstrates how to read and write files.
 */

import java.io.*;

public class FileCopyTest {

    public static void main(String args[]) {
        //signifies end of file
        final int EOF = -1;
        //stores each character as it is read
        int c;

        File original = new File("original.txt");
        File copy = new File("copy.txt");

        try {
```

```
            FileReader reader = new FileReader(original);
            FileWriter writer = new FileWriter(copy);

            while ( (c = reader.read()) != EOF) {
                writer.write(c);
            }

            reader.close();
            writer.close();

            System.out.println(
                "Copied \"original.txt\" to \"copy.txt\"");

        } catch (FileNotFoundException fnfe) {
            System.out.println("File not found: "
                + fnfe.getMessage());
        } catch (IOException ioe) {
            System.out.println("IOException: "
                + ioe.getMessage());
        }
    }

}
```

The `FileCopyTest` program instantiates two `File` objects, named `original` and `copy`. `original` is the file that `FileCopyTest` will read. The program constructs `original` object by passing in the `original.txt` filename. `copy` is the file that `FileCopyTest` will copy `original`'s data to. The filename for `copy` is `copy.txt`. To read the `original.txt` file, a new `FileReader` object, `reader`, is constructed with `original` as the parameter to `FileReader()`. There is another `FileReader()` constructor that accepts a `String` filename, which it uses to construct its own `File` object.

Because Java is going to be reading this file, the file must already exist. If the `FileReader()` constructors can't find the file passed in, they throw a `FileNotFoundException`. That's why the `FileCopyTest` program must handle `FileNotFoundException`.

The `FileCopyTest` program creates a `FileWriter` object, too. This object, `writer`, is used to write a new file. Because you pass in `copy` as the `File` argument to the `FileWriter()` constructor, the new file gets named `copy.txt`. The `FileCopyTest` program uses a `FileReader` and a `FileWriter` because the files are character files. You might consider also using `BufferedReader` and `BufferedWriter` to enhance performance here, as `FileReaders` and `FileWriters` are costly. For binary files, use `FileInputStream` and `FileOutputStream` instead of `FileReader` and `FileWriter`.

The `while` loop reads all of the characters from `original.txt` individually using the `read()` method. The `read()` method reads in a character and returns it as an `int`. Because you don't want the `while` loop to run forever, you need a way to know when you're all done reading the input. The `read()` method returns -1 when it reaches the end of the file (EOF). The `while` loop reads all characters from `original.txt` until it gets the EOF flag. Each time a character is read, the program immediately writes it to the `copy.txt` file. When the file is completely copied, both the input stream and the output stream are closed. Before running this program, the `original.txt` file should already exist. The result of running this program is that a new file, called `copy.txt`, will be created and will be an exact copy of `original.txt`. Figure 7.2 shows what should happen.

Using the JColorChooser Component

Ah, yes. Now you're ready to start adding some really cool features to the calculator application. Wouldn't it be cool to be able to set the colors of the `DigitalDisplay` while the program is running? Wouldn't it be even cooler to be able to save color preferences so that the calculator program remembers your favorite colors for you? That's what you're going to do.

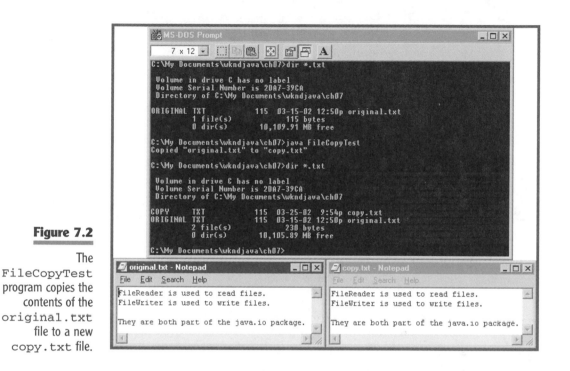

Figure 7.2

The
`FileCopyTest`
program copies the
contents of the
`original.txt`
file to a new
`copy.txt` file.

Oh, but I'm getting ahead of myself here a bit. First, you have to learn how to write code that allows for setting colors. The `JColorChooser` Swing component is a ready-made color-choosing component that will do this for you. This section shows you how to use the `JColorChooser` component. Later on, you'll use the `JColorChooser` component to change the three `DigitalDisplay` colors in real-time, while the calculator program is running.

The `JColorChooser` provides a pane that includes controls that allow a user to change and select colors. Figure 7.3 shows what the `JColor Chooser` component looks like.

The `JColorChooser` pane has three tabs, Swatches, HSB, and RGB. The Swatches pane lets you pick from a set of predefined colors. The HSB pane lets you create a color by specifying its hue, saturation, and brightness. The RGB pane lets you create a color by setting its red, green, and blue values.

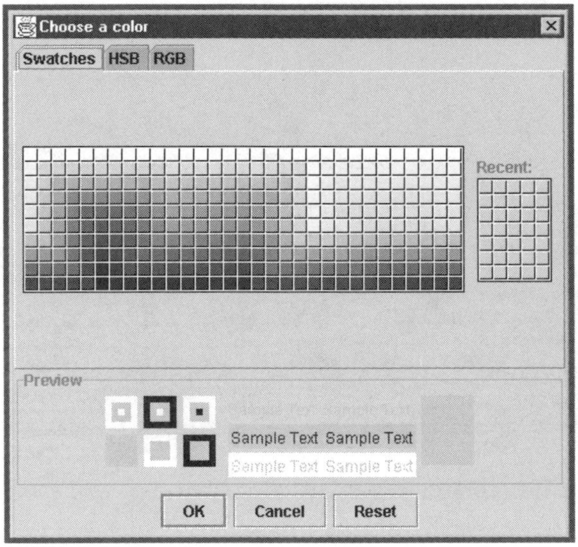

Figure 7.3

The JColor Chooser component lets you visually select a color.

The constructor that you're going to use accepts a Color object. The JColorChooser component uses the Color object as its initial color. For example, to instantiate a JColorChooser object that has its initial color set to black, you call the constructor like this:

```
JColorChooser myChooser = new JColorChooser(Color.black);
```

New JColorChooser components need to be added to containers. Because they are components, you can add JColorChoosers anywhere that other components can be added. In your case, you're going to want to add it to a dialog window, and not directly inside the calculator application frame. Because JColorChoosers are frequently added to dialog windows, the JColorChooser class provides a method that creates a dialog window for you. The createDialog() static method creates a specialized dialog window that contains a JColorChooser component. The createDialog() method accepts six arguments; they are (listed in the order that you pass them to the createDialg() method):

1. Component *c*. The parent component.
2. String *title*. The title for the dialog window.

3. `boolean` *modal*. Indicates whether the dialog window is modal.

4. `JColorChooser` *chooserPane*. The `JColorChooser` component for the dialog.

5. `ActionListener` *okListener*. Listens for OK button clicks.

6. `ActionListener` *cancelListener*. Listens for Cancel button clicks.

Here's an example:

```
JDialog c = JColorChooser.createDialog(this,
    "Select Color", true, myChooser, ok, null);
```

This example creates a new `JColorChooser` `JDialog` object, assuming that this method call appears in a subclass of `Component`. `JDialog` is the Swing version of a dialog window. The first argument is `this`, meaning that the `Component` itself is the parent component for the dialog. The `"Select Color"` argument is the title for the dialog window. `true` is passed to indicate that the dialog should be modal. `myChooser` is some `JColorChooser` object that would have been created somewhere previously in the program. The `ok` argument must be an object that implements the `ActionListener` interface for handling OK button events. The last argument is `null`, which would indicate that Cancel events are not being handled. You'll construct the dialog a bit differently for the calculator application. This was merely an example.

`ActionListener` objects implement their `actionPerformed()` methods to handle the button events. What will you want to do when the user clicks on OK? Well, you might want to get the selected color. That's what the `getColor()` method is for. As an example, the `ok` object from the previous example might have the following `actionPerformed()` method defined in its class:

```
public void actionPerformed(ActionEvent e) {
    myColor = myChooser.getColor();
}
```

This example assumes that the `actionPerformed()` method is only handling OK button events and that `myColor` is a `Color` object. It's easy to see why you'd want to handle OK button events, but why would you care if someone clicked on the Cancel button? Using `JColorChooser`, you can listen for color updates as the user is changing the color, and update your color accordingly. If the user clicks on Cancel, you'd probably want to change your current color back to its original color.

You can listen to `JColorChooser` updates by adding a `ChangeListener` to the `JColorChooser`'s `ColorSelectionModel` object. `ColorSelection Model` is just a class that supports selecting a color. You can get a `JColor Chooser`'s `ColorSelectionModel` object by calling the `getSelection Model()` method. Then you can add a `ChangeListener` to it. `Change Listener` is an interface defined in the `javax.swing.event` package. It only has one method, `stateChanged()`. `ChangeListener`'s only purpose is to listen for when things, such as the color you're interested in, change. That's it. Still, this might be confusing. Here is a code snippet that shows you how this is done:

```
JColorChooser chooser = new JColorChooser(Color.white);
chooser.getSelectionModel().addChangeListener(this);
```

This snippet creates a new `JColorChooser` object, called `chooser`. Next, the code gets access to the `ColorSelectionModel` by calling `getSelection Model()` and adds a `ChangeListener` to the model. The code passes `this` as the `ChangeListener`, which means that the class that this code is defined in must implement the `ChangeListener` interface and, therefore, must also implement the `stateChanged()` method. The `stateChanged()` method will be called every time the color changes. Take a look at this code to see how these events might be handled:

```
public void stateChanged(ChangeEvent e) {
    ColorSelectionModel csm = (ColorSelectionModel)e.getSource();
    Color c = csm.getSelectedColor();
}
```

`ChangeEvent` events are fired when the color changes. The source of these events will be a `ColorSelectionModel` object. You can get the selected color (so you can update whatever color you need) by calling `get SelectedColor()`.

Okay, now you know about the `JColorChooser` component. You're going to use it to allow `DigitalDisplay` colors to be changed on the fly. Not only that, you're going to be able to save the colors so that the calculator application will automatically start with the colors you've selected. You're not quite ready to update the calculator application files, because there are more features to go over, so I'll come back and revisit `JColorChooser` in a moment.

Take a Break

Now is a good time to take a little break. Relax for a bit. When you come back, you'll apply what you've just learned about file I/O and the `JColor Chooser` component to update the calculator application. After that, you'll learn about the `jar` tool and the `javadoc` tool. See 'ya in a few.

Saving Calculator Stuff

You should have all of the information that you need to start updating the calculator application code. The goal now is to be able to save two different things from the calculator application: the color preferences and the audit trail. The color preferences correspond to the three different colors of the `DigitalDisplay` panel—the background color, the unlit color, and the lit color. You'll use a `JColorChooser` to allow the user to select the colors while updating the `DigitalDisplay` and provide a menu option for saving those colors. Remember the audit trail from the creation of the `CalculatorHelper` class? The trail keeps track of all of the calculator application's mathematical operations in string form. You're going to add a dialog window that displays the audit trail for viewing. The calculator application will provide another menu option for saving the audit trail.

Revisiting the Audit Trail

Now, you're going to create the `AuditTrailView` class. The `AuditTrail View` class extends the `JDialog` class so that it is a dialog window. The purpose of the `AuditTrailView` dialog window is to give you a view of the calculator application's audit trail. It has a `JTextArea`, which is the Swing version of the `TextArea` component. The text area will display the actual audit trail text. `JTextAreas` are constructed a bit differently than `java.awt.TextAreas`; specifically, the way that scrollbars are created is different. Read over the code for the `AuditTrailView`, listed here:

```java
/*
 * AuditTrailView
 * A dialog window for viewing the calculator's audit trail
 */

package com.wkndjava.calculator.gui;

import java.awt.*;
import javax.swing.*;

public class AuditTrailView extends JDialog {
    private JTextArea trail;

    public AuditTrailView(Frame owner, String atText) {
        super(owner, "Audit Trail Viewer");

        trail = new JTextArea(atText, 25, 45);
        trail.setFont(new Font("Monospaced", Font.PLAIN, 10));
        trail.setEditable(false);

        JScrollPane scrollPane = new JScrollPane(trail);
```

```
        getContentPane().add(scrollPane, BorderLayout.CENTER);

        setDefaultCloseOperation(WindowConstants.HIDE_ON_CLOSE);
        pack();
    }

    public void setText(String atText) {
        trail.setText(atText);
    }

    public String getText() {
        return trail.getText();
    }

}
```

The `AuditTrailView` dialog window belongs in the `com.wkndjava.calculator.gui` package because it is a GUI component. The `AuditTrailView()` constructor accepts two arguments. The first argument is the `Frame` object that owns the instance of `AuditTrailView`. The second argument is the `String` object, which should be the audit trail text. The constructor calls `super()`, which is the `JDialog()` constructor. The super constructor accepts the `Frame` object as its first argument and a `String` title as its second. The title appears at the top of the dialog window. The `JTextField` object, `trail`, gets an instance by passing the text, the number of rows, and the number of columns to the `JTextField()` constructor. The font is "Monospaced" so that the audit trail text lines up properly.

To add scrollbars to the `JTextArea`, you have to put it in a `JScrollPane`. This is different from the AWT's `TextArea`, where you can specify the scrollbar visibility in the constructor. A `JScrollPane` is the Swing version of the AWT's `ScrollPane` component. Fortunately, there are `JScrollPane()`

constructors that accept a `Component` parameter. The `AuditTrailView` class passes in the `JTextArea` so that the `JScrollPane` will display the `JTextArea` with scrollbars when they are needed. The `AuditTrailView` class has two methods for getting and setting the text. If you're coding along with the book, make sure that you add the `AuditTrailView.java` source file in the `src\com\wkndjava\calculator\gui\` directory. Compile it with the following command from the `src` directory:

```
javac -d ..\classes com\wkndjava\calculator\gui\➡
AuditTrailView.java
```

Adding a Menu

To be able to tell the calculator application when you want to view the audit trail, when you want to set the colors, and when you want to save stuff, you use a menu system. The `CalculatorMenu` class extends `JMenu`, which—you guessed it—is the Swing version of a menu. You create `Jmenus` in the same basic way that you create AWT menus; the difference is that you use Swing components instead of AWT components. To create a menu, create a `JMenu` object. To add selection items to the menus, add `JMenuItems` to the `JMenu`. When you're done creating the menu, set it as a `Frame`'s menu bar. You'll be adding things to the menu. You'll later update the `CalculatorView` and `CalculatorApplet` classes to set the `Calculator Menu` as their menu bars. Here is a listing for `CalculatorMenu.java`:

```
/*
 * CalculatorMenu
 * The menu for the Calculator program
 */


package com.wkndjava.calculator.gui;


import com.wkndjava.calculator.Calculator;
import com.wkndjava.calculator.gui.*;
```

```java
import javax.swing.*;
import java.awt.event.*;
import java.util.*;


public class CalculatorMenu extends JMenuBar {
    private int appType;
    private Vector menuItems;
    //static constants represent menu items for event handling
    public final static String FILE_EXIT = "Exit";
    public final static String FILE_SAVE_AUDIT_TRAIL
        = "Save Audit Trail";
    public final static String FILE_SAVE_COLORS
        = "Save Color Preferences";
    public final static String VIEW_AUDIT_TRAIL = "Audit Trail";
    public final static String VIEW_COLOR_BACKGROUND
        = "Background Color";
    public final static String VIEW_COLOR_UNLIT = "Unlit Color";
    public final static String VIEW_COLOR_LIT = "Lit Color";

    /* The type is either Calculator.APPLICATION or
     * Calculator.APPLET and determines whether or not file
     * operations are enabled */
    public CalculatorMenu(int type) {
        super();

        switch (type) {
            case Calculator.APPLICATION:
            case Calculator.APPLET:
                appType = type;
                break;
```

```java
            default:
                appType = Calculator.APPLET;
        }


        populateMenu();
    }


    private void populateMenu() {
        menuItems = new Vector();


        // File menu
        JMenu file = new JMenu("File");
        if (appType == Calculator.APPLET) {
            file.setEnabled(false);
        }
        JMenuItem fileSaveAt
            = new JMenuItem(FILE_SAVE_AUDIT_TRAIL);
        menuItems.add(fileSaveAt);
        file.add(fileSaveAt);


        JMenuItem fileSaveColors = new ➥
        JMenuItem(FILE_SAVE_COLORS);
        menuItems.add(fileSaveColors);
        file.add(fileSaveColors);


        file.addSeparator();


        JMenuItem fileExit = new JMenuItem(FILE_EXIT);
        menuItems.add(fileExit);
        file.add(fileExit);
```

```java
        add(file);


        //view menu
        JMenu view = new JMenu("View");
        JMenuItem viewAt = new JMenuItem(VIEW_AUDIT_TRAIL);
        menuItems.add(viewAt);
        view.add(viewAt);


        //color submenu
        JMenu colors = new JMenu("Color");
        JMenuItem bkgColor = new JMenuItem(VIEW_COLOR_BACKGROUND);
        menuItems.add(bkgColor);
        colors.add(bkgColor);


        JMenuItem unlitColor = new JMenuItem(VIEW_COLOR_UNLIT);
        menuItems.add(unlitColor);
        colors.add(unlitColor);


        JMenuItem litColor = new JMenuItem(VIEW_COLOR_LIT);
        menuItems.add(litColor);
        colors.add(litColor);
        view.add(colors);
        add(view);
    }


public void addMenuActionListener(ActionListener listener) {
    Iterator itemIter = menuItems.iterator();
    while (itemIter.hasNext()) {
        ((JMenuItem)itemIter.next()).addActionListener(
            listener);
```

```
            }
        }


    }
```

The `CalculatorMenu` class has two instance variables. The `appType` variable is an `int` that keeps track of whether the menu is for an application or an applet. This means that its value should be either `Calculator`
`.APPLICATION` or `Calculator.APPLET`. The menu must be different for applets because applets are restricted from using the local file system. Therefore, if you run the calculator as an applet, you won't be able to read or write files. The second instance variable, `menuItems`, is a `Vector` of `JMenuItem` objects. The vector is used just as a convenient way of keeping track of all your menu items. The `CalculatorMenu` class also defines several static class constants, which are the `String` objects that are used for the menu item labels. As you'll see, when you have to handle the menu's events, having these constants around will be helpful.

The `CalculatorMenu()` constructor accepts only one argument, an `int`. The value passed into the constructor should be either `Calculator`
`.APPLICATION` or `Calculator.APPLET`. If it's not one of those two values, the default `Calculator.APPLET` is used. `Calculator.APPLET` is the default because the applet menu is more restrictive, and it's better to be safe than sorry. The constructor calls the private method, `populateMenu()`, which does all the work of adding all of the menu items to the menu. `populate Menu()` actually creates two submenus for the menu bar—`File` and `View`. The `File` menu is for the save options and also to exit the application. Because applets can't access the file system, the `File` menu is disabled for applets. The `View` menu is for viewing the audit trail, and also for setting the color preferences. Under `View` is the `Color` submenu, which gives you the three color options.

The `CalculatorMenu` class has one more method. The `addMenuAction Listener()` method is for event handling. It adds an `ActionListener` object to listen for menu item selection. The `ActionListener` is added to all of the `JMenuItems` in the `menuItems` `Vector`. The `ActionListener` implements the `actionPerformed()` method, which a `JMenuItem` will call when it gets selected, so you can handle the event.

The `CalculatorMenu` class goes in the `com.wkndjava.calculator.gui` package, so the source code belongs in the `src\com\wkndjava\calculator\gui\` directory. Compile it like this:

```
javac -d ..\classes
com\wkndjava\calculator\gui\CalculatorMenu.java
```

Updating CalculatorViewer

To handle the new menu system, you need to update the `Calculator Viewer` interface and the two classes that implement it. Basically, you're adding six methods. The new methods, as they should be defined in `CalculatorViewer.java`, are as follows:

```
public void addMenuActionListener(ActionListener al);

public void showAuditTrail(String atText);

public void updateAuditTrail(String atText);

public DigitalDisplay getDigitalDisplay();

public void showInfo(String message);
```

The `addMenuActionListener()` method complements the method of the same name in the `CalculatorMenu` class. It provides a way to register listeners to the menu through the `CalculatorViewer` object. The `showAuditTrail()` method calls the `AuditTrailView` component and displays the given audit trail text. The `updateAuditTrail()` method assumes that the `AuditTrailView` component is already showing and just updates the audit trail text. If the `AuditTrailView` isn't already showing, the `updateAuditTrail()` method does nothing. The `getDigitalDisplay()` method returns the `DigitalDisplay` object so you can handle changing its colors. The `showInfo()` method displays a message to the user.

Add the following two instance variables for the new menu and audit trail dialog window to `CalculatorView` and `CalculatorApplet`:

```
private CalculatorMenu menu;

private AuditTrailView auditTrailViewer;
```

Add the new `CalculatorViewer` methods to the `CalculatorView` and `CalculatorApplet` classes. Their implementations are as follows (they're the same for both classes):

```
public void addMenuActionListener(ActionListener al) {

    menu.addMenuActionListener(al);

}


public void showAuditTrail(String atText) {

    if (auditTrailViewer == null) {

        auditTrailViewer = new AuditTrailView(this, atText);

    }

    else {

        auditTrailViewer.setText(atText);

    }

    auditTrailViewer.setVisible(true);

}


public void updateAuditTrail(String atText) {

    if (auditTrailViewer != null && ➡
    auditTrailViewer.isVisible()) {

        auditTrailViewer.setText(atText);

    }

}


public DigitalDisplay getDigitalDisplay() {
```

```
      return display;

}


public void showInfo(String message) {

    JOptionPane.showMessageDialog(this, message);

}
```

The new methods are all pretty straightforward, except for the `show Info()` method. This method calls the static `JOptionPane.showMessage Dialog()` method. `JOptionPane` is a convenient way of popping up standard dialog windows, such as a confirmation dialog, which asks a yes/no question; an input dialog, which prompts you for text input; or some combination of the two. The `JOptionPane.showMessageDialog()` method simply pops up a dialog window that displays the text you pass as the second argument. The first argument is the parent for the dialog.

Instantiating the menu is easy. For the calculator application, add the following two lines of code to the `CalculatorView.java` source file (put it in the constructor right under the call to `super()`):

```
menu = new CalculatorMenu(Calculator.APPLICATION);

setJMenuBar(menu);
```

Do the same for `CalculatorApplet.java`, except pass in `Calculator .APPLET` as the application type to the `Calculator()` constructor:

```
menu = new CalculatorMenu(Calculator.APPLET);

setJMenuBar(menu);
```

That takes care of the `CalculatorViewer` updates. To compile the changes, simply recompile `CalculatorApplet.java`, which, if you remember, will compile everything.

```
javac -d ..\classes com\wkndjava\calculator\gui\➥
CalculatorApplet.java
```

Saving Color Preferences and the Audit Trail

Now you need to handle the menu events. This is a major update for the `Calculator` class. The new source code is listed below. Some of the parts of the `Calculator` class that remain unchanged have been omitted. You'll see that a big chunk of the `calculatorKeyPressed()` method and the entire `main()` method are not included. The code that is new is shown in bold.

```java
/*
 * Calculator
 * The Calculator application
 */


package com.wkndjava.calculator;


import com.wkndjava.calculator.event.*;
import com.wkndjava.calculator.exception.*;
import com.wkndjava.calculator.gui.*;


import java.awt.*;
import java.awt.event.*;
import java.applet.Applet;
import java.io.*;
import javax.swing.*;
import javax.swing.event.*;
import javax.swing.colorchooser.ColorSelectionModel;


public class Calculator implements CalculatorKeypadListener,
        ActionListener {
    private CalculatorViewer view;
    private CalculatorHelper helper;
```

```java
private boolean needNewNumber = false;
private int mode;
public final static int APPLICATION = 1;
public final static int APPLET = 2;


public Calculator(CalculatorViewer ui)
        throws CalculatorException {
    view = ui;
    helper = new CalculatorHelper();
    view.addCalculatorKeypadListener(this);
    view.addMenuActionListener(this);
    if (view instanceof Frame) {
        ((Frame)view).setVisible(true);
        mode = APPLICATION;
        //load saved colors
        System.out.println("Loading saved colors...");
        try {
            FileInputStream colorPrefs
                = new FileInputStream("colors.pref");
            ObjectInputStream colorIn
                = new ObjectInputStream(colorPrefs);
            DigitalDisplay display
                = view.getDigitalDisplay();
            display.setBackground(
                (Color) colorIn.readObject());
            display.setUnlitColor(
                (Color) colorIn.readObject());
            display.setForeground(
                (Color) colorIn.readObject());
            colorIn.close();
```

```
            } catch (FileNotFoundException fnfe) {
                System.out.println(
                    "No saved preferences... using defaults");
            } catch (Exception e) {
                //quit if any exceptions occur
                System.out.println(
                    "Error occurred... using default colors");
            }
        }
        else if (view instanceof Applet) {
            mode = APPLET;
        }
        else throw new CalculatorException(
            "CalculatorViewer must be an "
            + "instance of either Frame or Applet");

        System.out.println("The calculator is being started in "
            + (mode == APPLET ? "applet" : "application")
            + " mode");
    }


    public void calculatorKeyPressed(CalculatorKeypadEvent event) {
        view.updateAuditTrail(helper.getAuditTrail());
    }


    public void actionPerformed(ActionEvent event) {
        //these events should come from the view's menu
        if (event.getSource() instanceof JMenuItem) {
            String selection = (
                (JMenuItem)event.getSource()).getText();
```

```java
if (selection.equals(CalculatorMenu.FILE_EXIT)) {
    System.exit(0);
}
else if (selection.equals(
        CalculatorMenu.VIEW_AUDIT_TRAIL)) {
    view.showAuditTrail(helper.getAuditTrail());
}
else if (selection.equals(
        CalculatorMenu.VIEW_COLOR_BACKGROUND)) {
    DigitalDisplay display = ➡
    view.getDigitalDisplay();

    ColorUpdater colorUpd
        = new Calculator.ColorUpdater(
        ColorUpdater.BG, display.getBackground());
    colorUpd.updateColor();
}
else if (selection.equals(
        CalculatorMenu.VIEW_COLOR_UNLIT)) {
    DigitalDisplay display = ➡
    view.getDigitalDisplay();

    ColorUpdater colorUpd
        = new Calculator.ColorUpdater(
        ColorUpdater.UNLIT, ➡
        display.getUnlitColor());
    colorUpd.updateColor();
}
else if (selection.equals(
        CalculatorMenu.VIEW_COLOR_LIT)) {
    DigitalDisplay display = ➡
    view.getDigitalDisplay();

    ColorUpdater colorUpd
```

```java
                    = new Calculator.ColorUpdater(
                        ColorUpdater.LIT, display.getForeground());
                colorUpd.updateColor();
            }
            else if (selection.equals(
                    CalculatorMenu.FILE_SAVE_AUDIT_TRAIL)) {
                StringBuffer at
                    = new StringBuffer(helper.getAuditTrail());
                String nl = System.getProperty("line.separator");
                int nlIndex, place = 0;
                while ( (nlIndex = at.toString().indexOf('\n',
                        place)) != -1) {
                    at.replace(nlIndex, nlIndex + 1, nl);
                    place = nlIndex + nl.length();
                }
                try {
                    FileWriter writer
                        = new FileWriter("audittrail.txt");
                    writer.write(at.toString());
                    writer.close();
                    view.showInfo(
                        "Saved audit trail as audittrail.txt");
                } catch (IOException e) {
                    System.out.println(
                        "Unable to save audit trail: "
                        + e.getMessage());
                    view.showInfo("Unable to save audit trail");
                }
            }
            else if (selection.equals(
```

```
                CalculatorMenu.FILE_SAVE_COLORS)) {
        System.out.println("Saving color preferences...");
        try {
            DigitalDisplay display
                = view.getDigitalDisplay();
            FileOutputStream cp
                = new FileOutputStream("colors.pref");
            ObjectOutputStream colorOut
                = new ObjectOutputStream(cp);
            colorOut.writeObject(display.getBackground());
            colorOut.writeObject(display.getUnlitColor());
            colorOut.writeObject(display.getForeground());
            colorOut.flush();
            colorOut.close();
            view.showInfo(
                "Color preferences saved successfully");
        } catch (Exception e) {
            System.out.println(
                "Unable to save color preferences: "
                + e.getMessage());
            view.showInfo(
                "Unable to save color preferences");
        }
    }
  }
}


private class ColorUpdater implements ChangeListener,
        ActionListener {
  private final static int BG = 0;
```

```java
private final static int UNLIT = 1;
private final static int LIT = 2;
private int type;
private Color initialColor;
private JColorChooser chooser;
private DigitalDisplay display;

private ColorUpdater(int whichColor, Color initial) {
  type = whichColor;
  initialColor = new Color(initial.getRGB());
  chooser = new JColorChooser(initialColor);
  chooser.getSelectionModel().addChangeListener(this);
    display = view.getDigitalDisplay();
}


public void updateColor() {
    JDialog colorDialog
      = JColorChooser.createDialog((Component)view,
          "Choose a color", true, chooser, null, this);
    colorDialog.setVisible(true);
    colorDialog.dispose();
}


/* cancel listener for color chooser */
public void actionPerformed(ActionEvent e) {
    updateDisplayColor(initialColor);
}


/* listens for color chooser updates */
public void stateChanged(ChangeEvent e) {
```

```java
            if (e.getSource() instanceof ColorSelectionModel) {
                ColorSelectionModel csm
                    = (ColorSelectionModel)e.getSource();
                updateDisplayColor(csm.getSelectedColor());
            }
        }


        private void updateDisplayColor(Color newColor) {
            switch(type) {
                case BG:
                    display.setBackground(newColor);
                    break;
                case UNLIT:
                    display.setUnlitColor(newColor);
                    break;
                case LIT:
                    display.setForeground(newColor);
            }
        }
    }
}
```

To handle the color changes, you have to import the `javax.swing.event` package and the `javax.swing.colorchooser.ColorSelectionModel` class and implement the `ActionListener` interface. To register as a listener for menu events, you need to call the `addMenuActionListener()` method, passing `this` as the `ActionListener` object in the `Calculator()` constructor method. Because the calculator allows the colors to be saved, when the calculator application starts, it looks for any saved colors and, if the save file is there, uses them. The file that contains these colors is named `colors.pref`. A `FileInputStream` opens to this file. You should expect `Color` objects to be in the `colors.pref` file.

To read in objects, wrap the `FileInputStream` with a new `Object InputStream` object, `colorIn`. To read a single object from the file, call the `colorIn`'s `readObject()` method. The `readObject()` method returns an `Object`, so you must cast it to a `Color` object before setting the `DigitalDisplay`'s colors. The order in which the `colors.pref` file stores the colors is background color, unlit color, and lit color. The code gets a reference to the `DigitalDisplay` component by calling the new `get DigitalDisplay()` method that is defined in the `CalculatorViewer` interface. The colors read in from the file are set to the `DigitalDisplay` by calling the appropriate color-setting methods. After the colors are all set, the `ObjectInputStream` should close.

There's a possibility that the `colors.pref` file doesn't exist yet, so you need to handle the `FileNotFoundException`. If the file isn't there, `Calculator` simply prints a message to standard output and uses the default colors (by not explicitly setting any). If any other `Exception` occurs, again, just use the default colors. `Calculator` only looks for the `colors.pref` file if the calculator is running in application mode, as applets can't read files unless certain steps are taken (which I won't get into here).

The only line added to the `calculatorKeyPressed()` method updates the audit trail as keys are pressed so that the `AuditTrailView` component displays the most recent updates to the audit trail, as they are made.

The `actionPerformed()` method is completely new and handles all of the `CalculatorMenu` events. Just to be safe, the `actionPerformed()` method checks to make sure that the source of the event is, in fact, a `JMenuItem`. If the event source is a `JMenuItem`, the code sets up a `String` variable, called `selection`, with the menu text. A big `if-else` statement compares the menu text against the `CalcluatorMenu` static constants to see which menu item triggered the event. For example, if the menu item text is `CalculatorMenu.FILE_EXIT`, the `System.exit()` method terminates the application. The `actionPerformed()` method handles all of the menu events, which are for exiting the application, viewing the audit trail, viewing the colors, saving the audit trail, and saving the color preferences.

To view the audit trail, The `Calculator` class simply calls `Calculator Viewer`'s `showAuditTrail()` method. The `helper` instance variable, which is the `CalculatorHelper` object, keeps track of the audit trail, so you get a copy of it by calling `getAuditTrail()` on `helper`. To view and change the colors, `Calculator` uses an inner class called `ColorUpdater`. The `actionPerformed()` method gets the specified color from the `Digital Display` object, creates a new `ColorUpdater` object, called `colorUpd`, and puts it to work by calling `colorUpd.updateColor()`. (I'll explain exactly how the `ColorUpdater` inner class works in a bit. First, I want to finish the rest of the menu options.) The `Calculator` class saves the audit trail in a file named `audittrail.txt`. If you remember, the audit trail is built line by line, ending each line with the `\n` character. That's fine for Java programs, but as I mentioned before, line separators are different among operating systems. To get the line separator for the underlying operating system, you can make the following method call:

```
String nl = System.getProperty("line.separator");
```

This method looks at a properties file that is specific to the SDK installation for your operating system. A properties file ends with the extension `.properties` and contains key-value pairs. In this instance, there is a key called "`line.separator`" whose value is the string that your operating system uses to separate new lines, such as a new line and/or carriage return. Before saving the audit trail, the `Calculator` class replaces all of the `\n` character occurrences with the line separator string. This will ensure that new lines are created properly. If you don't do this, and are running Windows Notepad to view the saved audit trail, you will see black squares where the line breaks should be. The `while` loop that does the replacing uses two variables. The `nlIndex` is used to find the location of each `\n` character. The `place` variable keeps track of where you are in the audit trail string. You need to do this because the line separator might itself include a `\n` character. If the loop didn't keep track of where it is, it would infinitely loop as it replaces the first occurrence of `\n` with another `\n`. Once the audit trail is fitted with the line separator strings, the calculator application is ready to save it. A `FileWriter` object, `writer`, opens to the `audittrail.txt` file, writes the audit trail text to it, and then closes the stream. As a convenience to the user, the `view` pops up a message dialog to indicate whether the audit trail was saved successfully.

To save the current `DigitalDisplay` colors, a `FileOutputStream` opens to the `colors.pref` file. An `ObjectOutputStream`, `colorOut`, wraps the `FileOutputStream` so that it can write objects to the file. `colorOut` writes the three color objects and then closes the stream. Again, a message dialog indicates whether the colors were saved.

Now, I'll get back to the `ColorUpdater` inner class. The `ColorUpdater` class is responsible for using a `JColorChooser` to update the `Digital Display`'s three colors. `ColorUpdater` updates only one color at a time. It has three constants, `BG`, `UNLIT`, and `LIT`, which are used to indicate which color to update. Pass in one of these three values to the `ColorUpdater()` constructor's first parameter. The constructor saves the given value in the `type` variable. The `initialColor` variable keeps track of the original color before the user starts messing with the `JColorChooser` controls. This variable gets its value from the second argument in the constructor method. The other two variables, `chooser` and `display`, are the `JColorChooser` component and the `DigitalDisplay` object, respectively.

The `ColorUpdater` class implements `ChangeListener` to listen for color changes. It also implements `ActionListener` to listen for an event fired by the `JColorChooser`'s Cancel button (triggered by the button being pressed).

The `updateColor()` method opens the `JColorChooser` component in a dialog window in a way similar to the one you learned earlier. To create the `JDialog` object, the `updateColor()` method passes `view` as the parent component for the dialog, passes `true` to make the dialog modal, and passes itself as the cancel listener to the `createDialog()` method. The Cancel button listener simply resets the color to the initial color when the user presses the Cancel button. There is no need to listen for OK button events because `ColorUpdater` constantly updates the color as the `JColorChooser` components are played with.

Each time the `JColorChooser` changes the color (for example, by sliding one of the RGB sliders), the `stateChanged()` method is called. Here, you need to update the `DigitalDisplay` color so that you can see the effects on the calculator screen. To do this, pass the new color, which you can get from the `ColorSelectionModel` object, to the `updateDisplayColor()` method. The `updateDisplayColor()` method checks which color to update (`BG`, `UNLIT`, or `LIT`) and calls the appropriate color-setting method on the `display` object.

You compile the `Calculator.java` source code like this:

```
javac -d ..\classes com\wkndjava\calculator\Calculator.java
```

At this point, the calculator application is able to do what you need it to do. The menu system causes the calculator application to behave appropriately, and now you can view and save the audit trail, and view, change, and save the `DigitalDisplay` colors. Figure 7.4 shows how the audit trail looks and demonstrates that the calculator application can save the audit trail text.

Figure 7.5 shows that the color preferences are being saved.

Figure 7.6 shows that the new files, `colors.pref` and `audittrail.txt`, are indeed created for you when you select the appropriate menu options. A listing of the `src` directory should include the two new files.

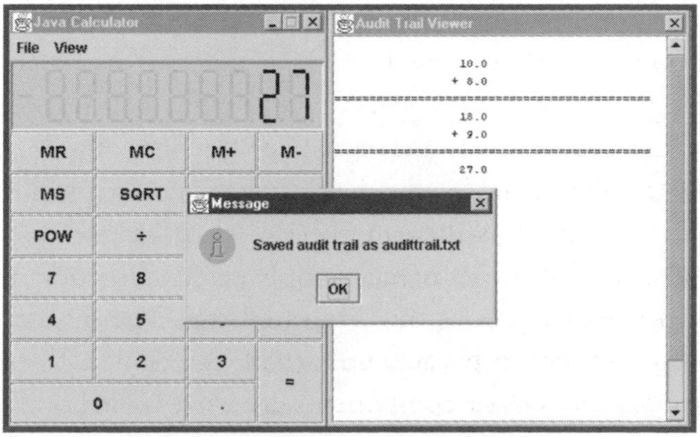

Figure 7.4

The calculator application has the ability to save the audit trail.

Figure 7.5

If you save your color preferences, the calculator application will remember them when you restart the application.

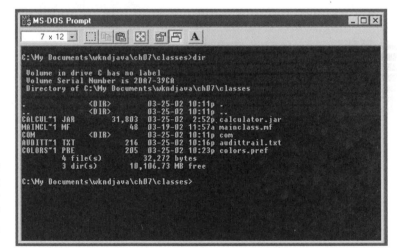

Figure 7.6

You can see that the calculator application really did create the new save files.

The jar Tool

The jar tool is a Java application that groups multiple files together into a single JAR (Java ARchive) file. The jar tool compresses the files so that the resulting JAR file uses less disk space than the sum of the individual uncompressed files use. The jar tool compression is based on ZIP compression. First, you'll learn about the basics of using the jar tool, and then you'll move on to JAR the calculator application.

How to Use the jar Tool

To use the jar tool, you need to run the jar program that is part of the SDK installation. The actual program file resides in the bin folder, under the directory where you installed the SDK. If you set up your PATH variable correctly, you should be able to run the jar program from any directory. To get a quick description of how to use the jar tool, simply type **jar** at your command prompt and then press the Enter key. This should give you a usage summary, along with a listing of options and their corresponding descriptions. If you get an error when you type jar, refer to Friday Evening's session for information about setting up your path. The output should look something like this:

```
Usage: jar {ctxu}[vfm0M] [jar-file] [manifest-file] [-C dir] files
Options:
    -c  create new archive
    -t  list table of contents for archive
    -x  extract named (or all) files from archive
    -u  update existing archive
    -v  generate verbose output on standard output
    -f  specify archive file name
    -m  include manifest information from specified manifest file
    -0  store only; use no ZIP compression
    -M  do not create a manifest file for the entries
    -i  generate index information for the specified jar files
    -C  change to the specified directory and include the following
        file
If any file is a directory then it is processed recursively.
The manifest file name and the archive file name needs to be
specified in the same order the 'm' and 'f' flags are
specified.
```

```
Example 1: to archive two class files into an archive called
          classes.jar:
      jar cvf classes.jar Foo.class Bar.class
Example 2: use an existing manifest file 'mymanifest' and
          archive all the files in the foo/ directory
          into 'classes.jar':
      jar cvfm classes.jar mymanifest -C foo/ .
```

If you want to list the contents of the JAR file, simply type

```
jar tf classes.jar
```

You might also need to un-JAR (extract) the file. You can do that with the
-x option, like this:

```
jar xf classes.jar
```

If you JAR a directory, the directory structure will remain intact. The `jar`
tool leaves the original files where they are and just creates copies of them
to archive. Also, when you use the `jar` tool, it automatically creates a
directory called `META-INF` for you. This directory holds the `MANIFEST.MF`
manifest file, which the `jar` tool also creates for you. The manifest file is
where meta-information about the archive goes. You'll actually work with
the manifest file when you create the `calculator.jar` file for the calculator application.

Creating the calculator.jar File

The calculator application has 25 class files, including the class files that are
created for inner classes. Using the `jar` tool, you can JAR all of these classes
into a single JAR file. You'll use the `jar` tool to create the `calculator.jar`
file. The `calculator.jar` file will contain everything you need to run
the application; you will actually be able to run the JAR file by itself
(independent of the source files and original class files).

When you run a JAR file, Java needs a way to know which class's `main()`
method to run, so you have to provide that information. How? You add

this information to the manifest file. The good news is that you don't have to manually edit the generated `MANIFEST.MF` file, but you do have to do a small amount of legwork. You have to create your own manifest file, name it whatever you want to, provide the information that you want to add to the manifest file, and then tell the `jar` tool to include your information when it creates the `MANIFEST.MF` file.

To do this, first create a file called `mainclass.mf` (open a text editor and save the file as `mainclass.mf`). The name of the file is actually not important, but whatever its name, make sure you remember it. Put the file in the `classes` directory, because you'll be archiving the class files. Add the following line of text in the file:

```
Main-Class: com.wkndjava.calculator.Calculator
```

It is very important that you press Enter at the end of the line to insert a new line. If the last line of a manifest file does not end with a carriage return, the `jar` tool will not parse it correctly. The `Main-Class` attribute of a manifest file specifies which class to run when you run the JAR file. In this case, you want to start the calculator application using the `com.wkndjava.calculator.Calculator` class. The `.class` extension must be omitted. Make sure that you save the `mainclass.mf` file now.

Now, you're ready to run the `jar` tool to create `calculator.jar`. Get into the `classes` directory and type the following command:

```
jar cmfv mainclass.mf calculator.jar com
```

The options you need to use are `c` to create a new JAR file, `m` to include the manifest information you just created, `f` to specify the JAR filename, and `v` to generate verbose output (just so you can see what's going on). The `m` option corresponds to the `mainclass.mf` file that you created, and the `f` option corresponds to the JAR filename, which is `calculator.jar`. The order in which you list these filenames must be the same order as their corresponding option letters. If the `f` came before the `m`, then you'd have to list `calculator.jar` before `mainclass.mf`. The final argument to the `jar` tool is the `com` directory name. The `jar` tool will traverse this directory and all of its subdirectories and add all of the files they contain to the `calculator.jar` file.

Now, just to make sure it worked, verify that the `calculator.jar` file was created. You should also check its contents by typing the command

```
jar tf calculator.jar
```

When you do that, you should get a listing of all the files that the `jar` tool added to the `calculator.jar` file, including their directories. The listing should look like this:

```
META-INF/

META-INF/MANIFEST.MF

com/

com/wkndjava/

com/wkndjava/calculator/

com/wkndjava/calculator/Calculator$1.class

com/wkndjava/calculator/Calculator$ColorUpdater.class

com/wkndjava/calculator/Calculator.class

com/wkndjava/calculator/event/

com/wkndjava/calculator/event/CalculatorKeyMap.class

com/wkndjava/calculator/event/CalculatorKeypadEvent.class

com/wkndjava/calculator/event/CalculatorKeypadListener.class

com/wkndjava/calculator/exception/

com/wkndjava/calculator/exception/CalculatorException.class

com/wkndjava/calculator/exception/
     DigitalDisplayOverflowException.class

com/wkndjava/calculator/gui/

com/wkndjava/calculator/gui/AuditTrailView.class

com/wkndjava/calculator/gui/CalculatorApplet.class

com/wkndjava/calculator/gui/CalculatorHelper.class

com/wkndjava/calculator/gui/CalculatorKeypad$1.class
```

```
com/wkndjava/calculator/gui/
    CalculatorKeypad$ActionEventHandler.class
com/wkndjava/calculator/gui/CalculatorKeypad$KeyEventListener.class
com/wkndjava/calculator/gui/CalculatorKeypad.class
com/wkndjava/calculator/gui/CalculatorMenu.class
com/wkndjava/calculator/gui/CalculatorModel.class
com/wkndjava/calculator/gui/CalculatorView.class
com/wkndjava/calculator/gui/CalculatorViewer.class
com/wkndjava/calculator/gui/DigitalDisplay$1.class
com/wkndjava/calculator/gui/
    DigitalDisplay$DigitalDisplayFormat.class
com/wkndjava/calculator/gui/DigitalDisplay.class
com/wkndjava/calculator/gui/LiquidCrystalComponent.class
com/wkndjava/calculator/gui/LiquidCrystalDigit.class
com/wkndjava/calculator/gui/LiquidCrystalNegative.class
```

Running JAR Files

Once you have verified that the `calculator.jar` file is okay, create a new directory, called `jar`, at the same level as your `src` and `classes` directory. Then move the `calculator.jar` file from the `classes` directory to the `jar` directory. Doing this gives you a clean slate on which to test that the `calculator.jar` file can be run independently of the original files. Once you do that, you're ready to run the `calculator.jar` file, which will start the calculator application. To run a `jar` file, specify the main class in the manifest file, which you already did, use the `-jar` option of the `java` program, and specify the JAR filename. So, to run the `calculator.jar` file, use the following command:

```
java -jar calculator.jar
```

When you run this command, the calculator application should start up normally and all of its features should work correctly.

Using JAR Files from Applets

Towards the beginning of this evening's session, you broke the calculator applet by moving the files around to create packages. Just a second ago, you broke it even more by putting all of the class files into a JAR file. It's time to fix it! To fix the package problem, you have to fully specify the class by adding the package name in front of it. To fix the JAR problem, you have to specify the JAR filename where the `CalculatorApplet` and other class files are. Use the `archive` attribute of the `APPLET` tag. The value of this attribute should be the JAR filename. Your new `APPLET` tag needs to look like this:

```
<APPLET code='com.wkndjava.calculator.gui.CalculatorApplet.class'
        archive='calculator.jar' width=268 height=334>

    Your browser does not support applets

</APPLET>
```

Copy the `calculator.html` file into the `jar` directory and make these changes. Now, when you run the applet using the `appletviewer` tool or your internet browser application, it should work. Be sure to note that, because the file is running as an applet, the `File` menu should be disabled.

This is a good time to tell you about a major benefit of the `jar` tool. When you have an applet and all of the classes it uses together in a JAR file, you gain certain benefits. The first benefit is that the JAR file is easier to upload to your Web server as one file is always easier to upload than many files. Plus, you don't have to worry about the associated directory structures. Another benefit you reap is download time. Because the class files are compressed, they download faster when someone is trying to run your applet. Not only that, but also because all of the class files belong to a single JAR file, your whole set of classes can be retrieved using a single HTTP request/response, which saves time.

Using the javadoc Tool

The javadoc tool generates HTML API documentation from Java source files. API stands for *Application Program Interface.* In fact, the Java Language API Documentation was generated with the javadoc tool. In this section, you'll learn how to create your own API documentation and how to use the javadoc tool to generate the HTML documentation for you.

Writing javadoc Comments

In order to prepare to use the javadoc tool, you need to write javadoc comments in your Java source code files. To write javadoc comments, you use specialized multi-line comments. Normally, multi-comments look like this:

```
/*

This is a comment.

This is another comment.

*/
```

You start multi-line comments with /* and end them with */. javadoc comments, on the other hand, use two asterisks after the forward-slash /** to start the comment and use the same */ to end it.

```
/**

 * This is a javadoc comment.

 */
```

The javadoc tool looks for these sort of comments when generating the HTML documents. The text found within javadoc comments will be included in the API documentation. Because the generated documentation is in HTML format, you can include HTML tags inside javadoc comments to format the generated text however you like.

javadoc Tags

When you write `javadoc` comments, you can include special tags, which the `javadoc` tool parses for you to perform special tasks. Table 7.7 lists the `javadoc` tags that the calculator application source files use. (For a description of the other tags and a rather lengthy description about using the `javadoc` tool, refer to the "Tools" section of the Java API Documentation.) Comments that apply to the class as a whole go directly above the class declaration line. Comments that are specific to members or methods go directly above the corresponding methods or members.

	TABLE 7.7 JAVADOC TAGS	
javadoc Tag	**Syntax**	**Description**
`@author`	`@author name`	Specifies the author's name.
`{@link}`	`{@link package.class#member label}`	Adds an HTML link to the specified class or member using the given label.
`@param`	`@param name description`	Adds a description for the specified method parameter.
`@return`	`@return description`	Adds a description for the returned value of a method.
`@see`	`@see package.class#member label`	Adds a "See Also" label and a link to the specified class or member.
`@throws`	`@throws class-name description`	Adds an entry for an exception, specified by *class name*, that a method throws using the given description.
`@version`	`@version version-info`	Adds version information so you can specify version numbers for classes.

I've included an example that uses `javadoc` comments with `javadoc` tags. The following code snippet is the `javadoc` comments for the `setDoubleValue()` method of the `DigitalDisplay` class. Only the method signature is provided (not the entire method), but the whole `javadoc` comment is listed.

```
/**
 * Sets the display value to the given <code>double</code>.
 * Calling this method does not repaint the new number.
 * To display this number, you should call
 * {@link #updateDisplay() <code>updateDisplay()</code>}
 *
 * @param dValue The number to display
 *
 * @throws DigitalDisplayOverflowException if the given
 * number is too
 * large to be displayed by this <code>DigitalDisplay</code>
 *
 * @see #updateDisplay()
 */
public void setDoubleValue(double dValue) throws
        DigitalDisplayOverflowException {
```

The first line of a `javadoc` comment is used as the summary description for whatever appears underneath the comment. The entire comment is used as the full description. You can see that I used an HTML tag, called code. This tag uses a monospace font to distinguish code words from regular words. I also used the following `javadoc` tags: `{@link}`, `@param`, `@throws`, and `@see`. In the `{@link}` and `@see` tags, I didn't have to specify the package name or class name because I'm linking to elements within the same class. Figure 7.7 shows what the generated HTML documents look like for this `javadoc` comment.

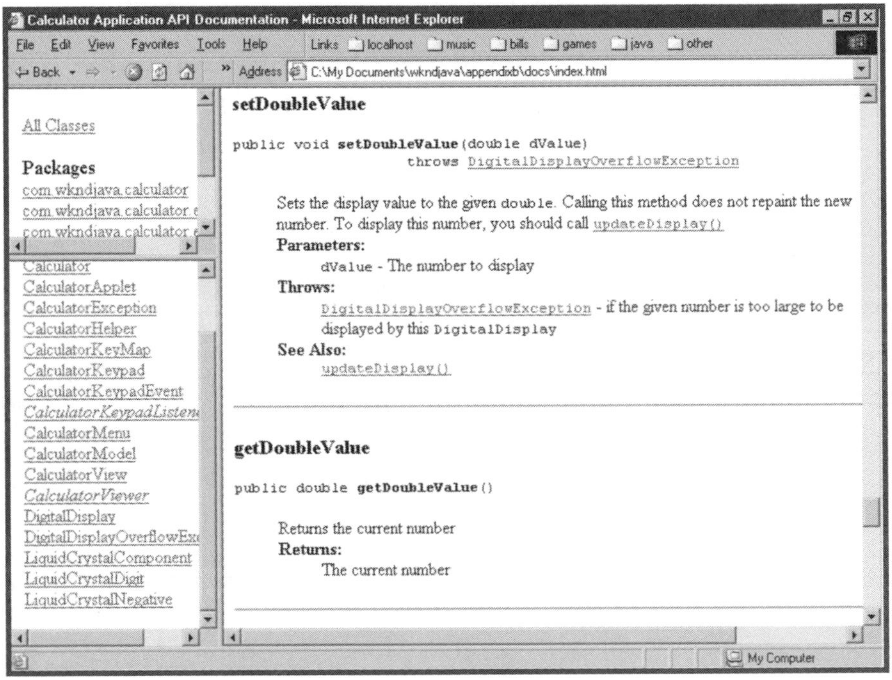

Figure 7.7

The generated `javadoc` documentation for the `setDouble Value()` method looks like this when you view it with Microsoft Internet Explorer.

Running the javadoc Tool

Like the `jar` tool, the `javadoc` tool's program file is located in the Java bin file, which should be included in your PATH by now so that you can run it from any directory. To run the `javadoc` tool, use the `javadoc` command at your command prompt. To run the `javadoc` tool over one or more packages, do this:

```
javadoc [options] package-names
```

You use options to affect the way `javadoc` generates your documentation. Four commonly used options are listed here:

➤ -d. Specifies the output directory for the generated documentation.

➤ -windowtitle. Specifies the main title for the generated documentation.

➤ `-author`. Includes the author information specified by the `@author` tags.

➤ `-version`. Includes the version information specified by the `@version` tags.

`javadoc` comments are not used to specify package documentation. Instead, if you want to have a description for each package, you have to create a file named `package.html` in each individual package. The `package.html` file should be in the same directories as the `.java` source files. Each `package.html` file should contain HTML code, including a BODY tag. The `javadoc` tool will insert everything that it finds between the opening and closing body tags (`<BODY>` and `</BODY>`) into the generated documentation as the package descriptions. For example, here are the contents of the `package.html` file for the `com.wkndjava.calculator` package, located in the `com\wkndjava\calculator\` folder.

```
<body>

Contains the Calculator application main file

</body>
```

If you are up to adding the `javadoc` comments, take a look at Appendix B (which you can find on the Web at http://www.premierpressbooks. com/downloads.asp). Appendix B lists the full source code for all the calculator application programs, including the `javadoc` comments. Here is the command that runs the `javadoc` tool over all of the calculator application's packages (the `-d` comment specifies a directory named `docs`, so make sure you create that directory before running this command):

```
javadoc -d docs -windowtitle "Calculator Application API➡
Documentation" -author -version com.wkndjava.calculator➡
com.wkndjava.calculator.event com.wkndjava.calculator.exception➡
com.wkndjava.calculator.gui
```

After you run this command, you can take a look through the generated documentation by opening your browser and viewing the `docs\index.html` file.

Wrapping Up

This evening, you learned some advanced Java concepts. First, you learned about packages. You learned how to create packages and how access modifiers affect how classes can access other classes. You applied this knowledge to package the calculator application. Next, you learned about the `java.io` package and you learned how to read and write files and serialize objects. After that, you created a menu system for the calculator application using the `JColorChooser` component and applying what you learned about the `java.io` package to save the audit trail and color preferences. You also learned about the `jar` tool. You archived the calculator application and learned how to run it from the command line. Finally, you learned how to use the `javadoc` tool to generate HTML documentation for the calculator application code.

Congratulations! You've completed the book. Hopefully, you learned a great deal from this book in a short amount of time. If you used this book to prepare for an interview or an exam, I wish you good luck. At this point, you're on track to start writing your own programs or to start learning even more advanced Java programming. Whatever you do next in life, just make sure you have fun.

The stars appear every night in the sky. All is well.

INDEX

Symbols

‘ (single quotes), 39-40
“ (double quotes), 39-40
- (subtraction operator), 48
-- (decrement operator), 50-51
! (logical compliment operator), 107-108
!= (not equal to operator), 101-103
% (modulus operator), 48-50
& (logical AND operator), 104-107
&& (conditional AND operator), 103-105
() (parentheses), 23
* (asterisk)
   comments, 21-22
   multiplication operator, 48
. (dot notation), 74
/ (division operator), 48
// (single-line comments), 22
; (semicolon), 24
[ ] (brackets), 54, 59
\ (backslash escape code), 40
^ (logical XOR operator), 104-107
{} (braces), 23, 138
| (logical OR operator), 104-107
|| (conditional OR operator), 103-105
+
   addition operator, 48
   strings, 42
++ (increment operator), 50-51
< (less than operator), 100-103
<= (less than or equal to operator),
   100-103
= (assignment operator), 43
== (equal to operator), 101-103
> (greater than operator), 100-103
>= (greater than or equal to operator),
   100-103

A

abstract classes, 272
abstract method, 272
Abstract Windowing Toolkit. *See* AWT
access modifiers. *See* modifiers

acronym (Java), 5
ActionEvent events, 212, 222
ActionListener interface, 193, 211, 299
actionPerformed method, 193, 211, 222,
   431, 452-453
actions, 212
adapter classes, 302
add method, 65-67, 93, 152-153, 190, 398
addActionListener method, 193
addAll method, 152
addCalculatorKeypadListener method,
   346, 358-359, 377
addition operator (+), 48
   strings, 42
addSeparator method, 211
addTax method, 64-67
addWindowListener method, 186, 303
AdjustmentEvents events, 214-217
AdjustmentListener interface, 217
adjustmentValueChanged method, 217
advantages, interfaces, 340-341
alpha values, 247
AND operator
   && (conditional AND), 103-105
   logical AND (&), 104-107
anonymous inner classes, 300-301
   event handling, 301-303
APIs (application programming
      interfaces). *See also* interfaces
   AWT documentation, 223
   collection, 150-155
   documentation. *See* javadoc tool
   operating systems, 6
   programs, 6
   Swing, 291-295
appendDecimal method, 325
appendDigit method, 325
appendDisplayDecimal method, 359
appendDisplayDigit method, 359
Applet class methods, 379-381
APPLET constant, 376
<applet> tag, 27-28, 381-383
   attributes, 383

applets
   jar tool, 462
   overview, 378-379
   panels comparison, 381
   parameters, passing, 383-385
   running, 28-30
   security, 25
   Swing, 387-390
   testing, 29
   writing, 25-26
appletviewer tool, 29, 385-386
APPLICATION constant, 376
application exceptions, 313-314
application programming interfaces.
      See APIs
applications, Swing/AWT comparison, 295
archiving. *See* jar tool
arcs, 258-261
args[] array, 143-144
ArgsTest program, 143-144
arguments. *See also* parameters
   () parentheses, 23
   args[] array, 143-144
   boolean, 199
   command-line, 141-143
   methods, 63-64
   overloading, 84
   str, 266-268
   verbose, 141-142
ArrayIndexOutOfBoundsException
   exception, 313
arrays. *See also* variables
   args[], 143-144
   declaring, 54
   elements, 56-58
   initializing, 54-56
   litPattern[], 284-285
   multidimensional, 59-61
   size, 55
   values, troubleshooting, 56
ArrayTest program, 56-58
assembly languages, 4
assigning floating point literals, 47